MW00583279

PENDAR

A FATHER AND SON'S EXTRAORDINARY JOURNEY TO FREEDOM

PENDAR MALEK

Pendar

Copyright © 2023 by Pendar Malek

All rights reserved.

Published by Red Penguin Books

Bellerose Village, New York

ISBN

Print 978-1-63777-436-6 / 978-1-63777-437-3 / 978-1-63777-442-7 / 978-1-63777-443-4

Digital 978-1-63777-438-0

For my father who never gave up. To my dedicated wife who has supported me. To my beautiful children who always motivate me. And to the millions of immigrants who travel to America by any means necessary.

CONTENTS

PROLOGUE

March 4th, 1987

t was well past midnight when we started our journey. The night air held a slight chill, and the aroma of sand and pine was all around us. I lay as still as I could, my face pressed against the hard dirt, trying to make myself invisible. I didn't dare move, nor sneak a glance at my father and the others who were traveling with us. After a few tense moments, I heard the tires of a vehicle pass by where we were hiding.

Pedro, our "coyote," or "smuggler," waited until it was completely out of view before instructing us, "Let's go!" he whispered, motioning us onward.

We obliged. Baba and I had our doubts about Pedro when we first caught sight of him earlier that evening, dressed in mud-caked jeans, a ripped gray T-shirt covered in dirt, his jet-black hair uncombed. But we were beginning to sense that we were in experienced hands.

Sprinting ahead, I prayed for the pain in my legs to subside, thankful when Pedro again directed us to halt. "Stop, down! Stop, down!" he said forcefully.

Thrusting us into thick foliage, he gave us the quiet signal, then disappeared beneath a nearby bush with the other traveler.

My heart was pounding, and I was drawing ragged breaths from the excessive climbing.

Our midnight journey had been full of starts and stops. But it now felt as if we were taking a longer break than usual. I was so weakened that I put my elbows together to create a makeshift pillow and rested my head on my forearms. At thirteen, I should have been at home in bed, resting up for another school day. But it had been months since I'd slept in my own bed, and even longer since I'd been in a classroom. Baba and I had been on the road for what seemed an eternity, applying for a student visa to enter the United States. My father was determined to keep me safe. We'd been away from home, visiting countries across the Middle East, Europe, and Asia. We had visited American embassies in five countries and traveled to multiple cities around the world, but it was all in vain. My father's unwavering attempts were interrupted by fate and destiny, but now Pedro was our last hope.

The pungent smell of pine hung in the night air, and the endless croaking of crickets, the hoot of the owls, and the distant sound of rushing water lulled me into a deep sleep, dreaming about the new life that awaited me. The crackling of voices on walkie-talkies startled me awake. It sounded as though they were mere feet away. My father covered my mouth with the palm of his hand, his eyes widening in fear of being spotted. I feared it was border patrol officers calling for backup and that soon we'd be arrested by the American authorities.

I made myself as flat to the ground as I could, nervously listening to the muffled voice of a man squawking into the transceiver. I sensed him coming closer, the sound of dirt being crushed under his boots grew louder while his bright flashlight illuminated the bushes right next to us. "I don't see any movement in this area," he related. "I'll keep searching and report back."

The night was eerie; I could hear something, a small insect, a mouse, perhaps a snake, rattling the leaves close to where we laid. The hair on my arms and the back of my neck, bristled as if called to attention, but I didn't dare make a move, I was frozen in terror. I held my breath, praying for this tense moment to be over.

"Negative. Nothing here, sir, 'BLEEP, BLEEP,'" the man said, clicking the button on his walkie-talkie. I could barely hear him over the booming of my heart, erratically beating out of my chest.

We heard his footsteps getting farther and farther away, and eventually, the sound of an engine as the vehicle drove off. Pedro and the other traveler slowly crawled out from the bushes, and with a huge sigh of relief, he waved us forward. "Let's go!"

At that moment, Baba and I realized that American authorities were inspecting this entire area, but Pedro was vigilant, the perfect lookout, even with his lazy eye. Somehow, he knew exactly where the border patrol was and managed to stay one step ahead of them.

We climbed one ridge after another, advancing, then hiding. It seemed as though the night would never end. As we scaled another peak, I glimpsed the shimmering lights of a giant city directly ahead of us. I squeezed my father's hand tightly with renewed hope and optimism.

We stood for just a moment gazing at the incredible scene, mesmerized by its dazzling beauty. Under the glow of the moonlight, I sensed America humming beneath my feet. *How much longer would we have to walk? How much longer before we heard the wail of a siren or spotted the flashing lights of border patrol? How much longer before we were handcuffed and placed in the back of a police cruiser?* The odds were certainly stacked against us.

Overwhelmed with anger, regret, and grief, I silently asked God for forgiveness. What *have I done to deserve this punishment?* I asked Him. I was escaping the war, cheating death, and yet, perhaps it was my destiny to die all along. I could think of no other way to comprehend what we were going through or to explain the complex emotions I was feeling.

My cousin Shahin had flown to America on an airplane, having obtained an American visa stamped in his passport. But this seemingly simple task had proved far more difficult than anyone in my family could have ever predicted.

Why did my situation have to be so impossible? Did I do something wrong to justify my life's new direction? My legs, knees, feet, and back were weak, cramping like I'd never felt before. I didn't know if I had the physical capacity to continue. All I heard was the thumping of blood pounding in my head. If Baba was right and there was a God, then he'd let this be over. Every time my pace slowed down, Baba was there, pushing me forward, placing his hands on my shoulder, and encouraging me to continue walking.

The next uphill barrier came in the form of a steep sandy embankment that stretched for miles in every direction. Pedro effortlessly led the way up the hill, then crouched down on his stomach to crawl the last three or four feet, motioning us to follow. Loose sand and gravel rushed past us like a river. When we finally reached the top, Pedro raised his head slowly to peek over it. I braved a glance and saw a dirt road to the left, which led to a soaring guard tower, equipped with an enormous spotlight. It was manned, and through the night's grayish haze, I could see the silhouette of a uniformed officer holding a machine gun.

Pedro instructed the other traveler in Spanish, then turned to Baba and me. In his best broken English, he whispered, "Let's go fast. Police shoot, yelling freeze, you no stop. Only run! Very fast, okay?"

We shook our heads up and down and understood that no matter what, we were to run as fast as possible across the road and down the embankment. Even if the guard spotted us, shouted at us to stop, or even shot at us, we were to keep going, to run fast!

In the pale moonlight, I could see the terror on Baba's face. He looked as if he'd seen a ghost and was starting to hyperventilate when Pedro gave the command, "LET'S GO! LET'S GO!"

In unison, we sprang to our feet and raced across the dirt road. In the darkness, and in a hurry to cross, I hadn't noticed the steep drop on the other side. The ground dropped from under me as I fell. I started blindly tumbling, doing somersaults in the sand, and then…BOOM! I was lying flat on my back, in a state of semi-consciousness, staring up at the bright stars that filled the cloudless sky and wondering how I had ended up here.

ONE
A NIGHT AT THE MOVIES

I have so many memories of my childhood growing up in Tehran. But my earliest and perhaps my fondest happened just a few weeks shy of my fourth birthday.

It was late November 1977, and the orange glow of the sunset stretched across the skies over the city. Maman was in the kitchen cooking up another scrumptious dinner. I could hear the rapid clicking of her knife striking against the cutting board. Soon, the aroma of frying onions, garlic, meat, vegetables, and spices like turmeric and saffron filled the air, followed by the familiar, high-pitched hissing sound of her pressure cooker.

The fragrant scent could only mean one thing; she was cooking my favorite, *Baghali Polo* (rice with chopped dill weed and fava beans) topped with a savory, fall-off-the-bone lamb shank. I was in my room playing with Legos when I heard the jingling of Baba's keys in the apartment door.

"Pendar, I'm home!" he called to me excitedly.

I ran into the living room as soon as I heard his voice and leaped into his arms. "Salam, Baba!" I said. "I missed you, where were you?

"Salam azizam, chetori?" or, "Hi, my dear, how are you?" he asked.

"I missed you too, Pendar Jan!" he replied. ("Jan" is a term of endearment, a way to address a loved one.) "You know what? I have a special surprise for you tonight! Since you're turning four next month, I'm going to take you and Maman out to the movie theater tonight!" he declared.

My mind went wild with excitement, imagining a *real* movie house. I'd never watched a movie in an actual theater with a large screen.

My thoughts raced as Maman set the table and announced, "Dinner is ready! The *tahdig* is going to burn, Nader. Hurry up!"

Tahdig is the caramelized crispy crust that forms on the bottom of the pan and is the most prized part of Iranian rice dishes, often fought over as it's the first to disappear off the table.

Maman lovingly served up the steaming, tasty food, piling long-grain rice and meat on our plates. I had to finish every morsel, every last grain of rice; Maman wouldn't let me leave the table until my plate was spotless. At times, I would pretend to be full in hopes of hurrying back to my room to play. Maman wouldn't fall for it and would scoot her chair closer to force-feed me every remaining bite.

Over dinner, Baba told us a little about the movie we were going to see that evening. It was an American film called *Jaws* that was released in the United States a couple of years earlier. It had been dubbed into Farsi and was showing for the first time at Cinema Rivoli near our home.

"It's about a giant shark that attacks swimmers in a small town off the coast of New York," he explained. "It's a box office hit, a record-breaking blockbuster in many countries."

"What's a blockbuster, Baba?" I asked.

"It's when a movie sells lots of tickets and is really successful," Baba explained.

Maman looked incredulous. "Nader," she said, directing her question at my father, "are you sure this movie is age-appropriate for a four-year-old?"

Baba shrugged his shoulders. "It won't be that scary," he said with a chuckle. "Eat up quickly and let's hurry to the theater," he instructed. He was almost as excited as I was!

My father loved movies, especially action films. His all-time favorite character was James Bond. He knew every detail of every Bond movie ever made. He also liked Westerns, especially those starring Clint Eastwood, and he was a huge fan of Bruce Lee.

His love affair with the cinema had begun when he was just a young boy, and by the time he turned fourteen, he was spending his entire allowance on movie tickets. Back then, Iran was a constitutional monarchy ruled by The Shah (king), Mohammad Reza Pahlavi, a secular Muslim with Western-style leanings who was determined to pull Iran into the modern age with a series of bold initiatives from infrastructure to privatization of industry to the arts. Foreign films, dubbed into Farsi, were regularly shown at cinemas across the country.

And my father was always first in line when a new movie was released.

After the meal, we hurried to our respective bedrooms to get ready. Maman picked out my clothes for the evening, which she often did—a pair of corduroy pants, a button-down shirt, and a matching jacket—and laid them on my bed before leaving to get dressed herself.

Baba came into my room as I was struggling to button my shirt and wrestled me to the floor, tickling me on the ribs, as I kicked and giggled. We horsed around until he rolled onto one of the Lego pieces I'd been playing with earlier. That was enough to stop the action, and both of us decided to focus on getting dressed.

I could hear the whooshing of Maman's blow dryer coming from my parents' bedroom, and once I was dressed, I ran to join them.

Baba was outfitted and ready, and he was urging my mother to hurry things up with her hair and makeup. She looked beautiful in her short mini-skirt, low-cut blouse, knee-high boots, and leather jacket. She looked like a biker chick.

I scrutinized Baba as he admired how pretty she looked. Her makeup was immaculate, and she sprayed herself with his favorite perfume just before she headed out the bedroom door. Both of us caught the scent of her delicate and flowery fragrance as she slowly walked past us.

The evening was already feeling like a big event, and we hadn't even left the apartment. Minutes later, we were all climbing into Baba's green BMW 518i for the short ride to the movie theater. Foreign cars were a common sight on the streets of Tehran at the time. American models like the Ford Mustang, Dodge Charger, and Cadillacs were particularly coveted.

As we drove, I gazed out of the rear window, my chin resting on my palms, impatiently counting the traffic lights in anticipation of Baba's special surprise. The streets were congested; it was rush hour in Tehran, and traffic was heavy. Along with the American and German-made vehicles, there were plenty of French cars on the road, as well, mostly Renaults and Peugeots.

When we reached the movie theater, I could hardly retain my composure. I felt butterflies in my stomach as I clung to my parents' hands and headed for the box office, where we were greeted by a mob of anxious moviegoers. The giant marquee overhead, with its bright dazzling lights, entranced me. As we waited, Baba affectionately ran his fingers through Maman's hair, telling her how beautiful she looked. "Dooset daram," or "I love you," he whispered in her ear.

He lovingly caressed my face, too, and gave me soft kisses on the cheek. His mustache and beard were prickly, which made my skin itch, but I didn't care because it was one of my favorite things in the world. As we neared the ticket booth, I was greeted by a giant movie poster displaying the image of a spooky, massive great white shark, its mouth agape, showing rows of jagged teeth. It was swimming up from the murky depths, toward a young, female swimmer oblivious to the danger that lurked just feet below her. My eyes were as big as saucers; imagining the creepy images in the movie was ominous and terrifying to a four-year-old.

Baba purchased our tickets, and we followed the crowd into the lobby. The sweet smell of cotton candy and the buttery notes of popcorn stopped us in our tracks. Baba couldn't resist the temptation and ordered a large popcorn with extra butter, a package of Gummy Bears, and a giant fizzy soda from the concession stand. His face was joyful, and I could tell he was eager for my first movie experience to be a memorable event.

Entering the theater was like stepping into a whole new world. The enormous projection screen was unlike anything I had ever seen. It was as wide as the room and towered like a giant building. The sea of red upholstered chairs facing it stretched toward the top of the auditorium. Baba found seats for us in the center of the theater.

"Maman, can I sit on your lap, please?" I begged.

She quickly agreed and motioned me over to her seat.

I caught a glimpse of Baba's raised eyebrow and a hint of a jealous gaze as I climbed over him and into her lap. I was only toying with him; I would eventually switch to his lap once the movie got underway.

We ate our snacks and watched while people continued to file in. Maman sat with one arm wrapped around me, tightly holding Baba's hand with the other. Life couldn't get any better than watching a movie with Maman and Baba, buttery popcorn grease running down my tiny fingers and onto my shirt.

Soon, the theater was filled to capacity. As the doors closed and the ceiling lights started to dim, the crowd began applauding, cheering, and whistling. Seconds later, the auditorium plunged into complete darkness, which heightened the suspense before the humongous white vinyl screen lit up, illuminating Baba's face.

The excitement of the crowd and the anticipation of watching my first movie on the big screen was overwhelming.

The movie's score was haunting, just like the motion picture. Two minutes and forty-nine seconds of brass, strings, and drums building towards a crescendo, dun dun, dun dun, dun dun dun dun dun dun dun dun, the two-note musical score growing louder and louder as the audience braced itself. My heart began beating rapidly, my palms were getting sweaty, and my mouth was suddenly dry. I could feel goosebumps forming on my arms. Before long, Jaws brutally ravaged its first victim.

I clenched Baba's hand firmly throughout the scary parts, my eyes popping out of their sockets in disbelief as each blood-curdling scene unfolded.

At one point, Baba leaned over to ask me something, but I paid him no attention, I just rocked back and forth in my seat, enthralled and terrified, my face illuminated by the glow of the grisly images bouncing across the enormous screen.

Midway through the movie, a character named Hooper traversed beneath a broken-down boat in the dark of night, finding a shark's tooth embedded in the chewed-up hull. He received the shock of his life, and so did the audience, when the head of Victim Number Three, Ben Gardner, popped out of the underside, shaking up the entire theater.

Some movie-goers jumped in fright, sending popcorn flying throughout the auditorium. I had witnessed the most frightening images of my life, unsure how to feel about this amazing, yet alarming experience. I had no idea just how big an impact the movie *Jaws* would have on me; for years afterward, I harbored irrational fears of an imaginary shark that lay in wait at the bottom of every swimming pool.

On that night, sitting in a real theater to watch an American feature film, my father's love of movies was apparent. I snuggled into his chest and held Maman's hand, blissfully unaware of the changes that were about to befall us and our country.

No one in the theater that night could have dreamt that in just a few short months, doing something as mundane as going to the movies with your family would become an activity filled with peril. Starting in January of 1978, movie theaters across Iran would become targets of terrorists upset about the Shah's continued embrace of Western culture and his steps to modernize Iran.

TWO
THE FIRST BORN

My parents Nader 'Baba' and Ziba 'Maman' were still newlyweds, married just over a year, when I was born on December 25, 1973, a Christmas baby, although as Muslims, we didn't celebrate that holiday. Growing up in Tehran, they lovingly cared and provided for me in every way that a parent could. I lived without worries, and as their first child and first-born son, I was being spoiled rotten—though I certainly never saw it that way.

We lived in a spacious two-bedroom apartment in the center of the city, on a quiet side street, close to the main shopping boulevard, and within walking distance of all the neighborhood stores. Tehran was a large and thriving city at the time, with some five million inhabitants. It was a comfortable environment, and there was little if any violence. We felt free to walk through residential areas at night or visit a movie theater that might be showing a new release from Europe or even the United States.

The area where we lived was considered a middle-class neighborhood, and some of us were fortunate to own a car or two. The street on both sides was lined with five- and six-story walk-ups. We had a ground-floor unit with security bars on all the windows to deter intruders.

My maternal grandparents, Papa Jahan and Mama Goli, lived directly above us on the second floor, and I often ran upstairs to spend time with them.

Papa Jahan was a puzzle maker; he created crossword puzzles for several of Tehran's daily newspapers. He often worked on his puzzles at home and only went into the office to deliver the finished product.

I adored my grandfather. He was warm and loving, and he didn't mind my frequent visits. He was slightly overweight with a full head of white hair, bushy eyebrows, thick, black-framed eyeglasses, and a white mustache. I'd often find him at his desk in his pajamas, using a fountain pen and a ruler to methodically draw the boxes that would eventually be his weekly masterpiece. His office always smelled like fresh ink and the stench of the many old books that packed his sizable bookshelf.

He kept the room dark except for a single lamp that shone down on the center of his desk where he kept an assortment of dictionaries and other reference books that he used to write the clues for his puzzles.

Sometimes Mama Goli would lure me out with an invitation to accompany her on a trip to the local pastry shop. Like my grandfather, Mama Goli was also a little on the heavy side. She wore her brown hair coiffed just above her shoulders and dressed conservatively in ankle-length skirts and neatly pressed blouses. She was not as style-conscious as Maman, but she was far more progressive than her own mother, my great-grandmother, who, like many women of her generation, wore a hijab (a veil that is worn by certain Muslim women in the presence of any male outside of their immediate family that covered the head and chest) when out in public.

Mama Goli always held my hand as we strolled the two blocks to Farah Street named for the Shah's wife, our queen, Empress Farah. The sound of the running water in the *jubes*, the open sewers that ran along the curbs of many of the old streets, nearly drowned the noise of the bustling traffic on the busy thoroughfare. Most of the shopkeepers knew my grandmother and would respectfully wave or nod their heads up and down as we passed by.

Like most neighborhoods in Tehran, ours had everything we needed within walking distance of our apartment. Just next door to our building was a boutique specializing in clothes and shoes, but we did most of our shopping on Farah Street, the commercial boulevard. There was my favorite sandwich shop where Agha Jamsheed, the owner, would make fresh sandwiches on the blacktop grill. The sheep's brain sandwich was my favorite.

There was also a jeweler, a handful of restaurants, a mini-market, a shop that sold dried fruit and nuts, and a bakery making fresh Sangak bread. Once I grew older, Maman would often send me there to fetch a few for one of our meals.

Bread and rice are a must at every Iranian dinner table and are a staple of life. The Sangak bread is a flat bread cooked in an enormous traditional oven filled with rocks, where raw dough is laid directly over sweltering small river stones. Once cooked, a long hook is used to pull the baked bread out of the giant oven, which is then tossed onto a wire-mesh rack counter. That's where the few remaining hot river stones sticking to the bread were plucked off, usually by the patrons.

One time, I made the mistake of standing too close to the counter, which rose to the bottom of my chin, and when the bread was thrown from a distance by the baker, a few of the hot stones went flying into my collar and down my shirt, resulting in my chest and stomach receiving first-degree burns. I had big blistering welts on three separate spots. I was told to be careful the next time and not stand so close to the counter. Lesson learned.

I always ordered the more expensive Sangak topped with poppy and sesame seeds, usually with enough money left over to visit the mini-mart next door for a delicious candy or gum.

As much as I loved the fresh Sangak bread, the pastry shop was my favorite. As we rounded the corner, the irresistible, mouthwatering smell of freshly baked sweets filled the air. I followed my grandmother inside and marveled at the assortment of pastries on display in the tall, lit glass case, like watches and rings at a jewelry store. Freshly baked fruit tarts glowed brilliantly under the lights of the showcase and were glazed to perfection. Sweet bread, Nazook, almond and raisin cookies, Halva, chickpea cookies with pistachio and rose water, Zulbia Bamiyeh, Baklava, Qottab and so much more had me drooling like a starving puppy.

My favorite by far was Pirashki, a custard-filled sweet dough, fried to a golden crisp, then sprinkled with a boatload of powdered sugar. When served hot and fresh, it was to die for. This was the main reason I volunteered to accompany Mama Goli to the pastry shop—she always agreed to buy one for me. I would bite into it quickly, salivating and causing the hot custard filling to drip down my chin and sometimes onto my shirt. When we'd get home, Maman could always tell that I'd had a Pirashki from the obvious stains on my shirt and the fact that I looked like Al Pacino in *Scarface* with a face full of powdered sugar smeared all over my nose, mouth, chin, and hands.

Maman was a proud homemaker who relished shopping, cooking, and ensuring our home was constantly spotless. She was obsessive when it came to maintaining an orderly, hygienic home, and spent hours each day dusting, mopping, and vacuuming. She took her job as a homemaker seriously and proudly made our apartment shine before Baba came home from work every day.

She prepared all our meals from scratch and used the freshest ingredients found in Tehran. She cooked piping-hot, fresh dishes for dinner every night and made enough to have leftovers for lunch the following day. Most days, she took me along to gather the ingredients she needed for that night's supper. That meant stopping at several specialty stores—the butcher for fresh meat, the bakery for bread, and the produce market for veggies and fruit.

Often, I would complain and ask to go home (our forays were never as fun or rewarding as the ones with my grandmother), but my cries fell on deaf ears, as Maman had to buy every ingredient on her long shopping list. Most of the foods she cooked took long hours, sometimes even a day or two to prepare. It was the highly complicated art of Persian cuisine, which had been lovingly passed down to Maman from my grandmother, Mama Goli, and boy, were they both fantastic cooks!

The worst of it was when Maman took me to the Bazaar, which was like an all-day marathon event. It served as the city's central marketplace. It was vaulted or covered and stretched for more than a block, with both sides of the tightly packed alley lined with small shops and crowded stalls. Every vendor was an aggressive salesperson determined to sell his "deal of the day" to the thousands of customers passing through.

Maman loved to bargain with the seasoned merchants, and she was skilled at it. She'd listen as they quoted her a price, bat an eye, offer a displeased look, then ask for an additional discount. The negotiations went back and forth, my head on a swivel, switching from Maman to the vendor and back like I was watching a tennis match. She'd throw out a lowball offer, then threaten to walk out forcing the vendor to agree to her demand. She was a tough negotiator, and the satisfaction of getting a lower price for an item she desired was like winning some sort of game. She loved it so much; she'd repeat it at every store and stall we visited.

My father was an aspiring entrepreneur. When I was two, he left his job as a real estate agent to start his own food delivery business. It was 1975, and he had an idea for a residential grocery delivery service. He started with our neighborhood.

His marketing plan was simple—print up flyers that he could pass out around the neighborhood and hang on houses, businesses, and apartment doors. Soon the phone was ringing off the hook, and food orders were pouring in. Demand was so great he had to hire additional delivery drivers and purchased a fleet of trucks.

Being able to provide for his family was important to Baba, in part because he was eager to prove to my grandfather that he hadn't made a mistake when he'd reluctantly agreed to let him marry my mother.

Maman was fifteen years old when she met my father on the public bus one morning in 1969. She was on her way to school, and Baba was heading to his eldest brother's TV repair shop, where he worked as a delivery boy.

He first spotted her when she and her family moved into an apartment on the same block, just a few doors down from his building. But it would be weeks before the two found themselves traveling on the same bus and he finally mustered up the courage to introduce himself. They fell in love at first sight and began dating in secret, as couples who were not married or engaged were not permitted any form of courtship, wooing, or going out on dates. But Baba broke all the rules and took her out several times.

They arranged to meet at a spot far enough down the block not to be seen by any members of Maman's family, then took a taxi to a cafe for a meal or headed to the Moulin Rouge Cinema, the oldest theater in Tehran, to see a movie like *Love Story* or *The Poseidon Adventure*.

Of course, Maman never told my grandfather where she was really going. As far as he knew, she was out with her friends from school.

Not wanting my mother to get in trouble, Baba always respected her father's rules. He made sure they took a taxi wherever they went, and he always had her home before dark.

My parents kept their courtship a secret for three years until my mother turned eighteen and Baba found the bravery to go for "Khastegari," the first step in the traditional Iranian marriage process. "Khastegari," means suitor, lover, or wooer, the role of my father in this case.

For the aspiring groom, the first step was to identify a suitable bride, and it was customary to select a woman from the same cultural and economic background. Having chosen my mother, Baba was already on uneven footing.

Maman's family had a certain standing in the community because of Papa Jahan's job as a puzzle maker for Tehran's many newspapers. At twenty-one, my father had little to offer other than his everlasting love. He had completed high school, but he had not gone on to college. He had a job as a delivery boy, but this was not a profession. He didn't own his own apartment and was still living at home with his siblings.

To further complicate matters, it was expected that a potential groom be accompanied by his parents, or at least his father, when he made the ceremonial Khastegari visit. But both of Baba's parents were deceased, so he invited his eldest brother, Hafez, who was more like a parent than a sibling, to accompany him.

Hafez agreed and asked his then-wife, Sara, and their brother Ramin, who was the second eldest of the siblings, to come along.

Not surprisingly, the ceremony did not go as Baba had hoped, and he left Maman's house that night, heartbroken after hearing a resounding "No!" from Papa Jahan.

Unremarkably, the rejection did not deter him. As I would come to learn, my father had the mental strength and focus to achieve the impossible. Once he got an idea in his head, that was it. There was no way to divert him or convince him to pursue another option. He was a force to be reckoned with; that was apparent to anyone in his orbit. Perhaps that's why my grandfather finally agreed to his pleas to marry his daughter after unsuccessfully turning him away five more times. The two were married the following year in 1972, and I arrived a year later.

My father's strength lay in his tenacity. Throughout his life, he devoted all his efforts to providing the best for our family. Even when times became extraordinarily difficult, he pursued his goal and ultimately achieved the desired outcome. He taught me an important lesson about what could be done with patience and sustained effort. His undying resolve and focus are what would eventually save my life.

THREE
PENDAR

A few weeks after our trip to the movies, I celebrated my fourth birthday with a big party at our apartment with all our relatives and friends. My parents always went out of their way to make my birthdays special. There were lots of candles to blow out and a humongous pile of presents to open. But the best part of the festivities was the birthday cake that Maman special-ordered and customized with my name boldly written across the top in delicious buttercream icing.

Pendar was not a common name, and I often wondered why my parents had chosen it. No one in our family and none of my friends had that name.

On this special day, I decided to ask my father about it. "Baba, what does Pendar mean?"

Baba smiled. "It's a Persian word meaning thoughts or imagination," he said. "We chose it because we thought it was beautiful, unusual, unique, and different from all the other boys' names we were considering.

"If I was dubbing your name in a movie, I would translate it to 'ponder'," he added, looking at me lovingly.

Baba was forever referencing movies and movie terms to explain things. "There's even a popular Persian phrase 'pendare nik, goftare nik, kerdare nik', which means good thoughts, good words, good deeds,"he continued.

His explanation was meaningful, and I felt empowered by it. There was a multitude of boys named after the prophets in the holy book of

the Quran: Ali, Mohammad, Hamid, Hossein, or better-known traditional Persian names, but no one else was named Pendar. Now, hearing
Baba's justification, I took pride in my unusual name and its beautiful
translation.

In preparation for the evening's party, Maman needed to visit the
market, which meant that I was going along. Afterward, she insisted we
stop by her friend's house to drop off a gift. Her friend was not Muslim
like our family; she was Christian and celebrated a religious holiday
that fell on the same day as my birthday.

Back then, Iran was a secular society that accommodated followers
of many religions. Although most Iranians were Muslim, Baha'is,
Christians, Zoroastrians, Mandaeans and Jews all lived in comfort and
harmony and without fear of persecution.

The moment we arrived at the woman's house, Maman and her
friend became engrossed in gossip. Already bored, I scoped out the
place. Blinking lights drew my attention to the adjacent family room,
and I set off to investigate. There, next to the fireplace, stood a soaring,
green pine tree. It was so tall it was nearly scraping the ceiling. Shiny
objects and round multi-color spheres hung from its branches, which
were intertwined with strings of glowing green-red-and yellow-colored
lights. At the top, a sparkling star dazzled brightly.

It was magical.

Under the tree were several beautifully-wrapped gifts. *Was someone
celebrating a birthday, just like me?* I was fascinated and curious. *Why did
they have a tree inside the house?*

On the wall next to the tree was a framed picture of the Shah of
Iran, Mohammad Reza Pahlavi, dressed in his ritualistic monarch's
uniform. It was a typical sight in many homes, schools, businesses,
and government offices across Iran, a way of paying respect to our
king.

"Maman, why is there a tree in your friend's house? Why is it decorated like that?" I asked.

"That's a Christmas tree, Pendar. Christmas is a holiday celebrated
by Christians and the day Jesus Christ was born. Presents are opened on
the day of Christmas, which is the same day as your birthday," she
explained.

I felt special that Jesus and I shared the same birthday, which I later
learned was a holiday celebrated by millions around the world.

My grandparents, Papa Jahan and Mama Goli, were the first to arrive at my party that evening. They didn't have far to go, just down one flight of stairs!

For the next several hours, every time the doorbell rang, I jumped up to see who had arrived. My immediate family numbered more than fifty, and that wasn't even counting friends and acquaintances. Soon, our apartment was packed with revelers.

I had more than a dozen Amoos (uncles) alone, between my actual blood relatives and Baba's friends and colleagues, who were close enough to also earn the affectionate title of Amoo. I had too many Amoos, it was hard to keep track of them all.

Being surrounded by so many uncles, aunts, cousins, and close friends was comforting, soothing, and reassuring. My parents were always there for me, but family meant much more than just my mother and father. Spending time with relatives was simply a normal part of life for me. Most of the family lived close by, usually no more than a thirty-minute drive away, so it was easy to get everyone together.

My father, with a million watts of social charisma, was the introvert out of all his siblings. Like all Iranians, my parents loved to entertain; it is a cultural tradition embedded in all of us, and my mother and father were no different than anyone else in that respect. Generosity, warmth, and hospitality are customary, and Iranians often go to great lengths to outdo each other, all in the spirit of friendly competition.

Regular weekend gatherings featured lavish spreads of delectable and traditional Persian dishes, including Ghormeh Sabzi (herb and kidney bean stew), Gheimeh Bademjan (split pea stew with eggplant), Fesenjoon (pomegranate and walnut stew), always accompanied by huge mounds of white rice, a variety of appetizers, and desserts. Usually, there was enough food to feed a small army—even though, at times, only a handful of guests were invited to share the feast.

In Iran, Fridays were considered "the weekend," and we were often attending a party or holding one of our own. Hosts strove to present a variety of home-cooked foods, along with an array of other delicacies. It was normal for a family to spend many hours, sometimes even days, preparing their home for a gathering, not to be outdone.

People yearn to hear someone comment that one person or another really knew how to throw a party. That was a compliment of the utmost order and one that would elevate your social standing. All this was made more difficult by the fact that Iranians expected extravagant treatment from one another. It was as if it had been made part of their very DNA.

Of course, there was a negative side to this behavior, too. Guests could be ultra-critical of their hosts. Someone might shower praise on a host in public, then turn around and criticize them to others—perhaps complaining about how 'the food was too salty', or there wasn't enough, or the décor wasn't to their liking. There were just as many complaints as there were compliments, and my parents were guilty of it, too.

There was also the unspoken Iranian practice of PST. Typically, short for Pacific Standard Time, to most Iranians, PST stands for Persian Standard Time. To be fashionably late to any gathering was the norm, and everyone desperately avoided being the first guest to arrive at any party.

In summer, the family gatherings happened in Darya Kenar, the high-end coastal town in Northern Iran, where one of my father's brothers, Amoo Payam, owned a villa. My parents dreamt of one day buying property there, but for now, we enjoyed two weeks as guests of my uncle.

The seaside community was a four-hour drive from Tehran and located adjacent to the Caspian Sea. Sunbathing on the sandy shores or paddling out for a leisurely swim was only a ten-minute walk away.

Darya Kenar was the Hamptons of Iran, with its upscale homes, manicured lawns, lush vegetation, and a quaint village that stretched for one block and boasted a mix of restaurants, boutiques, a mini-mart and, of course, a bait and tackle shop. The community where my uncle lived was gated and patrolled 24 hours a day. There was even a residents-only sports center with billiards, ping pong tables, foosball tables, lighted tennis courts, a café, and an Olympic-size swimming pool with a high diving board. A tiny slice of heaven away from the bustling Tehran metropolis, I felt right at home. Even with the high humidity and foggy mornings, the well-trimmed bushes and immaculately groomed landscape portrayed a picture worthy of a postcard.

It was here at Seaside, as we all called it, that my love of swimming, boating, and fishing really took hold. Amoo Payam had a 20-foot pleasure boat, and he'd often take us out for daylong excursions. We didn't need a boat to go fishing. Amoo Payam's brother-in-law, Dayi Milad, taught me how to fish from the town's long pier, which stretched one-hundred feet into the sea. I didn't use a professional rod, just a simple hook and fishing line tied to the end of a long dried-up bamboo stick, which was easy to find in the heavy brush around the outskirts of the community.

I spent many hours casting my line and occasionally hooked a fish or two. Off the windy shores is where I also learned to fly cheap, plastic kites, the kind that normally lasted a day or two in the hands of a young boy, purchased with my allowance at the local mini-mart. On very windy days, the kite would break within the first hour, which meant I had to beg my cousin Roya, Amoo Hafez's eldest daughter, for money to buy another one.

Vacationing at Seaside was one of my favorite things, and I often wished time would stand still, and our two weeks would never end. The weather in summer was usually warm, with high humidity that cultivated a lush green landscape and an explosion of flowers—jasmine, lavender, and magnolias.

Our days were spent outdoors, either at the shore or splashing around in the community pool. Maman often took me to the pool in the afternoons, and while she hung out on a lounge chair, chatting with her friends, I plunged into the deep end of the chlorinated, turquoise water. She always wore a bikini and liked to sip on a refreshing beverage, mindfully watching me from the corner of her eye.

Boys and girls of all ages swam together, and we laughed, splashed, screamed, and enjoyed ourselves.

Some days, it was Baba who accompanied me for a swim. And it was on one of those afternoons that I found the courage to attempt a jump off the high dive. But first I had to obtain Baba's permission.

"Can I jump off the high dive, please?" I asked nervously.

"No Pendar, you're too young. It might be best for you to wait a couple of more years before trying it," he answered firmly.

Disappointed, I replied, "Okay, Baba, if you think that's best."

His response surprised me. "Well, don't give up so quickly. I only said no one time. Why don't you ask me again?"

"Baba, can I jump off the high dive, please?" I repeated, this time flashing puppy eyes at him. I was quite a little salesperson, using the subtle power of suggestion to exert my will over Baba, which wasn't all that difficult up until now.

"Nooooo, I don't think you're quite ready yet!"

Confused, I shrugged my shoulders in frustration. "I've changed my mind, Baba, I don't want to try it anymore," I said. "I'm going back to the pool."

As I turned to leave, Baba yelled after me. "Pendar, are you sure you don't want to jump off the high dive?"

I shook my head no and continued to walk away.

"Haven't you ever heard of *Ta se nashe, bazi nashe*? Third time's the charm?" he asked.

Exasperated, I yelled my request. "Baba, for the last time, can I please jump off the high dive?!"

Baba looked astonished. He stared at me for a few tense moments, then broke into a grin. "Only if I get to go up there with you," he proclaimed.

"Are you jumping with me, Baba?" I grew excited imagining the two of us standing together high above the pool.

"You go, we go!" Baba exclaimed. "If you're brave enough to jump, then I'm jumping in right after you. And remember, don't take no for an answer next time. Don't give up without a fight."

I followed Baba to the perilous metal stairs leading up to the high diving board. Climbing up was the easy part, although it took a little effort not to slip. Once at the platform, Baba reached for my hand and confidently led me to the front of the board. I was apprehensive and jittery, but my father reassured me, "There's nothing to it, Pendar. Don't be scared. Overcome your fear and jump!"

Standing twenty-five feet above the water, higher than I'd ever been, my toes securely hugged the frightening edge. I felt my heart pulsating and throbbing in my neck and my knees were shaking uncontrollably.

The surface of the water appeared quite distant from where I now stood. *What if I fall and hit the pool deck? Will I die instantly?* Feeling frightened, I turned toward the Caspian Sea and looked out to the edge of the horizon.

Baba leaned into my ear and whispered, "Everything's going to be alright, trust me!"

I trusted him with all my life. I didn't want to disappoint him, but I was petrified. An impatient queue of swimmers started to form behind us. This was my moment of truth, and I didn't want the decision to be made for me. I sensed Baba was itching to push me over the edge if I didn't find the courage to do it myself.

Although my family had never been religious, I nervously recited a silent prayer to the Almighty, asking him—no, begging him—not to take Baba away from my side. Then, I slowly let go of my father's hand and leaped. As I dropped toward the water, I imagined I had super-powers like Superman. But the surface came rushing toward me quicker than I expected, and I splashed into the cool water, entering butt-first.

The excitement at having taken the plunge was soon overshadowed by the pain I felt in my butt cheeks. It was as if a thousand bees had stung my behind! I quickly swam to the side and, as I climbed out of the water, I struggled to put on my bravest face. My butt was burning, and stinging, and had turned bright red from the impact.

Baba had jumped in a few seconds after me, just as he had promised, and urgently swam to my aid. He noticed my expression was not one of excitement or jubilance. "What's wrong, Pendar?"

I silently turned around and pointed to my butt.

Baba started chuckling, then making light of my discomfort, he encouraged me to jump again.

I wiped the tears streaming down my cheeks and bravely set off for the stairs, this time without Baba.

The second time was effortless, and I ended up jumping off the high dive repeatedly for the next couple of hours.

Baba stood on the cement pool deck and watched over me proudly, rays of sun reflecting off the water gently dancing onto his face.

I enjoyed our family gatherings at Seaside as much as our frequent get-togethers back home in Tehran. But my birthday celebrations remained my favorite. With so many attendees, all bearing gifts, I was unwrapping presents and playing with them for weeks to come. But the best part of the festivities was when Maman dimmed the lights, silenced the partygoers, and emerged from the kitchen carrying the vanilla sheet cake with the banana and strawberry filling alit with candles, and everyone gathered around to sing happy birthday, *"Tavalod, tavalod, talodet mobarak, mobarak, mobarak, tavalodet mobarak…"*

During those early years in Tehran, I was surrounded by family and spent time with my relatives every day. It was far, far different than here in the United States, where families tend to get together only to celebrate holidays, birthdays, and funerals.

I couldn't imagine life without my extended family. I always felt safe and protected knowing we were surrounded by loved ones. It was comforting, and sometimes even entertaining to interact with my relatives, so much so that I may have taken them for granted. Like most kids, I assumed this was the way life would always be.

Little did I know that one day everything would change, my world would be turned upside down, and I would no longer be enveloped by my large family or see many of them ever again.

FOUR
CHANGE IS AFOOT

On January 7, 1978, less than two weeks after I celebrated my fourth birthday, demonstrators took to the streets in the Shi'a holy city of Qom to protest an article published in Iran's oldest daily newspaper, *Ettela'at*, which was critical of a popular Iranian scholar by the name of Ruhollah Mousavi Khomeini.

Khomeini, a Shi'a Muslim religious leader known to the Western World as the Ayatollah Khomeini, had long been one of Shah Mohammad Reza Pahlavi's harshest and most vocal critics. His campaign of opposition dated back to the early days of the Shah's reign with the publication of a book that attacked both his and his father's attempts to westernize Iran.

Shah Mohammad was a secular Muslim who took the throne from his father, Reza Pahlavi, in 1941 when the Soviet Union and Great Britain invaded Iran. Their occupation was aimed at ensuring the safety of Allied supply lines to the USSR and securing the all-important Iranian oil fields.

With the occupation, Reza Shah was forced into exile and his eldest son, Mohammad Reza Pahlavi, better known as the Shah (King) of Iran, became the country's ruler at the age of twenty-one. In an age when so many monarchies had perished, the Shah was on the throne and Iran still adhered to constitutionalist traditions. With the oldest constitution in all of Asia, she remained a monarchy.

In 1943, just two years into the Shah's reign, the Tehran Conference, one of three World War II conferences of the "Big Three" Allied leaders (the Soviet Union, the United States and Great Britain) was held at the

Soviet Union's embassy in Tehran. The attendees were Britain Prime Minister Winston Churchill, Soviet Premier Joseph Stalin, and the President of the United States, Franklin D. Roosevelt, who were welcomed by the Shah.

The main objective of the meeting was to secure the Shah's commitment to open a second front against Nazi Germany in hopes of defeating Adolf Hitler. It was at this conference that the independence, sovereignty, and integrity of Iran was recognized by the allies in a solemn declaration.

Iran possessed natural riches that could help to develop the country, but the oil was exploited by the British, who were receiving the lion's share of the huge profits and who, for a long time, refused to grant a greater portion of those profits to the country from whose soil it was being extracted.

Five years after the Big Three Meeting in Tehran, the Shah traveled to London and attended the opening ceremony of the 1948 Summer Olympics, introducing Iran's presence on the international stage. But at home, support for his policies remained divided. Meanwhile, a group of nationalists, cleric, and non-communist left-wing parties, known as the National Front, began to coalesce under an Iranian lawyer named Mohammad Mosaddegh.

Mosaddegh was a politician and nationalist reformer who wanted to turn the country into a democracy and reduce Western influence, especially the exploitation of Iran's oil resources by the British and others. His growing popularity forced the Shah to appoint him prime minister in 1951. Mosaddegh gradually became the effective leader of Iran. However, during a power struggle with the Shah, he attempted to nationalize the Anglo Persian Oil Company or (APOC), which led to Britain and America conspiring to overthrow Mosaddegh and to reinstate the Shah.

On August 19, 1953, a coup d'état, orchestrated by the United States and the United Kingdom, overthrew Mosaddegh. The violent and bloody event returned the Shah to power, further strengthening his monarchical rule of the country.

After his overthrow, Mosaddegh was arrested, tried, and convicted of treason by the Shah's military court. On December 12, 1953, he was sentenced to three years in jail, then placed under house arrest, where he remained until his death in 1967.

After the coup, the Shah ruled the country as an absolute monarchy, but relied heavily on the United States and other foreign allies to retain his power. His authoritarianism appeared to stem from a belief that the harshness of his rule was necessary to change a backward country.

By 1955, the Shah's policies of independence and self-reliance required the know-how in modern equipment. The oil boom for the first time made it possible for Iran to make substantial investments abroad. He also took full advantage of his close relationship with the West and Iran's vast oil wealth to build up his armed forces and equip them with some of the latest Western weaponry.

Tanks were ordered and supplied by Britain, but the acquisition of the American F-14 Tomcat fighters demonstrated how close of an ally Washington was to Iran. Without a doubt, the F-14's were the premiere air force fighter jets at that time, not only in the Middle East, but around the world. This meant that Iran ruled the skies over the Middle East, with no other country in the region possessing an equivalent.

With help from the United States, the Shah established an intelligence service with police powers. Its goal was to strengthen his regime by placing political opponents under surveillance and repressing dissident movements. In 1957 the agency was eventually replaced by SAVAK, the Shah's own secret police, which grew over time to include more than 5,000 full time agents. Soon, rumors began to surface of torture being carried out by SAVAK on opponents of the Pahlavi regime.

In 1959, the Shah returned to Great Britain, this time for an official state visit during which he was greeted by Queen Elizabeth and joined her for an open carriage ride to Buckingham palace to the cheers of onlookers lining the streets. For the first time, the Shah was treated as an equal sovereign power.

That December, the Shah married for a third time. His new bride was twenty-one-year-old Farah Diba, and the fairytale royal wedding took place in Tehran and received world-wide attention, in part for its over-the-top opulence.

The King and Queen of Iran were frequently photographed in the company of some of the world's most influential people, often hosting parties of spectacular abundance. The beautiful and impeccably dressed Farah, the Shahbanou of Iran, was the first Empress ever to be crowned in history, our Queen. Her style and grace would earn her a nickname, with some in the media calling her the Jackie Kennedy of the Middle East.

In October of 1960, Queen Farah gave birth to a son, Crown Prince Reza, and the country rejoiced. The Shah's first two marriages had not produced an heir, necessary for royal succession, so the arrival of the Crown Prince was cause for celebration. The couple would go on to have three more children, a son and two daughters.

In 1963, the Shah introduced his "White (or Bloodless) Revolution," a six-point program of liberal reform that included infrastructure modernization, nationalization of the forests, land redistribution, voting rights for women, privatization of state-owned enterprises and a literacy campaign targeting Iran's large but isolated rural population. Queen Farah traveled widely within Iran to support her husband's social and economic reforms, which included the advancement of rights for women and children, and under the patronage of the Farah Pahlavi Foundation, she financially supported a network of museums, art centers and dozens of charities and worked tirelessly to champion Iranian culture and the arts. But her crowning achievement was Pahlavi University, the country's first American-style university, meant to improve the education of Iranian women.

But the royal couples' opulent lifestyle continued to draw negative attention. Oil was the basis of Iran's wealth, and many believed the Shah was robbing the country blind by laundering money to offshore accounts, mostly in the United States. Mohammad Reza Shah Pahlavi, the self-proclaimed king of kings or 'Shahanshah,' as he would coronate himself, lived extravagantly and flaunted his spending. This infuriated Iranians, many of whom were living in poverty. Many dubbed him "the puppet" or the "king who was manipulated," one who had made the mistake of not making most of the decisions. Instead, they were made by foreign counselors, especially the American counselors who had the fundamental role of planning things for the Shah.

His reforms were accepted by many secular Iranians but not embraced by all. Many Islamic clerics were outraged, arguing the liber-alization of women was against Islamic values. They were also concerned that the Shah's push for the development of secular courts and education would further erode their clerical power. This meant that much of the wealth was being stripped from regional Islamic religious leaders, who had ruled over generations. The program was to be used toward cultural and technological reforms, which many Iranians perceived as the Westernization of their culture. Opposition groups began to form, each with its own political or ideological agenda. Ruhollah Khomeini, a conservative cleric leader, emerged as the Shah's most outspoken critic.

Ayatollah Khomeini, a longtime opponent of secularism in govern-ment, insisted the reforms were aimed at bolstering future foreign inter-ests in Iran and would only serve to further erode its religious and cultural traditions. He believed that Iran should strive towards self-reliance and argued the Shah's White Revolution was being influenced by the White House. His criticisms were severe, uncompromising, and very public. Khomeini remained the Shah's strongest and most vocal critic. His attacks on the Shah and his support of western ideas, coupled with his staunch embrace of Islamic purity, earned him a huge following. He was bestowed the title of Grand Ayatollah, making him one of the supreme religious leaders of the country's Shi'a community, which was by far the largest religious group in Iran.

This gave Khomeini tremendous influence, and he issued a strongly-worded declaration from his home in Qom, the religious center of Shi'a learning, denouncing the Shah and his White Revolution. He followed this up with the publication of a manifesto that accused the Shah of being submissive to the United States and Israel and condemned the spread of moral corruption.

On June 5, 1963, Khomeini further angered the Shah with a warning he delivered during a speech at the historic Feyziyeh School: if the Shah did not change his ways, the day would come when the people of Iran would offer up thanks for his departure.

The Shah's response was swift and forceful. Two days after Khomeini's public denunciation, he traveled to Qom in an armored column where he delivered a speech harshly attacking the religious scholars, sparking protests, and leading to the arrest and imprisonment of Khomeini.

Fear of backlash from the clergy and for the fact that he was considered a holy man, Khomeini's life was spared from the execution squad. Instead, the Shah declared martial law to quell the unrest.

On November 4, 1964, Khomeini was exiled and secretly taken to Ankara, then Bursa, Turkey, before moving to the Shi'a holy city of Najaf, Iraq, the following September. But his expulsion did little to silence him. From Iraq, he started his own revolution, known as the Cassette Revolution. His phone calls into Iran were recorded on audio cassettes by his secret supporters, then duplicated and redistributed to mosques, schools, and large Islamic gatherings with a message of hatred for the Shah and his close, secret ties to Western governments, ensuring an increase in anti-American sentiments.

Khomeini was now the ultimate opposition to the monarchy and his popularity continued to grow. To his critics, the Shah appeared more concerned with cultivating an extravagant lifestyle than running the country.

In October 1971, Iran celebrated its 2500th anniversary, making it the oldest monarchy in the world with the youngest dynasty, the Pahlavi family. To mark the occasion and honor his own glory, he hosted "the most expensive party ever," a $200 million three-day event held amidst the ruins of Persepolis and attended by sheiks, emperors, kings, and presidents from around the world. Interior designers, architects and couturiers were flown in from France to create a luxurious tent city with guest accommodations and a huge banquet hall. The Shah flew in eighteen tons of food from abroad and treated his guests to Iranian caviar and bottles of 1945 Chateau Rothschild. No expense was spared in his quest to show the world the new face of the ancient empire, a more civilized Iran, a wealthy oil state, and not a provincial country run by Mullahs. But many Iranians disapproved of what Ayatollah Khomeini publicly referred to as the "Devil's Feast."

For a time, it seemed the Shah's reforms were working. The country was modernizing its infrastructure and Iranians were experiencing economic success. But the benefits were not equally distributed, with mostly the country's elite and those groups closely tied to the Shah appearing to be prospering, sowing further discontent. Oil revenues were high but other sectors of the economy were not experiencing the same growth. By the early 1970s, inflation set in. Opposition to the Shah and his policies grew to include conservatives, moderates, landowners, merchants, and the pro-Soviet Tudeh (Masses) Party.

Although still in exile, and within the safety of his refuge abroad, Khomeini was now calling for the overthrow of the Shah, emphasizing his close ties to the West to further alienate him from the people of Iran. Somehow, he managed to rally many of the opposition groups together, despite their vastly different grievances and agendas.

No one would have guessed that the religious scholars would have the ability to overthrow such a powerful government. Iran had been under the rule of the monarchy for 2,500 years. But the dynasty was destined to fall.

During the last ten years of his reign, the Shah thought he had bought security through his weapons and military. But neither the Shah nor his Western allies could have anticipated this immense force, which was older than the Shah himself. This was the power of the Church of Mohammad. Since there were millions of Iranians, who in one way or another were repressed by the regime, they found the only vehicle for this expression was the mosque. And against the mosque, the Shah, in essence, was powerless. It was the Achilles heel of the monarchy. The one body, the one faith, the one power against which the Shah could not maintain his rule.

But not everyone was calling for an Islamic state. In fact, most of the protestors were hoping that with the monarchy gone, a secular government would be formed. They wanted the Shah deposed and the monarchy replaced with a more democratic state, with the power returned to the people.

In response to the protests, repression by the Shah's regime increased and stories of brutality and torture at the hands of the Shah's secret police began to circulate.

By 1978, the Shah had already made several state visits to America, meeting with every president from Roosevelt to Carter. President Carter called Iran "an island of stability" under the leadership of the Shah. But his grip on power continued to wane.

Pockets of protests broke out in small cities across Iran, movie theaters became the main targets. Political unrest continued into the spring and at least four people died in those attacks and many more were injured.

Watching TV one day, the programming stopped broadcasting my kid-friendly shows and began showing images of protests and demonstrations. A single tragic event proved to be the tipping point or as they say, "the straw that broke the camel's back." It was August 19, 1978, and four terrorists in the port city of Abadan locked the doors to the Rex Cinema with 700 moviegoers inside and set the theater ablaze, killing approximately 400 innocent people.

Mothers, fathers, children, and grandmothers had been peacefully watching a movie called *Deer*, starring the most famous male Iranian actor at the time, Behrouz Vossoughi, when the theater went up in flames. It was one of the worst disasters of its kind in history, and until 9/11, the greatest terrorist attack in modern times—and one that most people know nothing about.

Iran's official news agency blamed the attack on "unidentified protestors" and saboteurs" and radio reports coming out of Abadan claimed that several suspects had been arrested. There was speculation, but no one knew for sure, and no group or individual came forward to claim responsibility.

I was too young to understand the magnitude of what was happening. Cinema owners in Tehran and several provincial neighborhoods closed their doors in protest. The horrific event marked the beginning of the end, provoking thousands of Iranians to march through the streets in all major cities across Iran. Citizens no longer supported the Shah of Iran and desperately demanded change.

Increasingly desperate, the Shah declared martial law in Iran on September 8, 1978, better known as Black Friday. That day, the military forces clashed with protesters and were soon committing atrocities leaving 64 protesters dead, along with another 30 government security forces. The deaths could be described as the pivotal event in the Iranian revolution that ended any hope of compromise between the protest movement and the regime. This helped to radicalize the movement and it vilified the Shah's regime. The government's violent attempt to squash the uprising only drew in more supporters.

In a desperate attempt to silence his most outspoken critic, the Shah convinced the vice president of Iraq and de facto leader at that time, the infamous Saddam Hussein, to deport and expel Khomeini from his country. The Shah believed that Khomeini's expulsion from Iraq would silence his nemesis, but he was gravely mistaken.

Khomeini continued to agitate the Iranian ruler even after being exiled to Paris, France. His expulsion from Iraq had only fueled the fire further, with Khomeini now determined to overthrow the powerful monarch. Encouraging the protests and igniting the fuel for a revolution that seemed inevitable was the only way nationalists could reassert any authority over Iran.

The protests grew ever more intense with the crowds no longer chanting, "the Shah must go", but "death to the Shah" becoming a common rallying cry in the streets of Tehran.

Things continued to go downhill. Time was running out for the Shah, his downfall seemed inevitable, especially when he witnessed on the news, portraits of the royal family being burned in many bonfires raging across Iran. He was deeply disturbed by the images and devastated to witness the intense hatred of the regime by the people. Almost every section in society was united in opposition to his reign and saw him as America's king, not their own.

Such a revolution by the people had never occurred before in our country's history, but the Islamic Revolution would take Iran along a new path. Even the clerics themselves, most of whom had been imprisoned with other political opponents, would have never believed that they would ultimately become the powers behind the throne, the leaders of the country, the rulers of Iran.

Like many Iranians, Baba thought this would be best for our country. With the encouragement of friends and family, Baba decided to join one of the protests at their insistence. It was as if he was innocently watching the storm overtaking the city, curiously unable to avoid being directly in its path of destruction.

In retrospect, maybe he had gotten too close, because the ferocity of the tornado unwillingly sucked him into the eye of the storm. He eventually succumbed to the overpowering forces, it all happened very fast and in a blink of an eye, he found himself feasting at what had become a feeding frenzy called 'revolution'.

A few months into intense and continuous protests, my family decided to take to the streets and support the opposition. Baba wanted to drive out to where the protestors were marching, to watch this historic event unfold. I was excited. I got to ride in Baba's car, joining my compatriots and yearning to be a part of the change that was overtaking our country. It was a time of change, a time of upheaval.

We reached a street that was closed off and couldn't proceed any farther. Before long, I heard a loud rumble in the near distance, edging closer and closer. The earth trembled as a massive wall of people slowly crept toward us; it looked frightening from my point of view.

The booming sound of the crowd was impressive, Baba's car engulfed with protestors who surrounded us, passing through the street where we had stopped. I was enthralled by what I was witnessing. The screams of hatred toward America and the Shah were passionate, compelling me to accompany the crowd and join the protest.

"Baba, can I join them?" I asked.

Baba nodded his head, "Yes, but only from the car, son."

He didn't allow me to exit the vehicle, which would've been like stepping out in front of a pack of stampeding wildebeests. Instead, I rolled down the back window, sat on the frame, stuck my torso out, and started mimicking the protestors.

Maman held my legs tightly, making sure I didn't slip out.

"MARG BAR AMERICA! MARG BAR SHAH!" ("DEATH TO AMERICA! DEATH TO THE SHAH!") I yelled along with the swarm of people chanting repeatedly. The crowd was carrying homemade signs, large banners, and even started lighting the American flag on fire. I didn't comprehend the commotion and only wished to support my fellow Iranians.

My family chuckled and got a kick out of my stunt.

I thought everyone had to respect the King, but now they were burning his portrait in the bonfires.

By the end of 1978, protests and demonstrations had spread across all of Iran, and an ever-growing tide of revolution was on the horizon. Government employees, factory workers, people from all walks of life and the contrasting classes came together with no demands other than liberty. Black-veiled women carrying Khomeini's pictures and seas of working-class men filled the streets. The shopkeepers from the bazaar, and eventually the westernized middle and upper-class, people like my parents who'd begun to think that this would be a positive shift of tides.

In January 1979, Iran was in complete turmoil, and after decades of royal rule, millions of Iranians took to the streets to let their voices be heard against a regime that was seen as brutal, corrupt, and illegitimate. Demanding democracy, none of the protestors, including my parents, went on strike for an Islamic revolution, Islamic rule, or Islamic government; they all wanted a secular government.

With the streets ablaze, weakened by his cancer which had been kept a secret, and his rule in tatters, the Shah fled Iran in tears, accompanied by the royal family, never to return. Two and a half thousand years of Persian monarchy had come to an end.

Within hours of the Shah's departure, all signs of the Pahlavi dynasty were destroyed, royal public statues were toppled, and street signs bearing the royal family's name were torn down and eventually renamed.

Shapour Bakhtiar, who was Iran's prime minister at the time, ordered SAVAK dissolved and freed all the political prisoners. The reign of the Shah was completely over, and a new era was about to begin. The stage was set for Khomeini's triumphant return, perceived as a ready-made leader in the public eye. Two weeks after the Shah fled, Khomeini and his entourage were on a flight from Paris bound for Tehran's Mehrabad International Airport.

On February 1, 1979, Khomeini's plane touched down, and after fourteen years in exile, he was welcomed by several million Iranians, an event that was televised and written about for weeks to follow.

I was young and didn't understand the concept of revolution. I didn't fathom the new leadership – too naïve to recognize the changes that would soon transform our country.

For the old Shah's guard, who were now seen as enemies of the Revolution, retribution was swift and often brutal. Many were imprisoned, some were executed, and others were forced into exile. Many of the Shah's hardcore supporters believed it was time to leave the country and voluntarily packed up, emigrating to Europe, or America. Terrified of retribution, some families fled the country illegally through the Turkish border on horseback or hiked for hours through the mountains to escape from their own country. Often leaving behind their businesses, land, vehicles, and any valuable assets or personal belongings.

Soon a revolutionary court was assembled, as well as a revolutionary council that wrote the laws and delivered the Islamic rulings.

Revolutionary forces under the Grand Ayatollah Khomeini had forced the Shah of Iran into exile, his government overthrown and replaced by a new Islamic order.

On March 8, 1979, an event planned to mark International Women's Day turned into a massive protest with thousands of women taking to the streets of Tehran to voice their discontent with the new Islamic Republic's policies toward women. Many had joined the revolution to oust the Shah, fighting alongside the religious forces that were now seeking to take away many of their freedoms and rights.

My cousin Roya, Amoo Hafez's eldest daughter, was a teenager at the time and, like many of her female classmates, was not in favor of the newly-imposed dress code for women and girls. When she learned of the protests, she and several of her friends decided to join in. They met after class and walked together to the area of the city where the marches were taking place.

She was surprised when members of the military armed with batons and whips showed up in force to quell the demonstrations. There were also counter-protesters, supporters of the new Islamic Republic, armed with knives, stones, brick and broken glass and women in chador shouting obscenities at the demonstrators.

At first, police and military issued warnings, instructing protestors to disperse and return to their homes. But as the hours passed and the crowds continued to grow, there were beatings and arrests of both women and girls. To shield the demonstrators from police, male supporters formed human chains on both sides of the women.

At one point, Roya and her friends found themselves amidst the hundreds of uniform-clad officers wielding batons. One of the girls managed to push my cousin out of the way just in time only to be struck in the head and knocked to the ground. When Roya witnessed the violent backlash, she and the other adolescent girls gathered up their injured friend and went running back to their homes in fright and panic.

The protests continued for six straight days and resulted in a temporary withdrawal of the government's declaration of mandatory veiling. But it would soon be reinstated, followed by the introduction of an Islamic Punishment Law that authorized corporal punishment for those who failed to comply.

The new edicts were particularly difficult for westernized women like my mother. Both she and my father had grown up under the Shah, with a more relaxed government when it came to matters of dress code and observing Islamic rules. They, like many who had joined the Revolution, had believed that deposing the Shah would clear the way for a secular government that would be officially neutral in matters of religion.

My mother, who was twenty-five at the time, was unaccustomed to veiling in public, having only worn a hijab to religious ceremonies and funerals.

With the Shah's former supporters out of the way, and the military having declared itself neutral, on April 1, 1979, the newly appointed government approved a referendum to transform into the Islamic Republic of Iran.

Khomeini's new Islamic Republic manifested not only his own deep rooted religious beliefs, but a lineage that dates back to the 19th century when religious authority dominated over secular power. His belief was that the power lay with the clergy, and at its head was the Supreme Leader, in this case Khomeini himself, who supposedly was chosen by God.

Following the victory of the Islamic Revolution, leaders of Khomeini's Revolutionary Movement formed the "Komiteh" or "Revolutionary Committees" to take the place of governmental institutions such as social services, security, and police. The Komiteh was also responsible for eliminating counter-revolutionary elements within the country, and soon it was feared much like the Shah's secret police. There were rumors of atrocities committed against the men and women who did not adhere to the new Islamic rules and regulations. Some punishments were meted out in plain sight, with those deemed sympathetic to the Shah subjected to torture, beatings, or even execution.

FIVE
A NEW RULE

n the spring of 1979, the Islamic Republic of Iran, with the Grand Ayatollah Khomeini as its Supreme Leader, issued many orders and rules of governance for all citizens to follow. Females above the age of twelve were now required to wear a *hijab* (headscarf) to cover their hair in public and a *chador* or *manto* (a full-body scarf) meant to hide the shape of the female figure.

Now, many of the rights women had become accustomed to under the Shah were being severely curtailed. In addition to veiling, women were no longer allowed to wear makeup or apply any colored nail polish. They were also not allowed to be accompanied in public by a member of the opposite sex, except for family members.

Public displays of affection such as kissing, hugging, holding hands, or putting your arm on your wife's shoulder or waist were now considered inappropriate and illegal. Alcohol, cigarettes, music, and dancing in public were prohibited for all citizens, both men and women.

Men could no longer wear shorts or short-sleeve shirts in public and were prohibited from starting a conversation or mingling with a strange woman. Furthermore, schools, colleges, public parks, and swimming areas were to enforce total separation of the sexes. For pools, beaches, and other combined activities, there were now two separate shifts; men and boys attended in the mornings; women and girls in the afternoons.

For weddings, birthday parties, and other large gatherings, men and women needed to be completely separated. Banquet halls and event centers were directed to install a curtain or wall to separate the sexes. The list went on and on.

For me, there was an upside. Mandatory hijab meant Maman no longer took forever to get dolled up to leave the house in the mornings. No more blow drying her hair, no more sifting through different outfits or being concerned that they didn't match, and no more 'beauty queen' makeup regiments. All she had to do was put on the *manto* over her pajamas, then cover her hair with the Hijab, and we could be out the door in seconds. The downside was that now Maman had more time to spend haggling with the vendors at the bazaar.

What I innocently didn't realize was that with the new laws, Maman no longer had the freedom to express herself through her ever-changing wardrobe and the carefully applied makeup she was accustomed to wearing. It was unusual for her not to blow dry her hair into the newest fashionable style or inspect her flawless attire before leaving the house. She no longer wore makeup or polished her nails. It was a sad turn of events for me to witness.

One evening, after a long day of shopping, she and I returned to the apartment where Baba was awaiting our arrival, but Maman was in a foul mood.

Sensing her despair, Baba greeted her with a devilish wink. "*Salam Ziba Jan, chetori azizam,* how are you?" he asked. "I hope you're not tired from shopping all day, are you? That's your favorite thing to do."

Aggravated and exhausted, Maman snapped back at him, "It's not the shopping I'm tired of Nader, it's this ridiculous uniform I'm forced to wear all day. I miss putting on different outfits and wearing makeup, and I miss our old way of life."

Maman's tone was filled with sadness. "I still have my old clothes," she continued, "I don't have the heart to get rid of them. I'm just hoping that one day things will return to the way they were before the Revolution."

I looked to my father, hoping he could brighten her disposition. "I miss it too, Ziba. Don't be upset, honey. I love you, and everything will be alright."

My father had comforted her, but I was saddened when I noticed a tear running down her cheek. She was clearly not happy about the new dress code. It was a somber moment, and for the first time, the consequences of the new policies were apparent, even to me.

That fall, amid all the changes, I started kindergarten. My school was a fifteen-minute drive from our apartment, and I looked forward to going each morning. I couldn't wait to play with my schoolmates and to see my teacher. She was young and pretty, with light eyes, and a kind, gentle manner, and I had a crush on her.

I'd been attending kindergarten for about two months when our country underwent another crisis. It was November 4, 1979. I had just arrived home from school and after grabbing a quick snack from the kitchen, I had disappeared to my room to play.

Maman was in the living room watching television, I could hear it from my room. The news started at the top of the hour, that's when she turned up the volume.

NEWS REPORTER ON TV: "Today, a group of militarized Iranian college students broke into the American embassy in Tehran and took over, seizing up to sixty hostages. Most of whom are American diplomats and citizens who have been taken against their will and now detained."

I heard Maman gasp, and I ran into the living room to see what had happened. Images flashed on the television screen, Americans in blindfolds with their hands cuffed behind their backs were being paraded before the cameras, their captivity proudly displayed for the rest of the country and world to see. This was the crisis that would provide the catalyst for decades of unresolved hostility between the two countries. I didn't know what it all meant, but from my mother's reaction, I sensed something was terribly wrong.

Baba already knew about the Americans who had been kidnapped by student activists when he arrived home from work that night. "This is a disaster," I overheard him telling Maman.

For many Westerners, the Islamic Revolution conjures up images of the hostages, an event above all else. But the events leading up to the taking of the hostages at the embassy are more obscure.

Upon leaving Iran aboard his royal jet on January 17, 1979, the Shah sought refuge in several countries, first Iraq and then Rome. But in October 1979, he was flown to America to receive cancer treatment at a hospital in New York City.

The visit was publicized and provoked an uproar in Iran, setting in motion a chain of events that would continue to reverberate four decades later. His prolonged stay in America for chemotherapy was interpreted by Iranians to be part of an American plot to reinstate him as their ruler. Described by Khomeini as the "Second Revolution," the taking of the hostages would transform the Islamic Revolution from an overthrow of a tyrant to something of worldwide significance—the storming of the U.S. Embassy in Tehran by student followers of Ayatollah Khomeini.

Everyone expected that negotiations would last three to five days, culminating in the release and safe return of the hostages. But Khomeini seized the opportunity to aggravate America. He saw a chance to humiliate them, a way to get the upper hand, a victory by Iran over

America. Nobody could have predicted the crisis would last 444 days, with the hostages finally released on January 20, 1981. But not before a failed rescue attempt conducted by the U.S. military resulted in the deaths of eight American servicemen and one civilian.

The event fatally damaged Iran's reputation abroad, but at home, Grand Ayatollah Khomeini, the supreme leader, grew more powerful and popular than ever. The Islamic Republic of Iran was firmly established, and the two nations previously so close, would become the archest of enemies.

The impact of the Revolution has been enormous on an international scale and transformed the Middle East region by removing a key ally to the United States. But it came at a high cost in limiting personal freedoms at home and in making powerful enemies abroad, none more so than the U.S.A.

This hostage-taking or second revolution was viewed as bigger than the first, and the world watched as the most important embassy in the whole of the Middle East fell under siege. In hindsight, this was one of the costliest decisions ever made by any government, one that has had long-lasting effects on Iran's economy and politics.

Iran's reputation was forever discolored by this crisis. Sadly, the sentiment of Iran being a country of hostage-takers exists even today. It's unfair to the people of Iran to be tagged as the supporters of terrorist organizations or hostage takers, as all of that was the government's doing.

Still, our world was turned upside down, and within a few short years, Khomeini's radical views would become official policy.

Baba took it hard. He knew from this point on the relationship between Iran and the United States, a country he had come to know and love through the movies, would never be the same. I was too young to understand what was happening around me, yet I felt helpless and disturbed by it all. *Perhaps I was sensing my parents' reaction to what was taking place.*

Not long after the Ayatollah took power, my father suffered a second blow. He was informed that he could no longer continue servicing the hospitals and commercial accounts he had painstakingly cultivated. The new regime was terminating the existing general managers and bringing in their own crew, consisting of unscrupulous characters, most of whom answered to the new government.

Baba was making a good living with his food delivery business, but now he would have to look for new work. Ever resourceful, he hit upon an idea. With foreign films no longer allowed to be shown in theaters, he believed there would be great demand for home videos. Soon, he set about learning the requirements and how to secure permission on importing and distributing foreign films.

In 1979, the new Islamic Republic formed the Ministry of Culture and Islamic Guidance, or CIG, better known as the "Ershad Ministry." Its role was to review, censor, and approve all foreign and domestic movies before they were allowed to be shown publicly. They also regulated television films, audio recordings, cassette tapes, and even books. Censorship was for nudity, kissing, sexual content, and any other subject matter deemed inappropriate by the Ershad Ministry which had to be censored before being approved for general consumption. That meant that a scene as innocent as Rocky Balboa and Adrian's first kiss in the 1976 film *Rocky* would end up on the cutting room floor.

Many Iranians viewed this censorship as an infringement on their freedom, but Baba saw an opportunity. His plan was to import mostly American films with the approval of the Ministry, dub them into Farsi, reproduce, and then distribute them across Iran. It was an exciting proposition that combined his passion for movies and his need to start a new business to support his family.

Everyone in the family knew of my father's love of movies. But I had no idea just how much until I heard my uncle, my father's eldest brother, Amoo Hafez, joke about it one afternoon.

Hafez was twenty years older than Baba and was already working outside of the house, operating his own TV repair shop when their mother died, and Hafez stepped in to fill the void. Every week, he would give my father, who was twelve at the time, a small allowance, which he used to buy the newspaper, not so much for the content, but for the crossword puzzles, all of which contained a theme. The movie-themed puzzles were the ones that interested him the most, and through which he learned all about the classic actors, the titles of movies, and American cinema.

When he was fourteen, something magical happened. *Dr. No*, a British spy movie, premiered in Tehran. Not only was it a hit across the country, but the entire world was introduced to the suave, secret agent with a license to kill—007, a.k.a. James Bond.

Excited, Baba and his best friend Kiya decided to make it their first-ever movie experience. The two boys attended the same junior high school, lived in the same neighborhood and both had 8 p.m. curfews, with a 15-minute grace period. That meant they needed to get tickets for the 6 p.m. show to make it home in time.

The line was exceptionally long, and they waited for hours before finally making it to the box office. But just as it was their turn, the metal screen on the window slammed shut—the 6 p.m. showing was sold-out!

Disappointed, they prepared to leave but turned back when they heard an announcement that tickets were now available for the 8 p.m. showing.

Not wanting to miss curfew, Kiya told Baba it was time to go. "C'mon, we'll see the movie another time."

"No way! I'm not leaving!" my father snapped back. "We've stood in line for too long just to give up. Let's stay and watch the 8 o'clock show, what do you say?"

Kiya grew concerned. "Don't you know what our fathers are going to do to us if we get home that late?"

"Whatever it is, Kiya, it will be well worth it. I've been dying to see this movie."

"No, Nader, let's go please!" Kiya begged some more.

"Look behind you," Baba said, pointing to the line of moviegoers that stretched around the block. "We're already at the front, and I'm staying. C'mon, stay and see the movie with me." Baba teased some more. He was too close to the front of the line and the desire to see *Dr. No* overpowered his common sense. He knew the consequences of this mischievous behavior, but he convinced his friend to stay.

After the film, they left the theater on a movie high, thinking not only about James Bond and his high-tech gadgets but Ursula Anderson emerging from the ocean in her two-piece white bikini. They ran all the way home, making only a few short stops to catch their breath. It was 10:15 p.m., two hours past curfew, when Kiya walked Baba to his front door, as he always did, and waited while he knocked.

When his father opened the door, his hand was already raised high in the air and came crashing across Baba's face with such ferocity that it knocked him to the ground. Kiya stood frozen in horror. Thankfully, Grandpa's new wife got involved before Baba took another strike. By then, Kiya was halfway home, terrified that the same fate was awaiting him.

After seeing *Dr. No*, my father was hooked. As soon as Amoo Hafez gave him his weekly allowance, he was out the door en route to the cinema. His passion and love of movies ran so deep that he opted to walk instead of taking the bus, and even bypassed the concession stand to save more money, so he would have enough to see two movies instead of one.

Now, my father was about to turn his longtime passion into a business that he hoped would be profitable. He was one of the first to apply to the Ershad Ministry for a license to import films, and he was ecstatic when he was granted permission. He quickly sold the trucks he had purchased for his grocery delivery business and used the proceeds to buy the equipment he would need for his video production company.

The newest technology at that time was the VCR and the recordable VHS tapes, and with the sale of the trucks, he had enough money for a handful of VCR machines and several hundred boxes of tapes.

In early 1980, he proudly opened his dream video business. To his delight, his new venture took off like a rocket vanishing from the earth's atmosphere. Within a short period, he hired over twenty employees and rented an additional floor in the building where he had started his company to house all the VCRs. There must have been over fifty of them, stacked on shelves lined up against every wall.

Once a film had received approval from the Ershad Ministry, Baba tasked his employees with making the duplicates for distribution. That entailed inserting the approved movie into a Master VCR that was hooked up to all the others. Once the "Play" button was pressed on the master VCR, employees had thirty seconds to push the record buttons on the other fifty VCRs to ensure the copies captured the production in its entirety. Like the ringing of a cash register, the exercise was repeated throughout the day to ensure there were plenty of movies ready for sale. It wasn't long before Baba's business was doing so well that he achieved one of his lifelong dreams—owning property at Seaside.

SIX
SEASIDE

We celebrated the summer of 1980 in our very own villa at Seaside. Baba purchased a three-bedroom model with a big yard in the same gated community as my uncle.

The air around our villa smelled like a pleasant mix of wet grass and the flowery scent of magnolias, roses, and jasmine blooming in the garden. Butterflies fluttered their colorful wings, and dragonflies floated in the air like mini helicopters. A profusion of brightly-colored chrysanthemums was neatly planted along the fence leading up to the front gate. And an overgrown lavender-colored bougainvillea glabra or 'paper flower'—Maman's favorite—covered the gate and entrance to our villa.

The sunsets were a magnificent sight to behold. In the cool evenings, distant rays of the sun turned the horizon into a swirling palette of pink, purple, orange, and blue. At night, a large moon hung over the Caspian Sea, while its ashy rays illuminated the tranquil community.

It felt good to be away from all the turmoil happening on the streets of Tehran. Seaside was beautiful as always, and more importantly, it was peaceful.

New hours permitted for swimming at the Seaside community pool and beaches varied considerably. Men and boys swam in the mornings, followed by the women and girls in the afternoon. In the early afternoon, the swimming area was shut down completely—men, boys, the lifeguard, and staff had to exit. Once it was verified that there were no men left at the facility, the female lifeguard, staff, and patrons would then enter.

Baba took me for my first swim after segregation. It was fun, but I missed being accompanied by all my female family members. Heck! I even missed the girls whom I didn't know, who would normally be swimming alongside me.

Family swimming at the beach was no longer allowed. Curtains had been installed at the beaches, and they stretched into the sea for one hundred feet on strong steel rods. A wheel on the end raised and lowered them. Men were permitted to swim in the mornings, but once the women's hours of operation began, the curtains were unrolled to ensure no Peeping Toms could peek at them in their swimwear.

On weekends, the pool was bustling with families out for a day of splashing in the surf and playing in the sun. Weekdays were quieter. With many returning to the city for work, we had the place all to ourselves. But we had to be out of the area at the appointed time when the facilities were available to women and girls.

One day, instead of exiting the pool area when we were supposed to, my cousin Shahin, Amoo Hafez's son and one of my frequent play-mates, and I decided to hang around and spy on the girls. When no one was watching, we tiptoed to an area of the fence surrounding the pool that was hidden by palm trees and foliage. Shahin was a few years older than me and was very mischievous, often getting into trouble. He was not the best role model, but being my older cousin, I looked up to him.

Not wanting to be spotted, we crouched behind some brush and silently watched as the pool started to fill up with women and girls. It was stimulating but felt wrong at the same time. Up until this summer, I had been allowed to swim alongside the girls we were now spying on! That it was now illegal, and taboo was difficult to fathom.

Our first day as Peeping Toms was so successful, we decided to do it again the following afternoon. We assumed our positions behind the fence and surveyed the action. We had been there only a short time when one of the young swimmers spotted us and ran to report our pres-ence to the female security guard charged with enforcing the new rules. Fearful, we hot-footed it back to the villa. It was a close call, but we made it home undetected. The following day, we returned to the pool to find that the fence had been covered with nettings and large tarps, effec-tively putting an end to our spying days.

No longer able to pal around with my female cousins outside the villa, I found myself spending a lot more time with Shahin, and my father's youngest brother, Sasan. He was technically Baba's half-sibling, one of two kids born to his father and his second wife. Ironically, he was closer in age to me than he was to my father. Baba was already seven-teen when Sasan was born, and I arrived six years later. He felt more like a cousin than an uncle. Still, out of respect, I addressed him as "Amoo" or "uncle."

Despite the age gap, he and Shahin, who was one year younger than Sasan, let me hang out with them, often playing ping pong and billiards at the sports center with the rest of the kids. One afternoon, I learned that some of my female family members were going to the community pool for a swim. I missed swimming with them and begged them to come along. At first, my Aunt Tara refused. But unwilling to take no for an answer, I pressed her until she finally relented. I was like my father in that way, I didn't stop until I got the answer I wanted.

It took lots of begging, but eventually, my cousin Roya handed me a girl's one-piece bathing suit and ordered me to wear it. That was the only way I would be permitted to tag along, and to the surprise of my aunt and cousins, I complied.

I wore a huge smirk as I accompanied them to the swimming pool that afternoon, part defiance, part embarrassment. On the way out, I threw a devilish wink at Shahin and Sasan, who were in the living room watching television and looked on with envy. It was amusing but also nerve-racking. There would be consequences if I were caught by the lifeguard or one of the security guards. My aunt instructed me to dive directly into the water without lingering and not to communicate with any of the girls outside our family.

Once in the pool, I was not permitted to exit the water, nor was I allowed to jump from the high diving board. I didn't mind. I was happy to be with them and spent the rest of the afternoon happily swimming and splashing around with my aunt and cousins. The sun was so strong I could feel it stinging the back of my neck like a hot iron.

Inhaling a deep breath, I submerged and swam toward the opposite end of the pool. The water felt cool and refreshing against my skin, although I went unnoticed by the group of young girls huddled together near the deep end. Eager for some attention, I lurked toward them under water, pretending I was Jaws. I gurgled "dun-dun, dun-dun" from the soundtrack as I swam closer. When I was upon them, I burst out of the water, disappointed by their startled, yet annoyed reaction. One of them shot me a nasty glare.

"Hey, little girl, what's your name?" she teased.

Without thinking, I inadvertently blurted out, "Pendar!"

"That's not a girl's name!" she retorted, drawing the attention of the others. "How'd you get in here?" she demanded.

Realizing I'd made a mistake, I immediately submerged and swam away as fast as my little arms would take me, terrified of being caught. Thankfully, the girls didn't react, scream, or make a scene, but one calmly exited the pool, headed directly for her mother, and began to whisper in her ear while pointing in my direction.

Convinced I had been found out, I plunged under the water and swam clear across the pool to where my cousins were sunbathing on lounge chairs. Barely coming up for air, I was out of breath by the time I reached them, but I knew I had to alert them to the unfolding drama. They swiftly gathered our belongings, and we hastened toward the exit.

On the way out, I observed the girl's mother speaking to the lifeguard and began to panic when I realized she was pointing me out to her. My heart raced as I trailed my aunt and cousins to the parking lot, where we quickly climbed into the car and sped away.

My fear quickly gave way to sadness as I began to understand what I had lost. Just one year earlier, we were blissfully swimming together in this same pool. Now activities like this could result in disciplinary action.

That night, Maman, and the rest of the women took a break from cooking. That's when Baba became the "chef." We enjoyed a huge feast prepared by my father, a master of the *manghal,* an old-school contraption like a BBQ pit, an open-faced, rectangular, metal box filled with charcoal briquettes.

While the charcoal was lit and getting ready, Baba speared the assortment of meats and vegetables with a metal skewer called "Siekh," then swiftly fanned the charcoal with his 'badbezan,' making sure every briquette was burning bright orange, like the color of the sun. Once satisfied, he'd lay the skewers atop the open scorching glow of the charcoal. The smell of barbecued meats coming from the manghal was intoxicating.

Smoke and an irresistible aroma consumed the air, like a Native American smoke signal, harkening us to the manghal in hopes of grabbing a steaming hot, freshly cooked piece of beef, chicken, or lamb.

Baba called the awaiting bunch 'ghongishka,' or 'little sparrows,' begging for a bite. I'd watch in awe as he fanned the meat to charbroiled perfection, then wrapped up a piece in *lavash,* or flatbread, before quickly sliding the readymade wraps off the skewers and onto our plates. He'd proudly hand out bite-size pieces to those eagerly waiting, like Santa Claus passing out presents on Christmas.

A tasty delicacy in our household was the internal organs of a freshly slaughtered lamb but not one bought at the slaughterhouse or your local supermarket. We have a tradition of sacrificing an animal (usually a lamb or sheep) after one of our prayers is answered, or when something we've yearned for a long time finally became a reality, like Baba's wish to own a villa at Seaside.

That summer, we celebrated the ritualistic custom with the "Sacrificial Lamb." One afternoon, an old, dilapidated truck showed up at the front of the villa. In the bed of the truck were a handful of live sheep, packed in and squished together to maximize the space. The driver was quite the multitasker—a shepherd, a delivery driver, a salesperson, and a skilled butcher in that exact order.

I accompanied Baba out to the curb and watched him pick out the sheep he wanted to have slaughtered based on the kilograms or weight. To display the animals, the shepherd slowly walked the sheep down a ramp out of the back of the truck, much like walking a pirate's plank before stepping off to certain death. The sheep happily obliged, unaware of their pending doom.

Once my father had made his selection, the salesperson placed a sugar cube in the sheep's mouth and shoved a hose down his throat with a last gulp of water before getting started. He then put on his bloody apron and utility belt and became the butcher.

He slowly stroked his knife against the sharpening stone, back and forth a few times, "Brrrriiiing, Brrrrriiiiing;" the swishing made a high-pitch clatter, echoing in my ear like the sound of death. He grabbed the hind leg of the sheep, flipped it onto its back, then raised the head towards him, exposing the neck. With one swift motion of the sharpened blade, he slit the animal's throat from ear to ear. I jumped back in horror as blood flew out of its carotid artery and sprayed onto the driveway.

Disturbed, but afraid to make a peep, I stood silently by as I witnessed the life go out of the sheep's eyes. The squirting of blood from the gaping wound matched the rhythm of the sheep's heartbeat, slowly coming to a stop as it was laid to rest. This is called Nazri, "The gift of God," or food offering, a religious commitment that Baba had vowed to fulfill when his prayers were heard. This was meant as an act of goodness, like feeding the poor because the 60-kilogram sheep Baba had chosen to be sacrificed was not for us.

After the slaughter, the butchering of the animal started, which should have been the signal for me to go back inside, as if watching the sheep nearly being beheaded wasn't bad enough. Although my brain was telling me to retreat, the message was somehow intercepted and never made it to my legs. I felt a mix of disgust and fascination watching this poor animal being carved to pieces by the experienced butcher. The dead carcass was hung from a nearby tree by a meat hook speared through the hoof, then skinned and slit open.

Twenty minutes later, the sheep was divided and placed on several platters ready to be disbursed. The innards were so fresh that some of the raw organs on the tray were still pulsating, moving to a rhythmic heartbeat, as if they were still attached to a living body. The wool, skin, meat, and all other edible parts were passed out to the poor and the needy. Every part would be given away, except for the internal organs. *Delojigar*, the fresh internal organs of a sheep, was considered a delicacy by many.

Baba considered the heart, liver, kidneys, and testicles a delectable treat. As the saying goes, "One man's disgust is another's delicacy!"

In our culture dating back thousands of years, no part of the animal was discarded. It was tradition, a custom passed along generations. Meat often thrown away in other cultures was consumed in many varieties of cooking. For instance, in Iran, we have a dish called *Kalle Pache*, meaning head and feet soup.

It starts with the hoof and the sheep's entire skeletal head boiled in a large pot. Then flesh is carefully picked apart and placed in a bowl full of liquid that contains the brain, tongue, eyes, facial meat, feet, and hooves – every part is eaten except the bones, but for a select few individuals, digging out or sucking on a lamb shank for the inaccessible bone marrow, is like searching for lost treasure.

I often witnessed family members struggling with the lamb shank for minutes on end. Like an Olympic sport, they'd battle with the bone; slamming the open end against a spoon, striking it, licking, sucking, scraping the inside with a narrow utensil, or until every bit of the bone marrow was carved out.

Baba was proud of our new summer home, and he was eager to share his good fortune with all those who wished to partake. Our villa had a revolving door, and as soon as one family's stay came to an end, another would be arriving, sometimes in a matter of hours.

Entering the villa on a hot summer day was like entering heaven, the air conditioning would hit my face like a splash of ice water. Like in Tehran, Baba enjoyed hosting group gatherings and extravagant parties at our new villa. Most visitors didn't want to leave the comfort and resort style living of Seaside and inevitably ended up extending their stay. Yet, Baba still worked hard. Despite the four-hour drive, he traveled back to Tehran during the week to tend to his business, leaving Maman and me and whomever else was visiting to vacation at the villa.

My father's work habits were impeccable, but he always made it back to Seaside for the weekend in anticipation of hosting the next big party. Our villa was two stories and had three bedrooms, in addition we kept nearly thirty sleeping pads in our storage room. Once the family spilled over the capacity of the three bedrooms, they utilized the sleeping pads, stretching out into every available corner of the villa. It was the ultimate sleepover party for our entire family!

At night it would be difficult to fall asleep with guests lying in every corner and across the middle of the room, with cousins cuddling on their designated sleeping pads. Once the lights were turned off, that was when the hysteria ensued. The tiniest noise would erupt unstoppable giggles that spread across the floor like an out-of-control brush fire.

Flatulence from any member would cause the entire first floor to erupt in loud laughter, resulting in Baba having to get out of bed with last minute warnings, "GO TO SLEEP OR ELSE!" He'd yell down to us from the second-floor balcony, which overlooked the ground floor. Even when the giggles and laughter stopped, the snoring from certain family members began, like Mr. Davani A.K.A. "Garlic Man."

"Garlic Man" was a colleague of Amoo Hafez's, who was adored as a lifelong family friend and earned the affectionate nickname because of his deep-rooted love affair with garlic. He knew everything there was to know about eating garlic. He ate it with everything; barbecued, broiled, baked, sauteed, kabobbed, pan-fried, deep-fried, stir-fried. He would even add it to his soups, stews, and sandwiches, and eat it raw or picked, with every meal. Even his fried eggs for breakfast were prepared with sautéed garlic. He often fell asleep in his customary position, a ski mask or beanie pulled over his eyes to the edge of his nose, his mouth wide open and his head tilted back, signaling the start of his rambunctious snoring.

His nonstop loud snorts, growls, and struggles to breathe would echo through the high ceilings of the villa like an orchestrated symphony. High notes, low notes, lots of belching and strange whistles, or eventually a big passing of air before the perpetrator turned over and readjusted on the sleeping pad in his deep slumber. Some family members' snores were so intense, we'd have to kick or yank them back to consciousness by any means necessary, only to have a break from the turbulent commotion. We'd usually have a good laugh about it in the mornings when the overnight stories were told at breakfast.

Affection and intimacy were felt throughout our villa. We broke bread in sync, and everyone did their part to complete the household chores. I fondly hold my days at Seaside as some of the best times of my life.

SEVEN
THE FIRST PERSIAN GULF WAR

Worldwide many overlook an essential chapter in my country's history—a story of political ambition and the cost of it all paid for with Iranian and Iraqi blood.

On September 22, 1980, Iraq invaded Iran with surprise airstrikes on ten Iranian airfields followed by a massive ground invasion the following day. This marked the start of the first Persian Gulf War, launched by now-Iraqi President Saddam Hussein. Several interactions between Khomeini and Hussein lit the fire, but it was Saddam Hussein who launched the war. Hussein had noticed the political instability in Iran after the revolution and the newfound hostility towards the Ayatollah from the international community, did not go unnoticed by Iran's regional adversary and neighbor.

Saddam Hussein was a dictator, and he may have sensed the opportunity for a preemptive strike. Citing historical claims over the land, he authorized military action to seize and secure both banks of Iran's oil-rich region in the Shatt al-Arab waterway that flowed into the Persian Gulf. His other ambitious goal was to rapidly destroy the Iranian Air Force by bombing the planes while still on the ground.

He calculated the Iranians had a limited window of time to coordinate a counterattack and that he could quickly force them to concede defeat. Although the Iraqi air strikes did extensive damage, the Iranian Air Force rose to meet the challenge. Within 24 hours, Iraqi Air Force bases were under attack by Iranian pilots.

On the ground, Iraq sent six armored divisions on three fronts, where some of the bloodiest fighting took place during the first battle.

Rather than the quick victory Saddam Hussein had promised, both sides settled in for a prolonged war of attrition. The Islamic Republic of Iran was now defending itself with the vast foreign military power it had accumulated under the Shah.

Much to his chagrin, the invasion of Iran had a negative side effect on the Iraqi leader. Historically, Iran had endured many invasions throughout the centuries. Always conquered but never colonized, the Iranians remained proud, conscious of their history and heritage. Khomeini was calling on the people of Iran to rally against the Iraqi invaders and his appeal sparked a major mobilization of its young men. A large part of Saddam Hussein's planning counted on the disorganization and the internal instability of the new Iranian regime. Instead, the invasion only served to unite Iran as a country against the foreign invader. The country had not yet acclimated to the new Islamic Republic of Iran when war broke out, but having a common enemy served to bring its people together. In essence, Saddam Hussein had given Ayatollah Khomeini precisely what he needed to stay in power and unwittingly secured the future of the Islamic Republic of Iran.

Word of the Iraqi invasion was broadcast on every television channel and radio station. When Maman turned on the news that evening, a look of horror came over her face.

"What's going on, Maman?" I asked worriedly.

"War, Pendar. War is one of the worst things that could happen to our country. As if the revolution and the hostage crisis weren't bad enough, and now this? she said, staring hopelessly at the television screen.

"Maman, do I have to go to war?" I asked with concern.

"No honey, you're way too young. Normally, soldiers have to be eighteen to join the army."

Baba arrived home that night feeling nervous, agitated, and frustrated by the news. He had completely lost his appetite for supper and with a defeated look, slumped onto the couch next to Maman. I knew little of our country's history or the previous wars we had fought and was too young to be concerned.

The expression on Baba's face, however, alarmed me. His eyes were filled with tears; I had never seen him cry. His somber mood and body language signaled that I needed to give him space and leave him alone for a while. No words were spoken for the rest of the evening.

As I lay in bed that night, I tried to imagine what war was like. *Was it comparable to what I had seen in the movies?* I was naive and confused but saw that the terrible news had a negative effect on my parents' outlook on life, not only for our country but for the future of our family.

I was seven years old watching the troops, tanks, and our entire military preparing for the forthcoming battle. Slowly, I understood the concept of war and recognized that thousands of people were going to die—on both sides. The thought was unsettling. *What if they call Baba to war?* I began to tremble thinking of Baba being sent off in one of those tanks, or worse. *What would I do?* The thought of someone I loved going to war terrified me.

———

In March of 1981, we traveled to Seaside to observe Nowruz, the Iranian New Year celebrated on the first day of spring each year. Amoo Payam rented a minibus that year, one that seated twenty passengers or more. We drove to Seaside as a big family, squeezing everyone tightly onto the minibus which resulted in creating some unforgettable moments. Along the way, we snacked on pumpkin and sunflower seeds, while different family members told funny jokes. While at one of many pitstops, homemade lunch was served, cold cuts, salad Olivier (Russian potato salad), and meat cutlet sandwiches. For dessert, fresh-cut fruits like watermelon, cantaloupe, honeydew melon, and an assortment of berries. Followed by an array of mouthwatering pastries served with hot black tea.

In the spring, Seaside underwent an explosion of flowers and contrasting colors—incredible shades of pink, purple, yellow, orange, and green. The Iranian New Year was like our Christmas, but we typically did not receive gifts. It was customary for adults to hand out cash, and not wrinkled old bills they found buried in their wallets. It was tradition to pass out freshly printed, uncirculated Iranian currency, "Rial," of different denominations. We called it "Eidi," and every kid in Iran looked forward to receiving a fist full of cash on this day. The bigger the family, the bigger the payout, since every adult was expected to participate.

Every family had its own special custom of handing out Eidi to the children. Some families put the money in envelopes to hand out like a birthday card. Religious families inserted the cash in pages of the holy book of Quran. Their kids had to say a religious prayer in Arabic just to get their Eidi. Some adults made the kids dance or do odd tricks to earn their Eidi. It was also tradition to visit the houses of family and acquaintances to wish them a happy and prosperous year to come.

As always, my family thought of a new way to distribute the cash on this special New Year. First, Baba and his three brothers, Amoo Hafez, Amoo Ramin, and Amoo Payam, cleared the furniture from the ground floor of the villa to create a wide-open space for all the kids, cousins and friends who had joined us at Seaside for the occasion. They then instructed everyone to gather there.

We watched as the four patriarchs climbed the stairs to the second-floor landing. They teased us, slowing their pace, and stopping and starting as we cheered and urged them on.

Once at the top, they assumed their positions, overlooking all the kids. We stood, each agonizing second ticking by while we waited in anticipation of their next move. Suddenly, they would start, and for the next thirty minutes, they took turns letting the Rials, crisp, newly minted bills fly down on us. It was like a slow-motion clip for those standing below. The money flapped through the air like a wounded bird, beating its wings to make a smooth landing. It was raining money, and bills flew everywhere, changing direction midair and throwing off us kids below eager to be the lucky recipient.

I felt like it was taking an eternity for each bill to reach us. We were not only having difficulty snatching them out of the air, but we toppled on top of each other trying.

When it was all over, the first floor looked like the aftermath of a battlefield thoroughly riddled with injured kids. Only Amoo Sasan and Cousin Shahin remained unscathed and stood laughing at the pathetic kids whimpering or crying to their parents. I was one of those kids and almost jumped into Maman's embrace after an injury, but their presence prevented me from doing so. I didn't want them to laugh at me or make fun, calling me, "Bache nanne," or "Momma's boy."

One of many celebratory meals consisted of fresh poultry. Maman was referred to a woman who lived on the outskirts of town and raised chickens in her backyard. Her husband worked for the city's mainte-nance department, which qualified the couple for subsidized housing. Selling chickens and eggs to the locals was her way of supplementing the household income.

I accompanied Maman and waited patiently as she ordered a half dozen birds from the chicken coop. We both assumed the woman would need time to prepare them and that we'd return later in the day to pick them up. But before Maman and I knew what was happening, the "chicken whisperer" pulled the birds out one by one from the coop and slit their throats with a sharp knife, beheading each one right in front of us.

Confused and reeling from the grisly display, I nearly burst out laughing when the now headless chickens started bouncing up and down, profusely bleeding all over their white feathers, helplessly flap-ping their wings in what looked like a final dance of death. I couldn't resist kicking a couple of them around like a soccer ball when they came bobbing my way.

Months earlier, I had watched a butcher behead, skin, and dismember a sheep, and now this. In a short period, I had become oddly immune to this type of brutality.

As I marveled at the show, I noticed Maman out of the corner of my eye, sitting on the front porch of the woman's house, weeping, and I ran over to console her. "What's the matter Maman?" I asked.

"Nothing Pendar Jan, I'm just sad to see the chickens bleeding out and dying right here in front of me."

At that moment, I understood. Soon the dead birds were gathered, plucked of their feathers, and cut into eight pieces with a large cleaver. Sometimes, images of those chickens, bloody, beheaded, and struggling for life, return to haunt me. I have sympathy for what happened to them now, but as a kid, it was my guilty pleasure, and I was amused by it.

About a year after the war began, my parents announced we were going on our first family vacation abroad. Not only a chance to vacation in a different country but a much-needed respite from the madness that had consumed our lives over the last couple of years. So far, the war had not affected the residents of Tehran. Most of the fighting and open warfare was being carried out in Western Iran, along the two countries' joint border some five hundred miles from Tehran. There were no travel restrictions for Iranian citizens, therefore my parents chose Europe as our destination.

We were going to be spending two weeks in Germany. The thought of my first airplane ride at eight years old was exciting, and I looked forward to visiting another country.

We landed in Munich, where Baba rented a car for us to drive through the countryside and on the famous Autobahn. Germany was very different from Iran—the language, the roads, the people, the culture, and the food. I was enthralled with new experiences, like my first visit to an amusement park. There were a multitude of rides that we didn't have back in Iran.

Our itinerary included an overnight stay in Hamburg, a major port city in the north of the country. At dinner that night, I overheard Baba whispering to Maman, "It's called the Red-Light District, and I only want to walk through there.

"Come on, Ziba. It's within walking distance of our hotel, and it's only going to take a few minutes. Come on, please?"

I wasn't sure where he was taking us, or why he was begging Maman, but the secretiveness of it made me excited, nonetheless. After the meal, we set off for the mystery destination, arriving at a dimly-lit street with storefronts lining both sides and a bright, red light shining above each window. I was expecting to see traditional clothing, jewelry, or Belgium chocolates on display but as we walked closer, I couldn't believe my eyes. Naked women were showcased in each store window as if they were items for sale! I stood frozen, mesmerized by what I was witnessing. Normally, when watching a movie that contained inappropriate scenes, I knew to cover my eyes or was instructed to look away.

That's what my brain was telling me to do, but strangely, my parents had no expectations. They, too, were staring into the windows and admiring the beautiful, naked women—Baba, in particular. I don't know how he convinced Maman to play along, but as usual, his persistence and charm had won her over.

While in Frankfurt, Baba took me to a movie theater where we watched a James Bond film called *Diamonds Are Forever*. To my dismay, seeing a Bond movie in a public theater was no longer possible back in Iran. It was during this trip that I became more conscious of other countries' cultures; made aware of the diverse worlds that existed outside of the city in which I lived, and of the freedoms no longer afforded to us back in Iran.

―――――

In the spring of 1982, a few months after returning to Tehran, my parents called me into the living room. They announced that Maman was pregnant, and I grew excited when they congratulated me on becoming a brother soon.

My sister Donya was born that October, and I was elated when my parents brought her home from the hospital. Her arrival was met by a steady stream of visitors, relatives, and friends eager to meet her and congratulate us. I felt overwhelming love for my new baby sister. I wanted to embrace her, but my parents wouldn't allow it.

Suddenly, I was no longer the center of attention. Everyone who came to visit only wanted to see the baby, hold the baby, kiss the baby, and fight over her. It was about my parents' unconditional love, the purest love of all, and up until now, I had been the only recipient on the receiving end of it. Even celebrating my ninth birthday that December felt different, with guests no longer focusing solely on me.

It took time for me to adapt to the concept of shared attention. My parents spoke to me often about my feelings of jealousy and always affirmed their never-ending love and affection for me.

Even as the war raged on and several thousand soldiers on both sides perished in battle, our lives remained unchanged in Tehran.

We spent the summer of 1983 vacationing in Seaside. My baby sister was now eight months old, and I was nine—and tall enough to reach the pedals of Maman's pink, stick-shift Paykan, the first car manufactured in Iran, and Baba took the opportunity to teach me how to drive. I was excited at the prospect and jumped whenever he or Maman invited me to chauffeur them to the market to pick up provisions. I could tell they were nervous, especially Maman, who mindfully watched my speed and monitored my every shift and turn.

This was a particularly happy time for our family. Baba's new video business was a huge success, with sales beyond his wildest imagination. To reward himself, he fulfilled another lifelong dream and purchased a Cadillac, an American model he had long coveted. He also surprised me with a gift that quickly became the envy of every kid in Seaside—a Honda Z50, a street-legal mini trail bike in Paw-paw green.

That Honda spoke to me; my new minibike ruled. My Z50 was what started it off for me, my addiction to two-wheel vehicles. It was a sophisticated toy, but so much more, with its plush, black leather seat, the chrome fenders, and a three-speed automatic transmission, which meant no clutch and was easy to ride. It was a thing of beauty and I coveted it daily.

From that day forward, I never went anywhere without it. Although my limits were each four corners of the Seaside community, this was my first motorized bike, and I loved the thrill of the ride. The experience was not without mishaps, but the scrapes I suffered were proud scars of riding. I rode everywhere on my Honda Z50; it made me feel like the king of Seaside. I even volunteered to ride to the grocery store or happily picked up bread for Maman at the local bakery, just another excuse to ride my bike.

The wind blowing in my hair and the freedom I felt riding my minibike were glorious. One unforgettable evening, the clear, cloudless sky was magnificent, boasting a brilliant full moon and a gentle warm breeze coming from the Caspian Sea. That night, I returned to the villa to find we had company visiting. My parents were hosting a small gathering of guests, some of whom I didn't recognize. It was normal for strangers to visit, usually accompanied by a relative or an acquaintance from the community.

That night, a neighbor had joined us, escorted by a friend, a peculiar woman we had never met. She was dressed like a gypsy, with enormous gold earrings and a gaudy gold necklace with a matching headpiece, its rim encircled with gold coins.

The mysterious woman was cordial throughout dinner, but once we finished, she hit us with a pronouncement. "I'm a psychic!" she announced. Then, looking directly at Baba, she said, "You must allow me to tell your fortune."

Baba didn't believe in this type of nonsense, but being the gracious host that he was, he politely agreed.

"Do you have any Turkish coffee?" the woman asked.

Maman grabbed the coffee from the kitchen cabinet and whipped out her special copper kettle. The psychic then spooned the ground beans into the pot and added water to the concoction before placing it atop the stove. She turned the burner on the highest setting, then waited while the kettle heated almost to the point of boiling over.

Meanwhile, Maman fetched her fancy, elegant coffee cups and matching saucers. The psychic poured the steaming mixture into one of the cups and delivered it to the table, placing it directly in front of Baba.

My father sipped on it leisurely, careful to drink only the liquid and none of the grinds. Once finished, he gripped the coffee cup by the handle and flipped it upside down onto the saucer beneath.

Turkish coffee grinds have the consistency of talcum powder. Once the liquid is consumed from the mixture, a mound of coffee grinds remains at the bottom of the cup. When it is turned over, gravity takes hold and gently shifts the grinds, "painting" a picture as the coffee slides down the sides of the cup, leaving a trail.

Psychics interpret this "painting" or "image," to somehow predict the future. It may sound hokey-pokey and fake, but I'd seen it occur at the homes of other family and friends. There was always someone at the gathering who believed he or she could call upon psychic powers. Ten minutes passed when the psychic declared, "It's time!" She then took hold of the cup with Baba's permission.

I was sitting on the floor when I heard her gasp, causing everyone to lean in, curious to know what she had seen. She tilted the cup so that everyone could see, then, in a calm and soothing voice she said, "I have never seen anything this clear in all my readings." We were all intrigued and drawn in by her words. She probably said that to all her anxious believers. Nevertheless, she had my full attention.

Looking at Baba dead in his eyes, she declared, "You have an immense, monumental task or mission that lies ahead of you. This is a challenge unlike anything you've ever experienced, and it will come as a surprise when you least expect it. Your endurance, perseverance, determination, and survival instincts will be provoked. The most demanding life confrontation you will ever face, but you must tolerate and endure the discomfort. Not giving up is the key to your triumph."

As I contemplated her words, I wondered to myself, "How does she know all this by merely looking inside a cup with leftover coffee grinds?"

She continued, "Do you see the image on the right? It's a vast mountain containing many valleys and dangerous peaks. Did you notice the panther?"

On the opposite side of the cup lay an outline of a large cat-like image. The mysterious panther was facing the ridge of the mountain and climbing at an almost vertical angle. The psychic pointed it out to Baba and proclaimed, "The panther is on a mission and determined to reach the top of the mountain."

"Looks like the panther is still climbing," Baba said with a chuckle. "Does he ever make it to the top?"

The woman looked at him with a convincing gleam and replied, "There is nothing that will stop the panther from reaching the top of the mountain; his mission is imperative, and his purpose is meaningful."

I was riveted. "Can I take a look?!" I asked curiously.

The mountain was clearly visible, and the conspicuous panther was gradually crawling toward the peak. I assumed this must be a magic trick and had difficulty believing that coffee grinds along with gravity had contrived this beautiful and symbolic painting. I couldn't help but wonder, *What is this absurd woman chattering about?* Unbeknownst to any of us, her predictions would not only come to fruition, but they would directly involve me.

Neither of my parents really believed in this type of fortune-telling, but like many Iranians, they were superstitious. They firmly believe in an old folklore called the "Evil Eye," a concept that goes back generations about being the victim of a curse on someone else's behalf. At times, Iranians tend to be secretive about their accomplishments, simply because they are afraid that someone will bestow them with the "evil eye." Or they will refrain from sharing aspects of their lives out of fear of "cheshm khordan," literally translated to mean "being struck by the eye."

For those who believe, there are remedies to fight off the spell and prevent oneself from being struck by the curse. *Esfand,* better known as *Peganum harmala,* is a preemptive strike to ward off the evil eye practiced not only in Iran but by people in many other cultures and countries. Esfand (wild rue seeds) are burned in special contraptions to allow the smoke to rise from the seeds. The sound of the popping and the earthy oakwood smell immediately brings back vivid memories of my grandmother and Maman, who would burn Esfand seeds anytime someone complimented us. The prayer they recited was meant to blind the jealous eye while waving the smoke from the burning seeds, circling it around everyone's head to ward off the evil eye.

For extra protection, Maman hung an evil-eye-shaped amulet close to the entryway to our home. Most Iranian households and businesses have one for all to see upon entering. The round form and blue color signify Heaven and Faith, while the representation in the middle indicates a sacred, vigilant eye. These anti-evil eye accessories are not only used to suppress negative energy and for personal safety but are meant to guard and protect against jealousy, warding off the evil eye even for those who unintentionally bestow bad wishes or negative thoughts upon you.

———

Now that Baba was in the video business, we got to screen all the films he received from abroad before they were distributed for public consumption. That summer, we enjoyed previewing lots of movies at our Seaside villa. *Earthquake, Rocky, Rambo, Superman, StarWars, Indiana Jones,* and *Scarface* were among the many American blockbusters we watched.

I loved movies like *Flashdance* and *Footloose,* but by far one of my favorites was *Grease.* I especially adored the final scene when Danny, played by John Travolta, chased Sandy, played by Olivia Newton-John, through the carnival singing the famous duet, "You're the One that I Want."

It was great having exclusive access to many foreign films. I'd watch them over and over. While most were from America, Baba got ahold of others like the Bruce Lee martial arts movies from Hong Kong, and Bollywood films from India. He even invented a game based on the movies we previewed. He'd whistle different theme songs in my ear, and I had to guess the title of the film they were from.

My earliest memory is of him whistling the score from *The Good, the Bad, and the Ugly.* The tune immediately conjured images of Clint Eastwood, blowing away multiple baddies with a quick fling of his Colt revolver. I loved and adored sharing my father's passion for the cinema with him. We'd spend hours conversing about movies, directors, or his latest film projects at work.

I often lost myself in movies and pretended I was one of the characters. My view of America and the lifestyle I envied never faded, changed, or swayed, even when I would be forced to scream such obscenities as "DEATH TO AMERICA" upon entering junior high school.

EIGHT
LEARNING NEW LESSONS

I was blessed to have my grandparents living directly above us. Their apartment was like my second home. With Baba away at work during the day, and Maman busy with household chores, I found myself spending a lot of time upstairs with my grandparents.

Back then, it was common in Iran to only bathe or shower once a week. And up until I was nine years old, it was Papa Jahan who gave me my weekly baths. It was out of love and adoration for his first-born grandson, and over the years our weekly ritual became a habit that neither of us wanted to give up. Dressed in underwear or swimwear, we'd carry out the bath-time ritual at the exact same time and on the exact same day every week. He would lather up the loofah, slip it over his hand and exfoliate my body from head to toe. The last pitcher of water he poured over my head was always the best, with all the filth and grime washing off before starting a new week.

In the fall of 1983, I started junior high school. At almost ten, I was now permitted to walk to school on my own. My daily routine began with Papa Jahan banging loudly on our metal front door, my wake-up call at 6:45 am. My parents always stayed up late, watching recently released movies into the early morning hours, and the intense rattling didn't faze them. By the time I dragged myself out of bed and waddled up the stairs to my grandparents' apartment, Papa Jahan had already prepared my breakfast, hot tea with two sugar cubes and three slices of toasted Sangak bread topped with butter and my favorite strawberry jelly, all neatly arranged on the kitchen table.

On days with heavy snowfall, I'd listen to the radio, while clasping my palms together, praying for the announcer to report the closure of school. After breakfast, I'd set off, the walk typically took around thirty minutes.

Papa Jahan would stand at the kitchen window, which overlooked the street, to wave me off. I remember glancing back over my shoulder at him until he disappeared out of sight. In the afternoons, I'd find him at that same window perched like a watchful owl waiting to welcome me home. His presence at that window was extremely reassuring and, to this day, remains a cherished memory of those early years.

Middle school was a lot different than elementary school. For one, it was segregated, meaning there were no girls. Back then, boys and girls attended elementary school together but were separated once they entered junior high. The homework was also a lot harder.

During my first week, I made friends with a boy named Mohammad. He was one year ahead of me, and he already knew his way around, which was an advantage for me. We met at nutrition time. We hit it off immediately, and from that point forward, we were inseparable. He often got to school early and eagerly awaited my arrival each day.

We had very different upbringings, I was from a comfortable middle-class family, and his family was quite poor. We also had contrasting religious beliefs. His was a devout family that prayed and obeyed all Islamic rules, while we were more Westernized and did not practice religion the same way. Still, at school, we were the best of friends. We hung out at nutrition time, played soccer in the schoolyard, and spent most of our free time together.

Sometimes it felt like it was Mohammad and me against the whole school. He looked out for me and made sure I was not bullied by any of the older kids. He was brave, gutsy, fearless, and didn't mind standing up to another student.

One thing we all knew not to do was disagree, disobey, disrespect a teacher, or fall behind on our classwork. Teachers had strict rules and guidelines, especially when it came to disciplining the students. Most of the faculty and administrators were unpleasant, ruthless, and ran the school with an iron fist.

My disregard for authority and my lethargic habit of not completing my homework assignments would eventually land me in trouble. Punishment was called "counseling," which often included being struck with a ruler or other object, even an open hand to the face and limbs, but thankfully, closed fists were not allowed.

In Middle School, teachers had the authority to physically "counsel," as in punish the students, even during class. If a student stopped paying attention or got out of line, he could be subject to the thwack of a ruler or worse. It was a daily occurrence to witness a student receiving a beating at the hands of one of the teachers. The school also enforced religious rules and regulations. Every morning before class, we lined up for roll call (attendance.) While in line, one of the teachers or the school principal would yell into a blowhorn, instructing us to recite absurd slogans. "Death to America" was their favorite, one I remember chanting when my family and I had joined the protests during the revolution.

Now I was older and understood what it meant, it felt awkward to wish death upon a country I envied and secretly hoped to live in someday. I certainly didn't mean the obscenities I was being forced to shout, but I didn't want to be singled out, so I recited them loudly to satisfy the faculty's demands.

After the chanting concluded, we followed our teacher to the prayer room. There, we were forced to pray. There was another prayer session in the afternoon, though it was optional if you had already attended morning prayer.

Every morning, we lined up in the dedicated prayer room, thirty kids at a time, all in rows, with a prayer rug already laid out on the floor in each spot. We'd find our place and morning prayer would begin, led by our teacher. In sync, we bowed our heads, got on our knees, and placed our foreheads on the 'mohr' (a clay tablet used during prayer). I would recite mostly forgotten verses from the holy book of Quran in Arabic, a language I didn't speak.

My family was not religious, therefore prayer felt like more of an inconvenience for me. I went through the motions and mouthed the words incorrectly, butchering every verse.

One morning, I spotted Mohammad across the prayer room. He was in a deep trance; it looked like he was communicating with the holy spirit. He proudly pronounced every verse in perfect Arabic. He took prayer very seriously, keeping his eyes tightly closed while speaking to the higher power. Mohammad was deeply religious. Even during our afternoon soccer games he would excuse himself in the middle of play and attend prayer for a second time.

I believed in God and was sure a higher power existed, but I never found comfort in religion as he did. Looking at Mohammad, I envied his unbreakable faith and certainty about his beliefs.

One day at lunch break, we were challenged to a game of soccer by a group of older boys. It was three against three. Mohammad, our friend Amir, and I were on one team, versus the other three boys. Mohammad struggled through their tough defense and scored a goal.

That made them angry and in retaliation, they started playing more aggressively.

Mohammad and Amir fended off some of the abuse, but I was not as fortunate. The other team sniffed out the weak link and started homing in on me like a pack of wild coyotes. I was protecting the goal, as one of the offenders started rushing toward it with the ball at his feet. I headed for him, our shadows dancing on the blacktop. We arrived simultaneously, and as I kicked the ball out of the way, the opposite player accidentally kicked me in the shin. I fell to the ground in pain, rolling side to side while gripping my leg.

Mohammad stood over me, and in a forceful tone he said, "Get up, let's keep playing."

"No, I don't want to play anymore!" I replied, fighting back tears.

Mohammad grew frustrated. "It was an accident, get up and play. I'm not going to let you give up."

As I lay on the ground, writhing in pain, I looked up at my friend. *You're gutless*, I thought. *That's how you were raised, never having to stand up for yourself.*

Pain ripped through my leg as I struggled to stand and return to my position at the goal. We continued to play, and the ball came in my direction a couple more times. I was tempted to rush toward the ball, but I was hesitant. At that moment, I realized that I was missing the fierce competitive edge and determination that other kids like Mohammad had mastered. He was more driven with an insatiable appetite for competition and victory-two attributes I was clearly lacking.

He and the others ran full speed, rushing the ball, full of confidence, not tentative like me. Even though Baba had tried to teach me these important life lessons, I still caved into loss, giving up and accepting failure as a fact of life. *Why was I complaisant and lazy?* I felt pathetic, like a blundering liability to my teammates when we played. But Mohammad never let me sit on the sidelines or allowed me to give up. He was always there for me, pushing me to do better.

After the game, I rushed to the bathroom and sat in one of the stalls, with knots in my stomach. I was there only a few minutes when I heard Mohammad, Amir and the three boys from the other team walk in.

"He's just a spoiled brat who's had everything handed to him in life," I heard Amir say, "born with a silver spoon in his mouth. He's never going to amount to anything without Mommy and Daddy protecting him all the time."

Mohammad interrupted him, "C'mon Amir, he just needs a push. Give him a break already!"

I was heartened that my friend was standing up for me. But I remained silent, not wanting them to know I was eavesdropping.

"Then you can keep him on your team next time," Amir shot back. "I don't want to play with a crybaby. He's a coward, and his laziness is getting on my nerves."

"Enough!" yelled Mohammad in anger. He took a deep breath, calmed his nerves, and continued, "The Quran teaches us and says..."

Curious, I peered out through the crack in the stall to watch him. "Help one another in acts of piety and righteousness," he recited. "Do not assist each other in acts of sinfulness and transgression. And beware of Allah. Verily, Allah is severe in punishment."

Mohammad seemed to have moral authority over the other boys, and they clearly respected him. Perhaps because he was brave and was a superior soccer player.

I waited for them to leave before exiting the stall. What I heard was enlightening. For the first time, I was seeing myself for who I really was, the way other kids saw my existence. It was an eye-opening experience that made me examine my upbringing. I felt grateful to have such a loyal and faithful friend as Mohammad. He had stood up for me, even when he didn't have to.

NINE
CHANGE OF HEART

I n the Winter of 1983, my father was dealt yet another blow. After several years of thriving at the helm of his new video business, he was ordered by the Ershad Ministry to close its doors. While the Ministry had approved his request to import and dub films back in 1980, they no longer deemed foreign films as appropriate for the Islamic Republic and terminated all imports.

Baba was heartbroken. He'd made a huge financial investment in this venture, and it had already paid tremendous dividends. *What would he do with all the video equipment he'd purchased?* He now owned more than fifty VCR machines that were essentially worthless and outlawed.

Most viewed this as a daunting defeat, but Baba remained positive. He'd been extremely happy earning a living with a business that also indulged his long-running passion for movies. He tried to think of potential ventures that allowed him to stay connected to the film industry, even if just peripherally. He decided to convert his offices to a photo lab. Initially, his intention was to print movie posters that he could sell to the public. He had to purchase new equipment and learn a new profession, but he was motivated and jumped right in.

Unfortunately, with the sale and viewing of foreign films now prohibited, there was little demand for movie posters. Baba changed his focus and began developing pictures for weddings, parties, and photo studios. His new business motto caught on, and he quickly became one of the top photo labs in Tehran.

Although home videos from abroad were now banned, sometimes

Baba got ahold of smuggled tapes through his old connections. The films were no longer dubbed into Farsi, and for the first time, I heard the characters' real voices. But we had to be discreet. These films were now considered contraband, and it was illegal to have one in your possession.

One of the smuggled films Baba brought home was the Michael Jackson *Thriller* video. We didn't have access to American television, or cable networks like MTV, which aired music videos like this one. I was amazed at how the music videos were built around a short story or a movie within the song. When Jackson transformed into a bloodsucking zombie and started dancing with other zombies, I felt compelled to imitate that scene and act it out. I learned every move, every jump, and every step, and imitated every nuance. Everyone got a big kick out of my shenanigans and encouraged me to dance at every party.

That December, I celebrated my tenth birthday with a big gathering, as usual. Baba had just purchased a home video recorder and on this night, he used it for the first time. It took him a while to figure out the zoom and focus, but he managed to film much of the party after placing the camcorder on a tripod.

I had prepared a dance that I was going to perform for our guests. My aunt Tara, Baba's only sister from his father's second marriage, would be performing with me. Together, we choreographed the ending of *Grease*, and as Danny, I dressed the part in a white button-down sweater I found in my closet that looked exactly like the one he wore in that final scene.

Aunt Tara would be dancing the part of Sandy.

After Maman brought out the cake, we dimmed the lights, and Aunt Tara and I took center stage in the living room. Baba cued up the sound-track on his record player and turned up the volume.

Aunt Tara held an unlit cigarette and pretended to be puffing on it while prancing toward me with a sexy stroll. I slowly mouthed the words to the song—albeit incorrectly, while taking off the white sweater, twirling it around in the air, then flinging it behind me just like John Travolta. I was "electrifying," throwing myself to the ground in front of her feet.

That's when Aunt Tara threw down the unlit cigarette, put it out with the sole of her shoe, then pressed her shoe to my chest and pushed me back before I chased her all over our apartment.

It was a blast pretending to be running through the imaginary carni-val. We acted out every move, which resulted in a big standing ovation from the family. From that day forward, my aunt and I were expected to perform the song and dance at every gathering and party; we were happy to do it. We both loved the attention.

———

In early 1984, midway through the school year, I learned we were moving. I was in my room when I heard Baba's voice traveling down the hallway of our apartment. I looked out and saw Maman in the family room gently rocking my baby sister Donya in her arms and crept closer to listen in.

"Now that our family is growing, we need to find a bigger place to live," Baba told her.

I eagerly ran to join the conversation. "Are we moving?" I asked.

Baba smiled at me, "We're going to start looking for a new home soon. This apartment is not going to be big enough for the five of us."

"What do you mean, five of us?" I asked with a look of bewilderment.

Maman rubbed the palm of her hand over her belly in circles, "Pendar, we're having another baby."

I frowned. I was confused and my expression reflected it.

"I'm pregnant again, Pendar," Maman told me cheerfully.

I couldn't explain how I felt about the news of her pregnancy. I was happy, yet sad. I put on a cheerful face, but there had been too many changes lately. *What about Papa Jahan and Mama Goli?* I would miss living so close to them.

"Before we start looking for a new home Pendar, we've got to say goodbye to Amoo Hafez and your cousin, Shahin. They'll be here soon," Baba said.

"Why are they coming over to say goodbye? Where are they going?" I asked.

"Amoo Hafez is taking Shahin to America. That is where he is going to continue his education. He'll be living with Azad and Star," he replied.

"Who are Azad and Star?" I asked. I'd never heard of them.

Baba explained that Azad and Star were our distant relatives who lived in the United States, and they'd agreed to become Shahin's legal guardians.

I was speechless. I couldn't imagine ever leaving my family to live with strangers, although I did aspire to move to America someday. I felt envious, yet sorry for Shahin. *Wouldn't he be lonely in America without his family?*

Our visit with Shahin lasted just fifteen minutes. He had a lot of relatives to see, it was little more than 'hello' and 'goodbye.' I was surprised to hear that Shahin was planning to stay in America after he completed school, with no intention of ever coming back to Iran.

"How easy is it to get to America?" I asked my cousin.

"First, we'll have to travel to Istanbul, Turkey, and apply for a student visa," Shahin explained.

"What's a visa?" I interrupted.

"A visa is a document required to enter America, it's like a permission slip," he said. "We'll visit the American Embassy in Istanbul, where we'll interview with the American Consul and get our visas."

"Why are you traveling that far for a visa? Why can't you just go to the American Embassy here in Tehran?"

He lightly cuffed me on the back of the head and said, "Don't you remember? The embassy was overtaken and permanently closed after the Revolution?"

The images of the blindfolded Americans being marched out of the embassy flashed before my eyes, and I nodded in remembrance.

Amoo Hafez leisurely sipped on the hot black tea Maman had served him, but soon it was time for them to leave. Next stop, Amoo Ramin's house to say farewell.

We said our goodbyes and wished them luck and safe travels. I watched from the sidewalk as he drove off into the sunset on his way to America. Later that night, I wished that I too could go to America, but not without my family.

———

My brother Amin was born in October 1984. We were permitted to visit the hospital where I met him for the first time. I was almost eleven years old and excited to embrace him in my arms. Once at the hospital, I rushed to Maman's bedside, gently hugging her. She moved slowly but still kissed me gently on my cheek and forehead. There were flowers in every corner of the room, sent from family and friends to congratulate us.

Moments later, the nurses rolled in a cart, inside was a tiny baby boy who had peculiar blonde hair. There must've been a mistake, I thought. Both my parents had dark hair. Later, I overheard various family members joking about how Amin belonged to another family and was accidentally switched in the nursery.

We took many photos and Baba brought his video camera to record the joyous event. It was a deeply warm and happy welcome party for my brother Amin.

Approximately one week later, my parents finally found a suitable new high-rise apartment complex called A.S.P. Towers, amongst the most well-known buildings in Tehran. The triplet towers were among the first residential high rises in Tehran and at twenty-four stories soared above everything else in the city. The apartments were luxurious, upscale, and a sight to behold.

My parents settled on a spacious three-bedroom apartment on the twentieth floor that had every amenity I could have dreamt of. We had a covered garage, 24-hour security, guarded elevators, a community outdoor/indoor heated swimming pool, a gym, a kindergarten, a supermarket, a hair salon, restaurants, and much more.

They chose the complex in part to shield our family from the increasingly restrictive public sphere. The upscale private facilities offered everything nearby, clearly another motivation, making my parents' life easier with multiple children.

What I remember most about our first visit is Maman's high heels clicking against the shiny marble floors, the sound echoing through the empty apartment before our furniture arrived. There were huge floor-to-ceiling sliding windows that led to a long balcony boasting breathtaking views of the city. There was also a giant luxurious kitchen outfitted with the most updated appliances, a separate maid's quarters, a jacuzzi tub in the master bathroom, and a bidet!

The first time I explored the buttons on the bidet, water shot across the room and hit the wall on the opposite side of the bathroom. Much to my wide-eyed astonishment. I'd never seen a contraption like it and needed an explanation of how it functioned. Meanwhile, Maman kept me plenty occupied. Soon after moving in, she signed me up for advanced swimming classes, ice skating classes, and winter skiing lessons.

In the first weeks after Amin was born, my great-grandmother 'Maman Bozorg' literal translation meaning Big Momma, (Papa Jahan's mother) agreed to live with us and to assist Maman with my siblings. Meanwhile, I attended the same school, Baba drove me in the mornings on his way to work, and I took a taxi and the bus back in the afternoons.

With my family's attention diverted more toward my infant baby brother and my sister who was a toddler, I started to slack off in school. I often procrastinated in completing my work in class, along with assigned homework.

One morning, I was daydreaming while the teacher was explaining an important geography lesson. I was blissfully pondering a Bruce Lee movie, manipulating my two pencils to imitate his karate moves.

Suddenly, I looked up to find my teacher standing over my desk; I was caught red-handed! My teacher had spotted me and ached to make an example out of me.

He slid one of my pencils between my ring and index finger. His one hand grasped my wrist when he started to close his other hand around my fingers. He was firmly pressing on the pencil, crushing my middle finger. With each passing second, the pressure intensified, along with the ludicrous smirk on his face. Each intense agonizing moment was surpassed by the level of pain I could withstand. He pushed harder and ultimately, I screamed out in misery, concerned that my finger was about to break. My outcry had finally brought him to a stop.

"Worse will happen to the next student who's not paying attention in my class," he shouted as a warning to all my classmates, who were watching, frozen in horror.

My fingers hurt for days, but I concealed the pain along with the incident from my parents, ashamed and avoiding further trouble at home. But every student in school was petrified of one particular teacher, and rightfully so. The ill-tempered math teacher, Mr. Hakimi, was a short, stocky man with a gruff voice and wrestler's ears that looked like crushed cauliflowers. He had a reputation for being ruthless and was infamous for viciously beating up students.

A week later, I was caught dozing off in his math class. Not because I was up late studying, but because I secretly watched a scary movie called *Halloween* and stayed up past midnight on a school night. Through the night I was haunted by visions of Michael Meyers, the psycho killer in the film, chasing me, wielding a large kitchen knife.

Our math class had gone a few days without altercations, but now I was entangled in his sight like a deer in the headlights.

He stood me up, "Why are you sleeping in my class?" He demanded an answer, shaming me in front of the class.

I couldn't dare be honest about what I had really done the night before. Movies were forbidden. Especially American ones like *Halloween*. I didn't have a good answer, standing there humiliated and speechless.

He then gently placed his fingers on my chin and started to position my face pointing it sideways as if we were getting ready to pose for a family portrait.

My heart started thumping inside my chest; the anticipation of being struck was stressful. Knowing what was to come, my palms started sweating. I was uneasy and frightened. My body tensed up, and tears started pooling in my eyes. He slowly raised his right arm high in the air as if to give me a high five.

My eyes followed it, but my head didn't move. He then intently held his meaty hand up in the air for a few seconds. Each second was separated by an eternity when he swung the hardened palm of his hand and hit me flush across the face. I saw a flash of light, blurry-eyed and dazed. It made a loud noise, and the stinging pings of pain sent shock waves through my body.

I looked at Mr. Hakimi, expecting to see an expression of satisfaction, but instead, he was shaking his head in disappointment. I gulped, struggling to collect my thoughts while still recovering from the hardest slap of my life.

I couldn't believe what he said next, "That didn't make a loud enough noise, did it, class?"

No one spoke or moved a muscle; afraid they might be next in line.

I held my breath, didn't make a peep, hoping for the nightmare to end. An uncontrollable sound escaped my lungs, a kind of half-sob, half-laugh.

"Really? Now you want to laugh at me, or do you think this is funny?" He innocently smiled, squinting his eyes and raising his eyebrows. He was insistent about repeating the process. He raised his hand up in the air again, aiming for my face.

I flinched from the agony and fear of another swing on the second round as he was about to hit me, but he didn't catch my face plush and missed the mark. That made him ever so furious, his lips quivered in anger, which he tried calmly to hide, and I stood there staring at him. His eyes widened, like a crazed serial killer, the psychotic gaze lingered. They bulged so far out of their sockets; he looked like a cartoon character about to explode.

Again, the same senseless comment came out of his filthy mouth. "That wasn't loud enough!" He exclaimed after the swing and a miss.

He slammed his open hand against my face three or four more times, increasing the pressure each time until he was satisfied. All I heard was a loud ringing in my ear and felt an intense stinging pain on my cheek. He had not counseled a student for days and decided to catch up that day using my face.

I got home with a noticeable welt on my face, Maman saw it as soon as I walked in. The next day she accompanied me to school and attempted to complain to the principal but was respectfully turned away.

The principal told her, "It's normal for students to be disciplined or reprimanded by our faculty. Especially if they are caught sleeping in class or disrespecting the teachers. Your son managed to do both, all in one day, with our most unforgiving teacher, Mr. Hakimi."

Maman looked at me suspiciously. I guess that's the part I forgot to mention to her. She surely felt bad for the welt on my face, but now knew I deserved it.

My parents never physically abused me. When I was younger, Maman chased me around our apartment when I brought home poor grades. She waved a clothes hanger and threatened to hit me, but always waved it in the air, close enough to feel and hear the quick whip of the wind, only inches from my arms or legs. She hardly ever hit me, but I screamed bloody murder, nevertheless.

I knew my grandparents would hear me from upstairs. It was an excuse to tattle tale the following morning at breakfast. I'd tell them how Maman had taken a clothes hanger to my legs and about the vicious whipping I had received, all for their sympathy and attention.

After the actual beating I received from Mr. Hakimi, I worked harder to complete my assignments on time and paid attention to my teachers in all my classes. It was an attempt to avoid another beating at any cost.

A month later, I inadvertently fell behind on my math homework again and needed additional tutoring at home to get caught up. My parents decided to hire a math tutor, which was necessary to avoid failing my math class.

Who did my parents think was the best candidate to tutor me at home? You guessed it, dear Mr. Hakimi. They realized I feared and respected him, therefore they hired him to tutor me after school. He agreed to meet at my grandparents' apartment, where my private lessons occurred at the dining room table.

That first day, I reluctantly greeted him at the door. When he extended out his hand, which was the size of a catcher's mitt, I shook it dutifully, but he didn't immediately let go, vigorously shaking my hand up and down. I was praying he wouldn't rip my arm out of its socket before he finally released me from his clutches.

I felt safe in my grandparents' home and trusted that he couldn't abuse me there, but I quickly learned otherwise. On the first day of tutoring, I tuned him out. Instead, I switched to a polite nodding mode and stopped keeping up with the lesson.

The millisecond he realized my attention was elsewhere, he stopped the lesson. Mr. Hakimi, the hundred fifty pounds of solid steel, sitting amicably next to me at the dinner table, was ready to smack me at the slightest provocation.

The hair stood stiff on the back of my neck, like a porcupine ready to defend itself. He rolled his beefy, thick, meaty hydrant of a neck and had the audacity to stretch before he started to slap me around like a rag doll. Screaming in agony, I was dazed and bleary-eyed after being smacked around by my sadistic teacher. I was loud enough for the neighbors to hear and hoped that my grandparents would barge in any minute to save me.

I waited, but my cries of misery went unnoticed. *How could this be?* They were just outside the other room, yet I waited. But they never came to my rescue from the monster who had invaded their home.

I was sitting at the table I had grown up at, the same one we ate family dinners on, but now I was demoralized by my least favorite teacher. There was no escaping his grasp, not at school or the shelter of my second home. I felt shocked, betrayed, and hurt by my grandparents' inaction to my cries.

After the lesson concluded and Mr. Hakimi left, I stared at my grandparents for answers. I didn't want to believe that they heard my bloody screams of anguish and listened to the whipping I received yet did nothing to intervene.

"Why didn't you do anything to stop him?" I asked them solemnly. Tears were still drying on my face.

"Mr. Hakimi wouldn't be here if you were doing your homework and if you hadn't fallen behind on your assignments," Papa Jahan said, "let alone fallen asleep in his class!" he smirked at me with one eyebrow raised. They did nothing because they knew this might be the best intervention for my failing grades.

To avoid future physical abuse at school or home, I showed immediate improvement in all my classes. Although many of my teachers were unforgiving and dreadful, soon that was the least of our worries.

Approximately one year after Baba had been forced to switch his business from video to photography, the Ershad Ministry decided to pay us a visit. It was a random raid, conducted in the middle of the night, where they forcefully entered our apartment armed with warrants, guns, and flashlights in hand. They were ensuring that Baba had not illegally resumed his video business from home.

Foreign films, dubbing, movie sales, reproduction, and distribution were all banned, but unfortunately during the search, they found around twenty VCRs stowed away in the closet. He had paid good money for those machines and with no way to recoup the investment, he held onto them. The machines were now considered to be contraband.

They handcuffed Baba and took him away from us in the middle of the night like a criminal. Maman was in tears, holding Amin in one arm, with Donya clinging to the other, afraid of what may happen to him. It was Baba's last thread of hope for his love and dedication to the movie business, which sadly had come to "THE END." This was pure madness.

Baba was released after a couple of days of intense questioning. I listened to his troubling story of how the police had also raided his office and seized boxes full of records. The authorities finally verified that he'd changed his business practices before removing him from the suspect list. My teacher's brutality or my father's imprisonment was nothing compared to what came next.

TEN
WAR COMES HOME

TEHRAN, MARCH 1985

"What does a bomb siren sound like?" Mohammad leaned over and asked me innocently.

I couldn't explain the high-pitched sound, but I knew the exact noise it made. I had heard it in *The Big Escape* and *Von Ryan's Express*, two movies Baba's company had translated into Farsi involving Germany's ruthless Nazis.

"It sounds like a high-pitched train siren that keeps going on forever," I told him. I put my hand to his ear and mimicked the sound of a bomb siren; "Waaaaaaaaaaaaauuuuuuuuuueeeeeeee, sounds like that," I told him.

Our teachers explained a procedure called "duck and cover" in case of daytime bombings. "I pray we never have to duck and cover or be close to any exploding bomb," Mohammad wished.

Luckily, we never got to exercise it at school. There weren't any daytime bombings, they only happened at night.

Until now, most of the fighting had taken place on the front line of the battlefield, but war was about to reach our city. Tehran was eventually going to be bombed by the Iraqi Air Force. It is referred to as the "war of the cities," and both sides planned to bomb each other's major cities.

The targets weren't designated military targets, but the goal was to cause mass carnage and demolish urban neighborhoods, killing as many civilians as possible. It was meant to demoralize the population and kill their spirit to keep fighting.

At home, we had different rules though. Living on the twentieth floor meant no bomb shelter, basement, or any type of sanctuary. Management instructed tenants on the upper floors to walk down the stairs to the tenth or eleventh floor of our building. That was our makeshift shelter, where the probability of survival was at its highest.

At the start of the bombing campaign in late March, several sleepless nights went by without a siren or explosions. Those nights were terrifying on their own, the fear and anticipation of the inevitable was unbearable.

My great-grandmother, Maman Bozorg, slept in my room and kept the radio on through the night, turned up loud. It was a silent broadcast that started announcing the bomb siren once the enemy airplanes were detected by radar. An early warning system provided precious time for citizens to seek shelter.

One evening, I kissed my parents and siblings, wishing them pleasant dreams before retiring to bed. At approximately three o'clock in the morning, the loud sound of the bomb siren started blaring through the radio speakers.

I sprang out of bed disoriented and confused. Immediately after the siren started, the electricity to the city was turned off, leaving us in a full blackout. I heard Maman Bozorg struggling to light matches for the kerosene lantern she kept by her bed. I heard my parents crawling out of their bedroom, dragging Donya and Amin with them.

Without electricity, taking the elevator was not an option. Baba was prepared with his battery-operated flashlight illuminating the stairs for us while carrying Donya. I was sluggish, lethargic, wishing to be back in my comfy bed. I heard Baba breathing heavily through his nose, Maman not far behind with Amin in her arms.

Approaching the eleventh floor, we noticed a large crowd of residents who had taken refuge as instructed. Everyone was concerned, horrified, and worried about our impending fate. The war was brewing closer, looming just over the horizon, heading for our doorsteps.

Families were scattered across every inch of the floor and lined up against the hallways. Some nervously standing, some sitting, others leaning on one another to rest or sleep. One thing we had in common; we were trapped, and helplessly waiting for the exploding bombs, dropped by the Iraqi Air Force. We were like sitting ducks along with the rest of Tehran.

The silence stretched on while everyone stayed whisper quiet. Suddenly the distant thunder and rumbling of a bomb were heard and felt. Chills ran down my spine, and my entire body, including the hair on my arms and the back of my neck, bristled as if called to attention. The crowd panicked, women and children screamed. Everyone was petrified. The sound was isolated and produced a mild shock wave, giving everyone a jolt.

There were more explosions in the distance, while the rumbling and tremors were felt throughout the city with each blast. The bombings resumed for around thirty minutes, but much to our relief, they were dropped a distance from our location. At last, the lights came back on, signaling that the bombings were over, and we could return to our homes.

Unfortunately, the elevators were still not operating, which meant a long climb back upstairs for a select few.

"How long is this going to continue, Baba?" I asked.

He shook his head in disappointment, "Hopefully, the bombings will end soon." Breathing heavily. He looked troubled and distracted; it was unsettling to witness Baba like that. He was the rock in my life, my protector, my security blanket, someone who was always in a positive, optimistic mood. The look on his face that night was one I hadn't seen before.

I started to feel insecure and unsafe for the first time in my life. I crawled back into bed, but my thoughts kept me awake, worried about our future and what the war meant for us.

The bombings went on for a couple of weeks, luckily the first wave didn't reach our part of town, although the distant sound of exploding bombs and sensing the mild shockwaves kept everyone on edge within the confines of their shelter.

We were not as fortunate on the second wave of attacks. This time the siren went off around 2 a.m. Approaching the tenth floor, the crowd was humming with casual conversation and normal chit-chat; everyone had become accustomed to seeking shelter in the middle of the night. The bombs had not yet reached our location, and everyone felt a false sense of security, but that changed quickly.

Suddenly, the thundering blast of an explosion deafened us all. The violent shockwave smashed against the building with ferocious intensity. The tower swayed back and forth as if there was an earthquake.

Everyone screamed in terror, petrified of losing their lives. The bombs were dropped much closer, tormenting the horrified crowd with each massive blast. The next bomb exploded even closer and was more rambunctious; it felt like the entire building was going to topple over from the immense force and magnitude of the shockwave. The whole world appeared to rock up and down, the building swooping from side to side like a Jenga set.

I witnessed neighbors praying, pushing their palms together, and asking God for mercy and compassion. It was a heart-wrenching affair, watching parents doing their best to create the slightest bit of comfort for their terrified children.

I trembled with fear while contemplating my own imminent death. My ears had become accustomed to the sound of explosions, my eyes familiar with the frightened look on the families' faces as they prayed for refuge from the falling armament. The erupting thunder got closer, and closer. Enough to think it was our last night on earth.

Families huddled together and started to weep softly. Some started saying farewell to each other. After what felt like hours of torment, the explosions and shockwaves finally faded away. The lights came back on; the relief in the air was palpable. The crowd started cheering and applauding out of pure jubilation at being alive and rejoicing to see another day.

On a future bombing raid, the siren started to blare prior to dawn, around six o'clock in the morning. It was barely light out, I was first to arrive in the living room. I gazed out from our twentieth-floor window, staring at the morning haze when suddenly a bomb dropped a few hundred feet in front of our building; A massive cloud of dust rose hundreds of feet into the sky. I was mesmerized. It was the first time I had seen an explosion right in front of me.

A dusty ring formed around the detonation site like a mushroom cloud and started to rapidly creep out in all directions. The intrigue and wonder soon turned to panic and horror when the wave began creeping towards our building and slammed down with the force of a thousand tons of dynamite...KABOOM! The giant sliding glass windows in our apartment almost came apart and made the loudest commotion slamming into one another from the shockwave. I ran in terror down to the tenth floor without waiting for the rest of my family that morning. I sprinted down the stairs so fast that I was one of the first residents to arrive. Death was knocking at our doorsteps, night after night, without discrimination. It was difficult to imagine the dismay.

The following day at school, Mohammad and I spotted a humongous circular bomb crater, where a bomb had exploded, in the middle of our schoolyard where we played soccer. His facial expression was one of deep concern and shock. He was furious. Not at the fact that we couldn't play soccer anymore but enraged with the Iraqi Air Force and what they had done to our school. He took it very personally.

The shockwave also caused the glass windows to shatter into a million pieces in every classroom, spreading broken glass all over the desks, furniture, and floors.

"I can't wait to join the military, so I can get some payback for what they've done to our school and city," he proudly proclaimed.

"You're too young to join the army, Mohammad," I reminded him.

"I know, but if there was ever a way, I would join in a heartbeat."

It didn't surprise me that Mohammad felt so dedicated to our country, and his passion to join the army. He was emphatic, proud, brave, and wasn't concerned about dying for Iran, in fact, he welcomed it and considered it an honor to martyr himself. He would frown upon those who didn't see it his way.

I was one of them; I had mixed feelings and was confused, but I kept quiet and politely agreed with him, not wanting to disappoint.

The bombings eventually slaughtered thousands of innocent civilians, killing men, women, and children. No one was safe, regardless of what part of the city they lived in. There was no escaping or dismissing the traumatic experience, which affected families from all levels of society, rich or poor, lower class, middle class, heck any class.

We had never been a religious family, though I did believe in God and often attempted to speak with him. It was never praying for God to save my life, never out of necessity. But witnessing the families praying together on bombing nights made me wonder; had I underestimated the true power of prayer? I vowed to practice, to take it more seriously, and hoped that Mohammad would help me.

The nightly bombings were a hair-raising experience, and everyone had their own way of dealing with it. For Baba, the bombings hit too close to home, literally. This may have been the first time he considered moving our family out of Iran.

During the past few years as the war raged on, many families we knew had moved out of the country and emigrated to Germany, Sweden, Canada, and America to name a few.

My father and I had never discussed the possibility of me going abroad to complete my education, much like Cousin Shahin. Perhaps I was too young to be a participant in that kind of decision. Unbeknownst to me, he'd started to set the wheels in motion for what came next.

ELEVEN
EXILE

TEHRAN, 1986

One night as I was walking out of my room, I overheard Baba on the phone, "Can you tell me more about the process of taking him to America?"

I stood in the hallway, hiding out of his view, eavesdropping. I couldn't hear the other person on the phone, but Baba was busy scribbling down information. I patiently waited until he hung up the phone, then casually walked into the room, "Who were you on the phone with Baba?" I asked.

"I was speaking to Amoo Hafez, Pendar."

"About what?"

"Oh, about how he took Cousin Shahin, to America. You remember that don't you?"

"Yeah, of course. But why are you asking him about that?"

"Well, I'm thinking about moving our family to America, what do you think?"

My ears perked up in excitement, eyes grew wide. "Are you serious Baba? We're moving to America?" I exclaimed, jumping up and down.

"Well, maybe not all at once, but let me talk to Maman to see if I can convince her. It's a big decision and we're only speaking about it right now, Okay?"

"All right, I won't act too excited," I said, trying not to sound gleeful.

The war had raged on for more than five years but now it was inching closer to our home; it was an unsettling feeling, too much for Baba to bear. He was looking for alternative options, as my parents' plan of remaining in Iran had become a questionable dilemma. Their decision would forever change the direction of our lives and alter my destiny. They were cautiously investigating every option, because of the repercussions it would have on the rest of our family.

Baba took weeks determining our best course of action. A few months later, is when I learned of his decision. We were sitting at the dining room table as a family, eating a tasty meal Maman had just prepared.

Maman was feeding Amin in his highchair, and Donya was seated next to me. Baba was at the head of the table, as usual, when Maman suddenly got noticeably quiet, and I spotted a single tear running down her cheek, leaving behind a trail of her black-colored mascara. Although women were not supposed to wear makeup in public, she continued to apply it in private.

"What's wrong, Maman?" I asked in concern.

Baba already knew but didn't divulge any information.

After a moment of containing herself, she said, "I was thinking about leaving our home for a strange country. How I'd miss our home and the rest of the family," Tears pooled in her eyes, but she urged to smile through the discomfort.

"Would you miss my cooking Pendar? The traditional foods I've always cooked for you?" she asked.

"Of course I would miss it Maman, your cooking is the best in the world, I wouldn't give it up for anything."

She cried harder and couldn't contain herself, having to step away from the table.

It was awkward, and I didn't comprehend her intense emotions. Baba stepped in, "She'll be okay, she needs some time to think it over. It is a big decision like I told you, remember?"

I nodded in agreement.

"Your uncle already explained the process. First, Amoo Hafez and Cousin Shahin went to Istanbul, Turkey and got their visas from the American Embassy. Afterwards, they traveled to America, where Shahin lives now with our relatives Azad and Star, who have become his legal guardians."

"Yeah Baba, I remember Shahin telling me about them when he came to say goodbye."

"That's right! Well, what do you think about going to America like your cousin Shahin?"

What? I did a double take and thought I misheard him, "Do you mean by myself?"

Baba put his hand on my shoulder and looked directly into my eyes. "It would just be for a little while."

His question surprised me, I'd always dreamt of going to America, but never without my family. Many kids I knew dreamed of going to America, but not all parents had the financial capacity. And some parents weren't lucky enough to have the connections.

Thoughts of living the American dream distracted me from the feelings of separation from my family. After all, they were going to join me soon after I arrived. My fantasies were filled with the American lifestyle like I'd seen in the movies, a way of life I'd always admired, muscle cars, tall palm trees, diverse music, fast food, beautiful girls, movies, and loud motorcycles.

I'd developed a love affair with America through the many films I'd watched over the years, beginning with Jaws at the Cinema Rivoli when I was four. I admired America through movies and could only imagine what my life would be like. The movie *Grease*, which I adored so much, may have given me a distorted sense of reality, and filled my head with unrealistic hopes and expectations.

"How long would I live there without you?" I asked.

"First, I'll take you to America, but will return to Iran shortly after you're settled. Then I will sell our home and business here in Tehran, pack our belongings and move out to join you. How does that sound?"

"That sounds great! Are we moving to Los Angeles, too?"

"No Pendar, we're going to live in Arlington, a city located in the state of Texas."

"Aweee Baba, why can't we move to Los Angeles? Visit with Cousin Shahin, go to Hollywood, where they make movies!"

"No son, we can't. We're going to live in Arlington where my friend Kiya lives right now," Baba explained. He was talking about his childhood friend, Kiya. The two had attended school together and when they were older, Kiya became Baba's trusted movie companion back when foreign films were still being shown in theaters. I didn't remember meeting him, but I remembered the funny story Baba told me of his and Kiya's misadventure back when they were fourteen and stayed out past curfew to see *Dr. No*.

Baba explained that Kiya had left Iran and moved to the States not long after the Revolution and was now living in Arlington, where he managed a bridal shop.

"Baba, where is Arlington? And where's Texas?" I asked, confused.

"The city of Arlington and the state of Texas are in a different part of America. Far from where Shahin lives," Baba said.

Baba next told me about a woman named Shirley Foster. "Shirley owns the bridal shop that Kiya now manages, and she has agreed to become your legal guardian. That means you can stay with Shirley in Texas while we get ready to join you."

I was excited and surprised to hear about this. Baba hardly had to twist my arm to say yes. I'd dreamed of emigrating to America for a long time and here was my opportunity.

Baba understood the degree of difficulty in obtaining a visa and sending me to America, but his concerns were overlooked due to Amoo Hafez and Cousin Shahin's successful attempt.

———

In the following months, Shirley, my soon-to-be legal guardian, prepared the necessary documents required by the American Embassy, signed them, and mailed them to us in Iran.

In preparation for my departure to America, I was sent to private English lessons. My parents believed a few months of learning how to write and speak English would benefit my education in America. Although I already knew many English words and phrases, because of all of the American movies and shows I had watched over the years.

I often despised my school homework, but I found the English classes enjoyable and was eager to learn. My teacher had previously lived in America and taught English lessons out of her home, and always with the correct pronunciation and a proper American accent.

English words were written "backwards" (left to right, instead of right to left) unlike in the Farsi language. My teacher explained that certain words were also pronounced differently than how they were written on paper. "The following English words are normally written as 'Get out of here,' but you'd hardly hear an American say it like that. They would pronounce it 'Getta reheeye.'"

The phrase and her accent were unrecognizable. I was suddenly baffled, but I attempted to pronounce the sentences like my teacher, mimicking her American accent and soon I began to recognize certain phrases and the way it would be pronounced with an American accent.

I was growing more excited with each day. I wanted to share the news with everyone. But I avoided telling Mohammad, fearful he would hate me for betraying our country and joining the dark side. He was so dedicated and ready to die for Iran, but I was running away to safety, like a coward from his perspective.

It took several weeks, but I finally told him. We were in the school yard when I cornered him. "Mohammad," I began. "Baba is taking me to America. Our whole family plans to move over there." I couldn't look at him while delivering the news.

"Why would you want to move to America?" he asked. "They're the DEVIL!" His disappointed gaze made me uncomfortable. I didn't have the guts to tell him that this was something I had always aspired to do.

With my father's acceptance of American pop culture, movies, and social mores, nothing Mohammad could say or do could convince me otherwise. The truth was, I didn't want to stay in war-torn Iran any longer.

TWELVE
LEAVING HOME

TEHRAN, NOVEMBER 1986

The news of Baba and I traveling to America spread like a brushfire throughout our family, and soon it wasn't just the two of us traveling anymore. Amoo Hafez, who had recently gotten a divorce from his wife, decided he would relocate to America.

Amoo Payam and his wife Aunt Saye also decided they would accompany us to Turkey, with hopes of applying for a visitor's visa to the States.

Since Amoo Hafez had previously visited the American Embassy in Turkey with Shahin to secure his visa, he would be our tour guide. He booked us rooms at the same hotel in Istanbul where he and Shahin had stayed. Amoo Hafez was a frugal man and chose the hotel not only to meet his budget, but it was located close to the American embassy.

As was customary, my parents planned a farewell party for me and invited all our relatives. This would be a way to give everyone a chance to say their goodbyes. Our final gathering was scheduled for the night before our flight out of Tehran. I was eager to be the center of attention one final time.

The mood was festive, and Baba snapped what felt like a hundred pictures. It felt good having everyone clambering for my attention.

As the party was winding down, I called Mohammad to say goodbye and to wish him well. He had always been there for me at school, and I was certainly going to miss him.

The phone at his home rang endlessly, but no one ever picked up. As if we were not meant to say goodbye and to silently grow apart.

At the end of the night, I said my tearful goodbyes to my extended family and friends. I awkwardly hugged my many cousins and listened to their advice. They wished us luck and safe travels; some even agreed to see us off at the airport the following morning.

Our trip, or "the journey," began in late-November 1986, just five weeks shy of my thirteenth birthday. With our suitcases loaded, the car pulled away from our apartment complex, while my great-grandmother poured a bowl of water behind the vehicle as we departed. The gesture of throwing water behind a traveler is believed to make their journey as smooth as possible and to wish them a happy return.

I turned back to take a long last look at my home, watching through the rearview window as the triplet towers disappeared into the horizon.

A crowd of close to fifty people, uncles, aunts, grandparents, cousins, and friends of the family, awaited us at the terminal.

Saying goodbye to so many loved ones was difficult, and I started to feel anxious. Each one hugged me tight for a long while, tears pooling in their eyes or running down their cheeks. I felt the loving hands of my family patting my back and tousling my hair.

It was heartbreaking saying goodbye to Maman and my siblings. Over the last few days, Maman had looked upset, but today she seemed on the verge of tears.

My mother had hardly spoken that morning, and I could tell she was struggling to contain her emotions. My attempt to stay calm and in control of my feelings was futile.

Maman and I locked eyes; I froze. She was visibly shaken, tears streaming down her face, and her nose was running. "Khodafez azizam 'bye my dear'. Be safe and take care of yourself!" she uttered with a sickened heart once we reached the front of the line.

For a moment, I couldn't fathom why she was crying so intensely; we were going to see each other again in America soon.

Baba had to forcibly remove her hand from mine because she wasn't willing to let go.

"We'll see each other again," I told her. "It won't be long, I promise, Maman."

As I followed my father, my two uncles and my aunt to the departure gate, I began to feel homesick. The mood was somber, the scene at the airport left me with a deep pain in the pit of my stomach, as I relived the intensity of Maman's cries.

My uncles were making jokes to cheer me up. I clung tightly to

Baba's hand, realizing that it may be a while before I was reunited with Maman, my siblings, and the rest of my family.

We were flying Iran Air, the official airline of the Islamic Republic of Iran. As the plane took off, with sadness in my heart, I leaned my head toward the tiny oval window and banged my head against it with a gentle thud. I watched the city of Tehran grow smaller and smaller while I silently said goodbye to the city I'd grown up in.

The glimmering lights soon disappeared out of sight, as we soared towards cruising altitude. Flight attendants were bustling about the cabin and started passing out toy airplane kits to all the children. I couldn't wait for my turn.

The Boeing 747-replica toy of the plane we were flying in kept me occupied during our flight. My imagination ran wild, as I mimicked the jet engine sound of an airplane, taking off from my food tray, but only to crash land into the seatbacks.

Passengers around us started to whisper in discomfort, as I had unintentionally triggered their unconscious fear of a plane crash.

Baba noticed and took the toy airplane away from me.

I was upset, breathing heavy through my nose, almost a light cry. To unknowing passengers, I was merely a spoiled brat, but Baba knew why I was grieving. The toy airplane symbolized the loss and separation I felt from the minute we left the airport. It was a temporary distraction, but Baba comforted me and cheered me up. He was good at that.

The flight to Istanbul took three and a half hours. The food service was provided, but when my tray was cleared, images of a tearful Maman returned.

Baba did his best to console me. "We're almost there," he soothed. "Less than 30 minutes before we land."

Soon, the plane began its descent, and rolling green mountains came into view through my window, quickly replaced by the lights of Istanbul. I could see the huge waves of the Black Sea crashing against the seawall just a few hundred feet away from the runway.

The bang of the landing gear dropping from the plane's belly startled me and was followed by the loud screech of the wheels hitting the runway. Once the "fasten seat belt" sign was turned off, Baba took my hand and told me, "We should be arriving at our hotel soon."

I imagined comfortable hotel sheets, plush carpets, and a luxurious lobby. I felt a glimmer of excitement, mixed with feelings of guilt remembering Maman's face, her eyes swelled and filled with tears. That image was seared into my memory and kept flashing before my eyes each time I thought of her.

———

Amoo Hafez was familiar with Istanbul Airport and navigated through it like a pro. We collected our luggage from the conveyor belt and went outside to hail a taxi to our hotel.

Amoo Hafez spoke broken Turkish and gave instructions to the taxi driver, a scrawny, dark-skinned man with a pencil-thin mustache, a few missing teeth, and wearing a royal-blue baseball cap that covered a few remaining strands of his gray hair.

The roads were congested, clogged with traffic all the way to the hotel. I rolled down my window and watched the bustle of the city blurring past me. I observed the people walking along the public streets, and suddenly I noticed that women were not wearing *hijabs* or *mantos*. It had been years since I'd seen a woman walking in public with her hair uncovered. When we stopped at a light, I could see that many of them were wearing makeup. Women were dressed in short-sleeved tops and miniskirts.

This was the first sign of freedom. I needed to get accustomed to the culture shock before arriving in America.

"The city seems more crowded than I can remember," Amoo Hafez remarked.

The taxi driver came to a stop along the curb where our hotel was located, but the street was narrow, and traffic rapidly piled up behind us.

We quickly pulled our bags from the back of the van and headed for the lobby.

When my parents and I traveled through Germany, we'd stayed at upscale hotels with uniformed door attendants. But looking at the nondescript façade and unadorned lobby door, I knew this was going to be a dissimilar experience. The decrepit building was only three stories tall and looked more like a hostel than a hotel. Once inside the lobby, we were unpleasantly met by a thick cloud of smoke and the pungent smell of cigarettes.

Baba whispered to Amoo Hafez, "Are we at the right hotel Dadash, (brother)?"

My uncle smiled, then said, "We sure are!"

We scanned the lobby, taken aback by the number of people crowding the small, sparsely furnished space. People from a multitude of nationalities were grouped together, stuffed into every corner of the room, some sitting on their luggage, some playing backgammon or card games, most of them smoking. People were literally squeezed across every couch, on every chair and along every inch of wall.

Baba looked perplexed, his head cocked to one side, thoughtfully rubbing his chin, as if he were trying to make sense of each person's role in this unusual scene.

Despite the crowd, there was no line at the check-in counter, where the manager, an older, grim-faced, balding man sat smoking a cigarette and sipping from a stained coffee mug. His dingy-white button-down shirt looked snug around his big belly, and a massive gaudy gold necklace hung from his thick neck, nestled in the long fur sticking out of his shirt. On his forearms was a thick coating of course, black hair that looked like it belonged on a grizzly bear. When he opened his mouth to speak, I saw that his teeth were stained brown, probably the result of an outrageous intake of nicotine and caffeine.

I leaned in close to the counter and was overcome by his stench, like feet not washed for weeks. The odor was so overpowering, it made me gag.

Amoo Hafez handed him payment for our rooms, and he shoved the bills into the beat-up cash register, then motioned with his chin to the staircase. There was no elevator in this old building; it was ancient-looking, I imagined it was probably built before the elevator was invented.

We lugged our suitcases up the creaky stairs to the second floor, then made our way down a dimly lit hallway to the last room on the left. We stood at the door, eyeing it with trepidation.

Baba turned to Amoo Hafez and asked, "Were the hotel conditions the same when you visited here last with Shahin?"

"No. Things were in better shape, and the lobby didn't look like that. I don't know what's going on!" Amoo Hafez replied, shrugging his shoulders.

We mustered the courage and unlocked the door. Baba glanced inside the room, blinked twice, and shook his head in disappointment. The accommodations looked crummy and felt more like a jail cell than a hotel room, with two single, steel-frame beds topped with thin, worn mattresses, ragged blankets, a wooden desk in the corner and a single window overlooking the noisy street below. It was dimly lit, cold, and filled with negative energy.

We sat on the wispy mattresses, the afternoon sunlight casting a rectangular wedge of light onto the cracked linoleum floor.

Baba sensed my unease and tried to reassure me. "Don't worry Pendar, this is going to be a short stay. I know we're not off to a great start, but everything is going to be alright! I promise!"

His words of encouragement and knowing about our planned visit to the American Embassy made it tolerable. Still, a wave of sadness hit me as I started to unpack my suitcase. I thought about how Maman had packed it with love and care, mindful to include all the necessities for my journey. At that moment, a slow reality began to overtake me. I would soon be living on my own and the responsibility of chores like this would fall on me.

I was a pampered child; Maman and Baba had always been there to support me. Suddenly, my bladder gave me signals of discomfort. I needed to use the bathroom, but I didn't see one in our room.

"Baba, where is the bathroom?"

Looking around the room, my father found a small closet, and with a horrified expression, he motioned for me to follow him out to the hallway, where we eventually located a singular lavatory that was shared by all the guests on the second floor.

It was disgusting and smelled worse. It was clear from the rancid stench that it hadn't been cleaned in days. I nearly vomited and held my nose to avoid inhaling the foul stink. There were cracks in the cement floor, cobwebs on the ceiling where the walls met and dead flies littering the windowsill. Baba waited for me in the hallway, he was eager to call Maman. We headed back down to the lobby in hopes of locating a public phone.

At the front desk, the manager sat reading a newspaper and looking annoyed to see us again. Baba put his thumb to his ear, and his pinky to his mouth, like a makeshift phone receiver. The manager picked up his cigarette from the overfilled ashtray and took a humongous drag, then pointed to the public phone across the lobby.

Another hotel guest was using it and there were a few other guests waiting in line. Baba counted the loose change in his pocket, hoping to have enough coins to complete the call.

The line for the phone moved slowly, but finally, it was our turn. First, Baba dialed the number, then we fed multiple coins into the payphone until the call was connected.

That's when I heard Maman's soft voice. "Hi Nader Jan, how was your flight? Is everything going well so far?"

"Everything is alright Ziba, we made it safely to our hotel, and we're going to the embassy first thing tomorrow morning."

I squeezed closer to my father and pressed my head against the receiver, hoping to hear her voice. I was already missing her, even though we'd only been apart for a brief time.

"Let me talk to Pendar please," I heard her say.

"Hello Maman," I said.

For a moment, there was silence, then a faint sob. I detected she was trying to contain her tears for my benefit, but as the conversation progressed, it became harder for her to get a word out without breaking down. The cracking in her voice made me heartsick, and all I could see was her tear-streaked face waving me off at the airport.

Fighting through my own tears, I told her, "Everything is good here, Maman, don't worry! I'm fine."

We spoke for a few minutes, and I blew her kisses, making big smooching sounds into the receiver. "I love you Maman, and I miss you so much already," I told her.

"Stay safe Pendar Jan, take care of yourself. Always stick by Baba and be a good boy!"

"Don't worry, Maman. We're going to be in America soon," I said confidently.

As we headed back towards the staircase, Baba noticed a few Iranian patrons hanging out in the lobby and struck up a conversation. We were surprised by what they told us. They had come to Turkey in hopes of securing an interview at the American Embassy. They'd been staying at the hotel but were scammed out of their life savings only to find themselves broke and homeless. The hotel manager allowed them to stay in the lobby for a few days while they waited for financial help in the form of a wire transfer, Western Union, or assistance from their attorney.

But their stories were not unique. Many had sold all their possessions in Iran in hopes of emigrating to America.

One of the men told Baba that there were no appointments available at the American Embassy in Istanbul anytime soon. "Don't even bother trying," he said. "Just getting an appointment or an interview at the embassy is almost impossible," another man told us. "And even if you do, chances of getting a visa are more unlikely. They're not giving anyone a visa!"

I took a deep breath and fought down the negativity.

Baba dismissed the warnings and told them, "We've prepared for months, we've got our documents and we're going to visit the Embassy regardless."

They warned us about unscrupulous characters that lurked around the embassy in search of new victims to con. "Don't get scammed by those scumbags, they're thieves!"

We learned that a group of conmen had convinced several families that they had a special connection to one of the American consuls and promised them not only an appointment, but a guaranteed visa to America for the whole family. Unfortunately for them, it was a false story to scam them out of their life savings.

As it turned out, this family and many others were now stuck in the lobby, stranded, with barely enough money to eat, waiting for a miracle. Obviously, we were not alone in our quest to obtain an American visa.

The stories were upsetting and heartbreaking, not to mention discouraging.

Later that night, the five of us stepped out of the hotel and went on our first adventure for supper. Not far from the hotel, we found ourselves on a bustling street lined with shops. It was a noisy lane in a maze of alleyways congested with pedestrians, bikes, and trucks. As we strolled along, I caught myself gawking at the newsstand. There were magazines and newspapers casually on display with images of nude women on the cover. Baba stopped, too, and was peeking, but Amoo Hafez coughed, "AHEM," as a reminder that it was not proper for a twelve-year-old to be looking at these types of images. We continued along until my senses were tickled by the appetizing aroma of roasted chicken that filled the air.

I was starving, and the mouthwatering smell captivated my senses. We followed our noses to a restaurant with towering rotisserie machines lined up in the front windows.

At my insistence, we settled on rotisserie chicken for dinner, ordering two whole birds, with fresh baked bread and all the fixings. The food tasted like heaven and the five of us attacked it like a pack of hungry hyenas.

After the meal, we headed back to our rooms, and rested for our early morning visit to the American Embassy. A succession of honking car horns and police sirens filled the night. I pushed the yellow mildewy curtains aside and pressed my forehead against the window-pane, fogging it up with each breath. With my index finger, I wrote the letters USA in the foggy glass. Baba missed it before it dissipated.

Our beds were uncomfortable, with mattresses so thin I could feel the steel of the bed frame against my back. Despite the discomfort, I gripped my pillow tight and said a prayer.

Though in school, they taught us to pray, I never bothered, and it made me think of Mohammad. How I admired him, and wished to be more enlightened, the way he felt while praying. Laying sleepless in bed, I asked God for guidance. A prayer, and a wish to obtain an appointment, to speak with a consul, and to find success at the embassy.

I laid my destiny in God's hands and asked that we would accomplish our mission the following day. I kept positive thoughts rotating in my head. Speculating that soon, I would be on my way to America, to meet my future legal guardian, Shirley Foster. I hoped.

THIRTEEN
SECURING AN APPOINTMENT

We met up in the lobby at seven-thirty the following morning, ready to head over to the embassy. Having heard the nightmare stories from the families now stranded in Istanbul, I was anxious and struggled to push the doubts out of my mind.

We arrived just before eight a.m., but there was already a massive line. A few hundred immigrants waited in the lengthy line that wrapped around the block.

Baba again, was quick to spot a few Iranians in the cue. He approached them immediately, "How long have you been waiting in line?" he asked.

One of them answered back, "We got here before dawn, but the line hasn't moved in the last two hours."

We waited patiently for the next few hours. In the passing time, we had moved only a few feet further ahead.

By the early afternoon, we spotted a group of distraught applicants who were walking away from the embassy. Baba flagged down another Iranian couple. "What happened in there? Is the embassy still open?" he asked.

They stopped in their tracks and said, "There are too many applicants requesting an appointment. They just announced the next availability for an interview will be in a month."

Amoo Hafez was willing to remain in line and wished to set up his appointment. He was confident based on his previous visit to the embassy in Istanbul that they'd issue him another visitor's visa. However, waiting for weeks was not an option for Amoo Payam, Aunt Saye, Baba, or me.

"When you get inside, ask them about other options," Baba told him. "Maybe they have another suggestion for us."

We stopped at a nearby café for lunch. After a couple of hours, Amoo Hafez came out of the embassy with developing news. "I got the next available appointment in four weeks! And the embassy employees recommended Ankara, it's rumored to be less crowded and shorter waiting period for appointments. It's a few hours away from Istanbul, about five hundred kilometers east of here."

I told myself 'It's not over yet'.

Amoo Hafez recommended traveling by train to Ankara, the most feasible option. While he made travel arrangements, I made friends with a few kids, stuck in the lobby of our hotel. We played backgammon, 'Hokm,' a different version of 'Spades', and told tales about our common goal of going to America.

In the days leading up to our departure, we discovered a local amusement park with carnival rides.

We also visited a few local landmarks. But it was an effort to pass the time and not think about the obvious; we didn't have an appointment yet, nor were we any closer to the next embassy.

To reach the train station, we had to take a boat ride to Izmit via two ferries. Once in Izmit, we boarded the luxurious train car with sleeping compartments lined up along one side. We had a private compartment shared between Amoo Hafez, Baba, and me. Our room was equipped with pull out beds, and a small bathroom that looked sanitary.

Amoo Payam and his wife got a separate compartment for privacy. Shortly after settling in, we walked to the next car, the one dedicated to the restaurant and dining area. We ate dinner while the train slowly made its way to Ankara, traveling through the night, an adventure that took nearly eighteen hours. Back in our cabin, Baba pulled out our beds, the gentle rocking motion of the train helped me sleep like a baby.

ANKARA, TURKEY, NOVEMBER 1986

We arrived at the train station in Ankara and hailed a taxi. Once again, Amoo Hafez relayed instructions to our driver in broken Turkish.

He took us to a hotel near the American Embassy, within walking distance. This hotel was a vast improvement over the one in Istanbul.

Our rooms were basic, but the sheets were clean, the carpet vacuumed, paint was not peeling off the walls, and there was an in-room bathroom. Baba was delighted to find a phone in our room as well.

It was early in the afternoon by the time we unpacked, but Baba was eager to get to the embassy. He didn't want to waste another day. It was only a fifteen-minute walk from our hotel, so we set off on foot.

Ankara was less congested than Istanbul, but a noticeable difference in late November was the icy wintry weather. The type of cold that burns your skin. Although Maman had packed plenty of warm clothes for me, nothing prepared us for the unforgiving frosty air.

We inched closer to the embassy, I spotted the American flag, waving high on top of a large white building, surrounded by a towering wrought iron fence. A substantial line of immigrants waited outside, but it was half as long as the one in Istanbul.

It was late in the day, and we decided to come back early the following morning. However, before we departed, Baba glanced over at an Iranian family that caught his attention.

The couple quietly waited in line, accompanied by their daughter who looked about my age. He started a conversation, asking about the wait time. The couple gladly informed us, "We've been in line since early morning, and it looks like we're going to make it in today. We heard appointment times are usually within a week once you make it inside."

This was the third time I witnessed Baba starting a conversation with total strangers, assuming they spoke Farsi. I thought it was interesting how he was able to pick out other Iranians from across the street. The connection amongst compatriots was an amazing phenomenon to witness. They were magnetically drawn to each other. It was as if they had a secret unspoken language that involved intricate eyebrow movements, facial expressions, and certain body language, which was how they communicated.

Often, they felt compelled to offer each other advice, guidance, grievance, sympathy, and even moral support.

Baba continued asking the family multiple questions and they eagerly obliged. Once satisfied, he wished them luck and we headed back towards our hotel.

For dinner, we ventured out to a restaurant nearby, one that served *doner kebabs*. They were delicious, savory, and it was another satisfying meal in a strange, foreign city.

After eating, we headed back to our room and called it a night. Once again, I put my hands together and prayed to God. I prayed for victory, my hands pressed together, looking up at the ceiling. I thought about

Mohammad often at nights, I missed playing soccer with him. I wondered what he was doing at that moment.

On November 27th, Baba and I woke up early, ate breakfast, and strolled towards the embassy. Amoo Payam and his wife stayed behind, planning on going the following day. Baba insisted we didn't apply in a group or draw more attention to ourselves.

We eagerly waited in line with the rest of the applicants – Baba stood with his hands stuffed in the pockets of his raincoat, avoiding the bitter iciness.

After waiting a couple of hours, my body, face, and limbs were numb from the unwelcoming cold. I stood there shivering, while the hair on my eyebrows started to frost. But with every passing second, with every step, we were closer to the entrance, the exact motivation we needed to continue. I leaned into Baba for warmth, but he was as frozen as I felt. Once close enough, I spotted the front lawn, just outside the embassy door, on the other side of the fence. The grass was neatly mowed, circular clusters of flowers neatly planted, bordered by razor straight hedges, the height of orderliness-which contrasted the disorder of our lives.

The embassy was extremely clean and well maintained. Finally, after hours of waiting in the bitter cold, we arrived at the guard shack in front of the security gate. An American soldier stood at attention, armed with an automatic machine gun.

The guard verified our documents and told us to wait. The list of documents required was several photos, copies of my school records translated into English, and the affidavit of support signed by Shirley Foster. Finally, the guard at the window said, "Your scheduled interview with the consul is set for December the 3rd at 10 a.m." whilst handing our document back.

Baba paid the application fee for both of us with jubilation. That was the first step in the right direction, we were delighted to finally have our appointments. We left the embassy with a feeling of accomplishment.

Baba was thrilled as we rushed back to call Maman and informed her about our upcoming appointment.

We spent the next four days touring the sights, and Baba had another surprise for me. One afternoon he asked me, "Do you want to see an American film, Pendar? In the movie theater?"

I raised my eyebrows high on my forehead and eagerly nodded, "YES!"

"The name of the movie is *Romancing the Stone*, and it's playing at a theater around the corner from our hotel."

The movie was about a cast of characters chasing after an enormous green emerald called "El Corazon" (The Heart). Watching it, I helplessly compared the big precious jewel to the elusive American visa we sought after.

I was still on a movie high when we got back to the hotel and started explaining the intense action to Amoo Hafez. He was my perfect audience, totally immersed in my tale, his face shifting with the changing tones of my story. I crawled on the floor beside his feet, next to the bed he was sitting on, acting out one of the scenes when a giant crocodile jumped out of the water, and bit off the hand of one of the bad guys. Suddenly with a loud, monstrous noise, I grabbed onto Amoo Hafez's leg with both arms, pretending they were the jaws of the crocodile clamping down on his legs. I thrashed around just like in the movie, the motion so violent, I accidentally pulled him right off the bed.

As he slid off, he hit the ground, butt-first, which resulted in a wide-eyed gaze from him. After a moment of silence, Baba and I looked at each other, then suddenly burst into hysterical laughter.

Amoo Hafez reluctantly joined in as well while struggling to get back on the bed. That came as a relief from the tension and stress we'd been feeling, while traveling through Turkey. The dilemma of our situation, the grimness of the armed guards, the long lines, the freezing cold, and the importance of our mission laid heavily on my mind. But at that moment, I got to act like a young boy again. It felt great to be laughing for a change, not concerned about a visa or our next step.

A trickle of hope fluttered in my chest leading up to our appointment date at the embassy. Followed by conflicting feelings of nervousness and anxiety. Foreseeing our triumph was my only refuge from the disparaging thoughts.

FOURTEEN
AT THE EMBASSY

ANKARA, TURKEY, DECEMBER 3RD, 1986.

Finally, it was appointment day - another brisk walk to the embassy. We felt optimistic and arrived two hours ahead of our scheduled appointment. Baba and I had separate files, I was applying for a student visa, while he applied for a visitor's visa.

Our applications required us to list all existing family members. Baba's application required him to submit documents on his business, plus an extensive background check.

"Why does the embassy ask for information about the rest of our family?" I asked Baba.

"It's like a hostage situation, son. If the embassy knows that Maman, Donya, and Amin are back in Iran, then there's a better chance that I'll return because of them." he explained.

While standing in line, I noticed a few individuals entering the embassy without waiting or the need for an appointment. A flash of their passport is all it took for them to enter the compound. Judging from their appearance, they looked American.

I peeked a quick glance at one of the American passports, spotting a bald eagle on the cover. To me, it was like a holy book that contained mystical and unexplained powers. In my mind, it glowed brightly, representing power and freedom.

The guards treated the American citizens like royalty. However, their attitude towards the immigrants standing in line was vastly different. Often, they were stone-faced, emotionless, and hardly spoke, military-like and had a lack of personality. But once an American citizen walked up, they lit up with an ear-to-ear smile and welcomed them in like an invited guest to their home.

Meanwhile, a few applicants who had entered the embassy ahead of us started to exit after their interviews. There was a young couple celebrating, screaming, jumping up and down with joy. Boasting about going to America with excitement. It was like hitting the jackpot or lottery.

Not long after, we saw another family exiting, but they had a defeated look on their faces. They were obviously dejected, disappointed, and couldn't find any motivation to hold their heads up, consoling each other in their moment of grief.

As we waited, I started to daydream. I could already imagine; Baba and I received our visas, wailing with elation. I daydreamed about arriving at the airport in Texas, embracing my legal guardian and starting a new chapter of my life.

Once they called our names, I was jolted out of my daydream when Baba yanked me to the security gate by my jacket. We announced ourselves to the guard; he confirmed our appointment and opened the gates to the embassy. We walked towards the entrance, admission beyond the tall wrought iron fence felt like a big accomplishment.

We were instructed to walk through a metal detector before entry. The security was tight, just like at the airport, while armed guards cautiously observed the crowd's movements.

Once inside, we were greeted by the pretty secretary sitting at a desk. A thirty-something, lean-faced, red-headed woman dressed in a burgundy blouse and beige slacks who smiled and asked for our paperwork. She stepped away for a moment, her high heels clicking on the polished floor. When she returned, she kindly pointed us to an adjacent room which sat 20 or so applicants, all waiting to be called for an interview.

We found two empty seats in the crowded room and sat down. Baba spotted the family we'd met days earlier in line and sprung out of his seat to connect with them. When he returned, he told me in a low whisper, the voice he took on when I embarrassed him in public, "Their daughter is going to be called any minute now. They think there's a good chance of getting her a visa."

I curiously glanced into the next room while the door opened and observed several windows, where interviews were being held, like a bank teller. Instead of bank employees, there were American consuls sitting opposite the bulletproof glass.

Soon after, the family Baba was speaking with was called into the interview room. I kept shifting in my seat, nervously untying, and retying my shoelaces. We waited another thirty minutes before our names were called.

I was nervous, my palms were sweaty, my heart was beating fast, and I broke out in a cold sweat before entering the interview area. Enormous effort had gone into getting to this moment, and I needed to seize the opportunity.

We made our way into the next room, as the other family was already on their way out. Just then I locked eyes with the young girl, who looked panic-stricken, her eyes gushing with sad tears.

Her body language and demeanor told me everything I needed to know. Crying hysterically, her parents embraced her, comforting her, both shaking their heads in disappointment.

Baba looked at her dad and nodded his head side to side, pinched his lips together with an understanding stare that said "I'm sorry" without saying a word.

My heart sank as I entered the adjacent room with trepidation, but I tried to let it go. In this room, tall partitions separated each applicant.

We appeared at the window and waited for the interview to commence. "Think positive, Pendar. Put those English lessons to good use, don't be nervous. Everything's going to be alright," Baba reassured me.

Most Iranian applicants required the use of a translator to communicate with the consul. In our case, I was the translator, which was another nerve-wracking responsibility. Baba saw it as an upper hand and believed it would set us apart from other applicants.

"Remember to tell the consul that you're going back to Iran after your education is completed. Tell them you promised Maman that you'd go back," Baba instructed me.

"But aren't you and Maman going to come to America like we talked about?" I asked in confusion.

"Yes Pendar, we are, but don't say anything about that to the consul!"

Baba had always been an honest businessman and he was never considered to be a deceitful person. But witnessing the other family's failed attempt must have pushed him over the edge. Now he was purposely instructing me to lie. I didn't have enough time to process or contemplate what he'd just asked of me.

Just then the consul walked up to the window and took a seat. We were greeted by a cordial, mild-mannered, middle-aged woman who had both our files. She was a tad overweight, her hair in a ponytail, and wore thinly rimmed eyeglasses. She introduced herself and asked us about the need for a translator.

I shifted on my feet, gulped, and cleared my throat, "I'm the translator." I announced proudly.

She tilted her head down, gave me a stare from over her eyeglasses and asked, "You're the translator? Are you sure about that young man?"

"Yes Miss! I've been taking English classes in Iran, and I want to continue the interview in English please," I said with confidence.

She pushed her lips to one side, raised her eyebrows at me and looked impressed. "Does your father need a translator?" she asked.

"No. I will translate for my father also," I told her.

She was taken aback by this unusual circumstance but agreed to proceed with the interview. She meticulously thumbed through our documents. She politely asked about my family and education before the tough questions started, "Why do you want to travel to America?"

I answered her honestly. "I've always dreamed of going to America, where I want to complete my education."

"And please tell me about your father's business and the purpose of his trip to America?" she asked Baba.

He answered in Farsi, then I translated back to her in English. Everything seemed to be going as planned thus far.

The interview continued with her asking us many more questions. Satisfied, she turned to Baba with a smile and said, "Congratulations on your successful visa application to the United States, you are approved at this time!"

I translated this for Baba, and he looked relieved. Like a big weight was lifted off his shoulders. She excused herself and stepped away from the counter with Baba's passport. Baba was elated and excited.

I waited for her to return with the good news regarding my visa. She came back shortly, and I was anxious to ask her. "Is my application approved?"

"No. Only your father's application is approved. After further consideration, your application for a student visa has been denied," she said matter-of-factly.

Baba stood there with a huge grin on his face, not comprehending what had just transpired. After a moment, and from the look on my face, the news settled in.

Baba's smile turned upside down in disbelief. We didn't understand how they'd approved his application but not mine.

Baba didn't take no for an answer and urged me to continue, "Tell her you're going back to Iran after graduation. Tell her you're not

staying in America; you're going back to Iran eventually. TELL HER!"
he yelled in frustration.

My pulse quickened, I repeated it back to her in English convincingly, but the Consul didn't react.

She kept flipping through my documents, but her decision didn't
change. Baba and I stood at the window, hopelessly stating our case to
her for a third time, but to no avail.

"I'll go back home; I promised my mother," I repeated, but our
efforts didn't affect the outcome. Even lying to her didn't help.

She blinked deliberately as to say, "that's enough out of you."

I could feel Baba tightening up next to me. He cleared his throat
several times, dropped his head, and grumbled something under his
breath which I couldn't make sense of.

I held my breath, hoping, praying, and I felt the collective eyes of the
embassy shifting to me. I imagined a complete silence falling, everyone
stopping mid-sentence, heads turning, and their eyes narrowing in on
me with keen interest when the woman finally started shaking her head
no and said, "Pendar, there's a considerable risk of you not leaving the
U.S. after entry. Your application for a U.S. visa will not be approved."
Muttered with a blank look on her face. No emotion, cold as ice.

My passport was then marked with a red stamp that read
"APPLICATION RECEIVED."

Once you received this stamp of rejection in your passport from an
American Embassy, you wouldn't be permitted to apply for another
visa for a period of 90 days.

Baba's passport was stamped with a visitor's visa to America which
expired on March 4, 1987, ninety days from the date received.

It took a few moments for reality to settle in, for us to accept defeat.
Soon, a wave of disappointment washed over me. It was devastating
and soon a waterfall of tears rolled down my cheeks. I dragged my
sleeve across my face, wiping away the snot and tears, something Baba
despised but he was silent.

Months of demanding work preparing for this interview, only to be
rejected in a matter of minutes. Being turned down hurt deeply.

On our way out, I heard a whimpering echo in the hallway and realized it was my own. My lips were salty with the ocean of tears that were
trickling down my face. I felt the eyes of everyone in the corridor,
staring at us while leaving. We were in a complete state of shock.

"What--" I said, gasping and hitching between sobs, "what now,
Baba?"

For a second, he said nothing, only shaking his head in disgust and
then, "it's not over yet, I'll find a way!'

In my simple mindset, we had been defeated and I was ready to give up and start heading home. In Baba's mind, we lost the battle, but the war had just begun.

Unbeknownst to me, Baba wasn't ready to give up, not even close. It wasn't in his nature to throw in the towel at the first sign of defeat. If anything, his acceptance, and my rejection is what fueled his motivation to continue.

That night, back at our hotel room, I admired Baba's visa for hours, running my fingers against it, caressing it with envy. Amoo Hafez snapped a photo of us with a 35-millimeter camera that my father had brought to document our trip. Through tiny snuffles, I smiled for the camera and tried to appear like the happy boy everyone knew, but it was all a façade.

Looking back at Baba's face in the picture, it told another story.

FIFTEEN
FLYING SOLO

The mood at the hotel was somber the morning after our failed visit to the consulate in Ankara. We waited for Amoo Payam and his wife, Aunt Saye, to complete their appointment in hopes of securing visitors' visas to the United States. Not surprisingly, they were both turned down.

That afternoon, we packed up and headed back to the train station for our trip back to Istanbul, where our return flight to Tehran was to be booked. During the train ride, I was withdrawn, my vision blurred by my excessive tears. I felt dejected, my dream of going to America was crushed.

In Istanbul, we ended up staying in the same crummy hotel we had left a week earlier. After depositing our luggage in our rooms, Baba suggested we meet in the lobby to reconvene.

"What are we going to do in the lobby?" I asked.

"We've come too far to give up now. We'll figure something out, Pendar." He gave a short laugh through his nose and tousled my hair, making light of our situation.

We headed back to the lobby to meet for a brainstorming session. Everyone looked dejected, and there weren't any suggestions until Baba had a moment of enlightenment. "What if we ask Shirley to travel and meet us somewhere?" he blurted out.

"WHAT?" Amoo Hafez looked at my father like he was mad. "Why would you do that, Nader?"

My father pointed out that at the embassy, American citizens didn't have to stand in line. They were permitted to walk in without an appointment. "What if Shirley agreed to meet us in another city, or country? She could accompany Pendar to the embassy without an appointment. They would surely issue him a visa then."

Everyone looked at my father in bewilderment, but he rambled on. "Think about it, what could be better than to have an American citizen march Pendar right into the embassy for his interview?"

"That actually doesn't sound like a bad plan, Nader," Amoo Hafez exclaimed. "But where would she travel to? What embassy are you thinking of?"

Amoo Payam interrupted. "How about Germany?"

All eyes shifted to my uncle.

"Germany?" Baba asked inquisitively.

"Yes, Germany, do you remember Karim?"

Baba shrugged his shoulders.

Amoo Payam explained, "He's an old friend who lives in Munich. I've always stayed with him when I travel there for business, remember him?"

"Are you talking about Karim, who's married to Mina?" Baba suddenly remembered.

"Yes, that's him. I'm sure we can ask him for a favor," Amoo Payam said.

All at once, a flash of inspiration—a spark of hope, which is what Baba needed before hurrying back to the phone. He called Kiya in Texas to ask if he could convince Shirley to get on board.

Kiya promised to get back to us within a day.

That night, I lay in bed with a feeling of renewed hope. I prayed that Shirley would agree to Baba's proposal and would travel abroad. After a day of anxious waiting, Baba called his friend Kiya, who gave us the incredible news.

I was bursting at the seams with excitement, Shirley had agreed to travel to Germany. More importantly, she'd agreed to personally escort me into the embassy for my interview.

The plan was to accompany me back to America once my student visa was received. And just like that, we were back on track.

Amoo Payam called Karim to make the necessary arrangements. Karim was a lifelong friend of Amoo Payam's from Tehran who now lived in Germany. He agreed to help.

The American Consulate was in Frankfurt. Karim lived in Munich, which was a four-hour drive away. Once we arrived in Munich, we would stay with Karim and his family for a week, until the time arrived when he would drive us to Frankfurt. He'd pick up Shirley at Frankfurt International Airport, then drop us off at the hotel where Shirley was scheduled to stay, close to the embassy. Karim didn't plan to stay in Frankfurt; he'd be returning to Munich.

With everyone's devotion to our cause, there could only be a victorious outcome. During the excitement and commotion of Shirley and Karim agreeing to help us, I overheard Baba speaking to Maman on the phone about my flight to Germany, Karim driving me to Frankfurt, my stay with Shirley, and how Shirley and I were going to visit the embassy.

I noticed that he did not mention his participation on the next leg of the journey and when he hung up with Maman, I asked him, "Aren't you going to Germany with me, Baba?"

"No, Pendar. You're going to Germany by yourself. Karim will be at the airport to pick you up and is going to travel with you the rest of the way to Frankfurt. That's where you'll meet up with Shirley," he explained.

Baba believed I was in good hands with Karim and Shirley the rest of the way. Plus, he thought his idea was so bulletproof, he didn't feel it was necessary to come along.

The thought of my first trip alone stirred unease in the pit of my stomach. I put on a brave face and agreed to travel unescorted to Munich. It was a city I had visited once before, only this time I would be traveling there without my parents.

"You'll stay in Munich until Shirley's flight from Dallas arrives in Frankfurt. Staying with Shirley in a fancy hotel will be your first chance to get to know her," Baba told me.

He always had a way with his words. The thought of meeting Shirley was exciting and tantalizing, otherwise thoughts of Maman constantly consumed my mind and now separating from Baba made it even worse. My parents were everything to me but now, I prepared myself for a new chapter of life, without their presence.

The following day, Baba made flight reservations, then arranged for Shirley and me to stay in Frankfurt for four nights.

Once I departed Istanbul for Germany, Baba, Amoo Payam and his wife, Aunt Saye, would travel back to Iran. Amoo Hafez will remain in Istanbul to await his upcoming appointment at the embassy.

For the next week, I kept busy playing with the kids in the lobby of our hotel. This time, I had my own sad story to share about being turned down for a visa, and we could relate furthermore. My story didn't seem so heartbreaking in comparison to some of the children that were stranded in Istanbul indefinitely.

My flight to Munich was scheduled for the morning of December 11th. My thirteenth birthday was only two weeks away on the 25th and I already imagined celebrating the milestone in America, becoming a teenager amongst my new family.

Anticipation of my birthday and my first Christmas in America filled me with contentment. I said farewell to Amoo Payam and Aunt Saye at the hotel the night before my flight. Before going to bed, Baba told me that a last-minute modification needed to be made in my passport.

He explained, "The embassy in Ankara marked your passport with a red 'APPLICATION RECEIVED' stamp. That means you can't apply for another visa for 90 days."

My eyes widened in surprise. Barely two weeks had elapsed since our failed attempt at the embassy in Ankara. *What was he thinking?* Shirley and I will be walking into the embassy in Frankfurt in less than three weeks from the time my passport was stamped.

"I need to do something about the "application received" stamp in your passport. I've seen lots of different passports and noticed some pages contain big Chinese stamps." He continued while reaching into his briefcase and pulling out four large stamps, covered with Chinese lettering.

"What are you going to do with those, Baba?" I asked curiously.

"You'll see, but you can't tell Shirley about this, do you under-stand?" Baba put his thumb and forefinger to his mouth, twisted it, then tossed away the imaginary key, as if to say, it'll be our little secret.

I nodded my head in agreement. I witnessed him meticulously lick the four large Chinese stamps one by one, then carefully placed them over the red "APPLICATION RECEIVED" and completely covered it up. Once he finished, it was like it was never there! Baba turned into a professional counterfeiter right in front of my eyes.

For the first time, and only in my head, I was questioning my father's tactics. I understood why it had to be done and out of respect, I never questioned him directly.

Under normal circumstances, my father would have never committed such an act. I also wondered, *why the rush? Why is he under such tremendous stress to secure a visa for me?* I figured we'd try again as a family when all of us endeavored to move to America, together. I knew hiding the rejection stamp in my passport was a necessary evil, if Shirley and I ever stood a chance to have an interview in Frankfurt.

"Desperate times call for desperate measures." Besides encouraging me to lie to the consul in Ankara, I'd witnessed Baba commit an act of perjury and forged government documents. He was always truthful; his word was his bond. But now I had to look the other way. I had to be understanding, not to hold it against him.

That night as I drifted off to sleep, I thought about Shirley and I, holding hands, boarding a flight to America, together. In the morning, Amoo Hafez and Baba took me to Istanbul Airport and saw me off to Munich, Germany.

At the boarding gate, I was confronted with saying goodbye to Baba. Suddenly, tears started rolling down my cheeks. I pressed my face into my father's chest, desperately trying to control the weeping.

"Everything is going to be fine son; this is all happening for a good reason."

"I'll be alright, I'll behave with Shirley and Karim, I promise Baba!" The weeping continued.

Baba was the rock of my life. He was my everything, separating from him was painful. He was the person I leaned on the most then. Now I was forced to say farewell to my hero, forced to continue alone. I had always imagined making the journey to America together, Baba by my side, every step of the way, but maybe that scenario wasn't meant to be.

He placed his finger under my chin, brought his face down to mine. "We're going to see each other real soon Pendar Jan, don't cry, azizam." He reassured me with a gentle grin.

His endearing smile always brightened my mood. I hugged him tightly for a few moments, I couldn't bring myself to let go, but eventually, time ran out, and I had to board the plane. I cried, coming apart from him, struggling to keep my composure.

Not sure when we would meet again, we locked eyes, and I kept looking at him until the very last second before he disappeared out of my sight behind a wall. For the first time on that trip, I couldn't bear the sadness. I felt naked and alone without Baba. His words of reassurance and unwillingness to give up, emphatically rang in my ears.

I boarded the Lufthansa flight on my way to Munich, Germany. It was a three-hour trip, but time passed rather quickly. Once in the air, the pilot executed a sharp left turn and brilliant rays of morning sunlight came streaming into the cabin.

The flight attendant was a young, gorgeous, blue-eyed knockout; especially the way her silky blonde hair fell on her navy-blue blouse. She wore a yellow silk handkerchief around her neck, a pair of sexy gold pilot's wings pinned just above her left breast, and her tight, blue skirt compressed her hips and those silky black panty hose made such a wonderful swooshing sound with each step. She was very friendly, bringing me extra snacks and drinks when she noticed that I was traveling alone.

Iran Air didn't have female flight attendants on any of our flights, and even if they did, they didn't look like that. She spoke a phrase in German, but I answered back in English. She was fluent in English as well and started to speak with the most seductive accent, asking me questions about my name, age, where I had come from, and wondered where I was going all by myself.

While politely answering her inquiries, I gazed into her soft blue eyes, she boosted my confidence to new heights. Back at the galley, she told the other pretty flight attendants about me, pointing in my direction while they giggled.

I imagined the flight attendants were gushing over my bravery of traveling alone. They must not have noticed; I was terrified deep down inside! I kept it cool on the outside, while worried and distressed below the surface. For the first time, I had no one to help me. I was on my own, and I had to continue regardless of my doubts, loneliness, and uncertainty.

SIXTEEN
INTERROGATION

MUNICH, GERMANY, DECEMBER 11ᵀᴴ, 1986.

deplaned at the Munich airport, restlessly waiting in line for passport control. I nervously presented my documents to the uniformed officer at the window. He asked me a few questions in German which I couldn't understand. "Do you speak English?"

I nodded my head.

"Come this way, you will have to follow my colleague," he said. He clenched my passport and summoned another officer who was standing by.

I followed him through back corridors, arriving at a distinct holding area. We entered what looked like an interrogation room; it was dark, no windows, no pictures, no clock, no telephones, nothing but two steel-gray chairs with a matching steel-gray desk in the middle of the room.

Immediately I got nervous, thinking I was in trouble. I imagined a scenario, like a scene right out of a movie: the Nazis were going to interrogate or even torture the twelve-year-old Iranian boy suspiciously trespassing alone.

Soon a fortyish man entered the room, he was about six-two, built like a Mack truck and was sporting a crew cut. He looked like the person in charge as the other officer saluted him. He looked irritable, in a foul, unpleasant mood. He was gruff, had laser piercing eyes, and an incredibly square jaw. His face was battle scarred with a line running down his cheek where he had likely been knifed.

He sat down in the chair across from me and leaned in. I started shaking, confused, uncertain of my fate or what to expect. He started shouting aggressively, spitting rapid fire questions at me in German.

I didn't understand a word spilling out of his mouth, but the growl of his voice and his outraged demeanor scared me half to death. I paused for a moment, gulped, then a massive wave of panic overtook me. My lips started to quiver, my knee bouncing up and down, and my body tensed up as if preparing to be struck by Mr. Hakimi. I started crying hysterically.

Apparently, he had no patience for my hysteria and once he realized I didn't speak German, he shouted directions at the other officer who promptly left the room. He leaned back in the chair, crossed his arms, and his steely blue eyes fixated on me with one eyebrow lifted into his forehead. My frazzled nerves went into a complete tailspin.

I was frantic and thought the worst – I may never see my family again. *Were they arresting me? Were they planning to torture me? Were they taking me to a German prison camp for the rest of my life? What was to become of me?* I was distraught, struggling to contain myself. I shifted in my seat uncomfortably. All these bizarre thoughts were roaring through my head with the ferocity of a Category 5 hurricane.

The door swung open; my suitcase was rolled in on a cart. The officer in charge picked up my suitcase and slammed it on the metal table. It made a loud ringing noise that startled me. He opened it, rummaging through my belongings as if there were contraband hidden inside.

I was ready to crawl into the fetal position. "Please, can you let me go, I haven't done anything wrong?" I begged, weeping with every other word.

But he didn't respond, only ignoring my hysteria. He forged ahead through every nook and cranny of my suitcase turning it inside out. I sat there, quietly sobbing, frightened at the unexpected turn of events.

I started praying, hoping they didn't find anything that could prolong my miserable existence. Once the inspection of my luggage wound down, a female officer walked through the door.

She noticed I was distressed, quickly pulling up the other chair beside mine. She started speaking in English. "What are you doing in Munich all by yourself, young man?" she asked me kindly.

I was still weeping, needing a moment to calm down, to catch my breath before the words could escape my mouth.

"Karim, who's a family friend, is picking me up. I'm staying with him for a few days, then he's going to drive me to Frankfurt to pick up Shirley Foster, who is my legal guardian from America." I rambled on and explained our plan in detail, holding back the tears.

"Calm down, breathe," she said softly. She took careful notes, then excused herself.

She explained the situation in German to her supervisor, who was standing in the corner, arms crossed, head turned sideways, and a snarl from the corner of his mouth.

I sat there, tears gushing out of my eyes, confused. I wished Baba could have been by my side, he'd know what to do. But I was all alone, nobody there to reassure me or to tell me that everything was going to be alright. I missed Baba dearly, even more so then.

I had to be brave, I kept telling myself. *It's all going to be over soon, you're going to meet Shirley soon, you'll be in America soon!* Nervously rocking back and forth in my chair, I remembered the pretty flight attendants who flirted with me, and thought I was brave. Only if they could see me now; the panic-stricken coward, ready to wet himself, crying like a baby.

The supervisor took a hold of my passport and started to inspect it closely, meticulously flipping through each page. My heart sank, thinking about the "APPLICATION RECEIVED" stamp, and how it was concealed. I prayed over and over that he wouldn't find what was underneath the enormous Chinese stamps. I was detained in the inter-rogation room for almost an hour, meanwhile they treated me like a terrorist or suicide bomber.

While ravaging through my documents, the supervisor stumbled across the affidavit of support signed by Shirley Foster.

Once the female officer translated, everyone immediately calmed down. My story had checked out, he knew I was in Munich for a valid reason. Once satisfied, he instructed me to repack my suitcase, and I was cleared to leave.

Relieved, I nervously stuffed my belongings back into the suitcase.

The lady officer handed back my documents and passport, then pointed to the exit with the open palm of her hand, "Have a good day!" she said.

I said thank you in a shaky voice and rapidly left the room. I kept nervously looking behind my shoulder to make sure I wasn't followed. I dashed quickly towards the exit, quickly making my escape from the imaginary Nazis. I scrambled to the arrivals area where Karim was waiting.

I caught sight of him waving in the distance, he walked straight towards me. He recognized me because of photos he had seen. It was a relief to see him.

Right away, Karim noticed my puffy eyes, runny nose, and the tears that had not dried off my face yet. I was in such a big rush to break out of that room, I'd forgotten to wipe down my face!

"What's wrong Pendar? Why did it take you so long to exit after your flight landed?" he asked me.

"For the last hour, the German police held me in a room, asking lots of questions. They opened my suitcase too and searched through it." I sputtered out.

He panicked and instructed me to scurry and exit the airport with him at once.

We hurried towards the parking area, Karim anxiously looking over his shoulder – he was spooked, thinking the police had set a trap for us. He opened the trunk, flung my suitcase in, then speedily drove away from the airport, screeching the tires of his car.

Once we entered the highway and confirmed that we were not followed, I breathed in a sigh of relief. Thirty minutes later, we arrived at Karim's home, which was a pleasant apartment located in a large complex. He lived in a one-bedroom unit with his lovely wife Mina and infant daughter.

The family was gracious for allowing me to stay with them for a week. Shirley will be flying to Frankfurt, arriving on the afternoon of December the 18th. Meanwhile, I was glad to be in the home of a happy family.

It was almost dinner time, and the aroma of fried onions, garlic and Iranian spices filled the apartment, vividly reminding me of home. I observed Mina cooking up a familiar stew, 'khoreshte bademjoon' , a stew prepared with eggplant, chicken, served with white rice. My mouth salivated eagerly waiting to devour the home cooked meal.

We sat around the dining room table, and although the food was tasty and mouthwatering, I couldn't help but to compare it to Maman's cooking. I realized that not only did I miss family dinners back home, but most importantly, I dearly missed my parents, siblings, and extended family. Our travels in Turkey had been intense, my thoughts constantly consumed by the struggle to enter America. I hadn't slowed down long enough to realize how much I deeply missed them all. I looked forward to the future, hoping my family would be reuniting with me soon.

I slept on the cozy couch in the living room and woke up the following morning to pleasant sounds. I heard laughter, giggling, and the commotion of children at play. I peeked through the family room window and realized that it had snowed through the night in Munich.

The cars in the parking lot, the trees, the rooftops, and the hills buried under three feet of fresh snow. It was white as far as my eyes could detect. The sky was seamless and blue, the reflection of the snow so bright, it made my eyes hurt.

Karim was sitting at the kitchen table reading a newspaper. I quickly ate my breakfast, but the whole time I was distracted by the sound of laughter and jubilation coming from outside. I gazed out the window again and observed a group of kids preparing for a snowball fight.

"Can I go outside and play with them, Amoo Karim?" I asked politely.

"As long as you promise you'll stay in the parking lot and not go past our apartment complex," he told me.

"I promise!" I said eagerly. However, once downstairs, I heard the kids speaking and realized there was a small obstacle to overcome, the language barrier.

Most were my age, but they were speaking in German. Timid and shy, I pushed myself, *'C'mon Pendar, just go play with them.'* I was reserved and intimidated but found the courage to casually stroll up to them, hands in my pockets.

The quiet morning was peaceful, the silence was broken by the kids, and the cawing of nearby crows. I shoveled a handful of fresh snow in my mouth, and quietly admired them at play. Two groups separated on each side of the parking lot, taking turns hurling snowballs at the opposing team. The fresh snow crunched under my tennis shoes as one of the kids noticed me standing by. He shouted a few words at me in German.

I looked behind me to make sure he wasn't talking to someone else. With my index finger pointed at my chest, I confirmed he was speaking to me.

He nodded his head yes and waved me over with the motion of his arm.

I was excited and ran to my team's side where another intense wave of snowballs rained down on us. I tried communicating with the kids in English, but none of them understood me, only a blank stare in response.

It didn't matter, during the intermission, our captain drew a diagram in the snow with his index finger, ordering us to rotate positions. Then he helped me make an arsenal of snowballs for our teammates. The language barrier went unnoticed, not hindering our game.

An abundance of fresh snow kept us busy into the late afternoon. Enjoying my snowy play day, I lost track of time, *'Time flies when you're having a good time!'* Frigid and exhausted, we said goodbye and headed back to our apartments.

In our makeshift sign language, I was invited to play the next day as well. I headed back upstairs feeling joyful and delighted to have played with kids my own age. It was a much-deserved break after weeks of being cooped up in hotel rooms, standing in line for an appointment, topped by the rejection I felt after being denied in Ankara. We played for the next few days, it was the perfect distraction for me, not thinking about the visa or America for a short while.

On the 18ᵗʰ of December, Karim and I prepared to make the four-hour drive to Frankfurt and planned to pick up Shirley at the airport. I said goodbye to Karim's wife and daughter, sincerely thanking her for the hospitality.

Thoughts of meeting Shirley were reassuring – her presence could be the winning advantage, an upper hand, something other applicants didn't possess. With Shirley by my side, there was no way the embassy would deny me a visa.

My confidence soared with eager anticipation. On the drive to the airport, I imagined our first encounter and wondered what it would be like. *Does she have a pleasant personality? Is she easy to talk to?* Hoping and praying for the best outcome was all I could do.

———

We reached Frankfurt International Airport just as Shirley's plane was touching down. Recognizing her at the Arrivals Gate would be easy; Kiya had provided a good description. Besides, knowing that her bad hip necessitated the use of a walking cane would help me distinguish her.

Promptly after her plane landed, I identified a female passenger with a cane. I recognized her short gray hair and slim eyeglasses from the description; she looked lovely in her burgundy business suit and cashmere overcoat. We made eye contact, and from her smile, I knew it was Shirley.

"PENDAR!" she shouted, waving her arm.

I bounced toward her, unsure how to handle our initial encounter, I contemplated shaking her hand, giving her a hug, or maybe a polite kiss on the cheek. Before I could act, she planted her arms around me and drew me in for a tight squeeze. She embraced me as though we had been acquainted for years.

"I've been dying to meet you!" she said, her voice sincere. The heady scent of her perfume resonated in the air. It was aromatic, soft, and accurately matched her warm, bubbly personality.

"Hello Shirley. It's nice to meet you. How was your flight?" I said in my best English.

Karim shook hands with Shirley and introduced himself. Karim spoke fluent German, but he was obligated to rely on me for communicating with Shirley in English.

Instantly she was amazed by how well I spoke English.

"Pendar! I know you were takin' classes, but I had no idea you'd be speakin' English so well," she said in a heavy Southern accent.

"Thank you, Shirley," I replied, politely smiling back at her.

Our initial encounter felt special, her charismatic personality instantly resonated with me. I was in awe of her strong American accent, peppered with a Texas drawl, which required some getting used to. She was kind, polite, and attentive towards me. The maternal love and affection that I'd missed during the trip was oozing from her, just like her perfume.

Shirley's suitcase arrived on the conveyor belt.

"Can I help you with your luggage?" I asked, eager to make a good impression.

She raised her eyebrows, reacting to my considerate gesture: "And a gentleman, too!"

"It's no problem, Shirley." I felt my ears redden. It was the least I could do in return for her help.

Once in the parking lot, I politely offered her the front passenger seat.

She smiled and said, "No Mister, I insist on sitting in the back with you."

I was happy to sit next to her for the ride to our hotel.

"Are you ready to go to the embassy tomorrow?" she asked.

"Of course, I'm looking forward to it," I said.

"I'm going to make sure you get your visa. Afterwards, we'll fly back to America, together. How's that sound?"

"I can't wait Shirley!"

"Such a handsome boy you are," she said while tussling my hair.

"Thank you very much for helping."

"You don't need to thank me. I'm glad I can help."

I was elated.

Karim dropped us off in front of the hotel, "Thank you Amoo Karim for all your help, have a safe trip back to Munich," I told him.

Shirley and I stood on the curb next to our luggage for a moment when suddenly a bellman in a teal-green uniform with gold buttons and

matching cap scampered up to us. "Willkommen!" he said enthusiastically in German.

He insisted on placing our suitcases onto the shiny, gold, luggage
cart he had wheeled over.

"Excuse me, where are you taking our things?" I asked.

"To your room, sir, you are a guest of the hotel, right?"

I nodded in the affirmative.

It was a pleasant surprise, a bellman to transport our suitcases right
up to our room. It felt fancy even before walking inside. I grasped
Shirley's hand and together we advanced towards the lobby. The
towering glass doors were guarded by another uniformed hotel
employee who, with a warm smile, gently opened them and welcomed
us into the lobby. The hotel was elegant, modern, and newly built. The
clean, fresh smell throughout the lobby was a welcome change after the
questionable establishments Baba and I had stayed in during our journey. The employees were professional, cordial, and respectfully greeted
each guest with a tilt of the head.

Check-in was swift, and soon Shirley and I were aboard the
mahogany-paneled elevator, ascending to the fifth floor. My eyes grew
wide, and I let out an excited gasp when Shirley opened the door to our
room. It was huge, fancy, and well-appointed with many amenities.

There were two queen-size beds, a large television set, a minibar
with snacks and a balcony overlooking the street below. In the bathroom was a marble jacuzzi tub. I was astonished by the miniature
shampoo bottles, bars of soap in tiny boxes, bathrobes and freshly
folded towels that smelled like lemons.

I pounced onto the bouncy mattress; it was the most comfortable
cushion I'd ever laid on. The pillows were fluffy, and the linens were
silky smooth to the touch.

Before long, my suitcase was unpacked, and I asked Shirley for
permission to watch television. She allowed it while unpacking herself
and freshening up from her long trip. I was entertained flipping
through various channels which were in German.

"Are you hungry yet?" she asked.

I had been excited about finally meeting Shirley and was so taken
with our room that I hadn't even thought about food. "Yes!" I replied.

"I know just the place, Pendar, I think you're going to love it, we
passed it on our way here," she said.

While walking to the restaurant, Shirley asked me lots of questions
about my family.

Disheartened and homesick, I told her about Baba, Maman, my two
siblings and my extended family.

She was inquisitive and kept drawing closer to me. As we walked, I imagined my life with her in America. I looked up to her like a mentor, soaking up her fascinating tales about Arlington, soon-to—be my new home.

Up ahead, I spotted the distinctive yellow arches, displaying the letter "M," soaring above the bustling streets of Frankfurt. I'd seen this familiar logo in American movies, it meant a symbol of freedom to me. Enchanted, I asked, "Is *that* where we're eating tonight?"

"Yes! Would you like that?"

"Absolutely!" I could hardly contain my enthusiasm. My wish to dine at a McDonald's was becoming a reality.

The mouthwatering aroma of French fries filled the air once we stepped inside. Shirley directed my attention to the menu on the board. "Pendar, would you like a Big Mac Meal?"

"What's that?" I asked befuddled.

"A Big Mac Meal includes a double cheeseburger, French fries, and a soda. It's like a package." "Okay, I will have that," I said.

"Do you want errthing on it?"

I looked at her with a dumbfounded expression.

She repeated, "Do you want errthing on it?"

Again, I couldn't make out what she was saying.

"Dooo yooooou waaaaant errrthing on your burger? You know like lettuce, tomatoes, or onions?"

Then, it dawned on me. Because of her thick Southern accent with a Texas twist, I couldn't comprehend what she was asking me. I nodded in agreement to all the trimmings, and she ordered the food, taking the liberty to include dessert, fried apple pie, with a side of vanilla ice cream.

The first bite of my Big Mac was scrumptious, just as I'd imagined. I shoveled crunchy, hot French fries, dipped in ketchup, into my mouth and washed them down with a bubbly soda. The combination was tasty, delivering a flavor explosion in my mouth. Then came the desert. The flaky crust of the fried apple pie melted in my mouth, while heated cinnamon filling dripped on my chin, reminiscent of my visits to the pastry shop with my grandmother. This meal tasted like a small piece of heaven and made me feel as though we were closer to America.

"This is the best-tasting burger I've ever had in my life," I enthusiastically told Shirley.

My imagination ran wild about my first meal in America. *Would it be McDonald's or some other delectable food?* I couldn't wait to find out.

After our feast, we walked back to the hotel. I was eager to plunge into the jacuzzi tub in our bathroom. Overzealous, I accidentally poured an exorbitant amount of liquid soap into the bathwater, causing an overflow of bubbles. Not wanting Shirley to find out, I tidied up my mess before exiting the bathroom.

Shirley was on her bed flipping through a magazine. Timidly, I sat on the edge, itching to ask her a favor. I didn't know how she would react. My eyes kept drifting to her purse, where she kept what, in my opinion, was the "holy" book.

"I've been meaning to ask," I said hesitantly. "Can I ask you a question Shirley?"

"Of course, Pendar, what is it?"

"Can I take a look at your passport please?"

She smiled lovingly, removed the passport from her handbag, and placed it in the palm of my hand.

In my head, angels from the heavens were singing 'Hallelujah' as she handed it to me. Once in my grasp, the small, blue passport illuminated with an angelic light that only I could see. I admired it, running my fingers over the eagle, encircled by the seal of the United States. I thought of it as a sacred book, containing special powers. My wish was to have an American passport of my own someday.

At bedtime, I said goodnight and crawled under the plush, cozy sheets. I sank into the soft mattress while my head dissolved onto the pillow. Shirley rolled to face me and curled her arms under her head. "I'm gonna help you get that visa, Pendar!".

After putting her palms together, she said a prayer and requested for me to repeat after her, "Now I lay me down to sleep, I pray the Lord my Soul to keep…"

I repeated it verbatim, although I didn't understand its meaning. Then I said a silent prayer of my own, hoping for a positive outcome at the embassy the following day. Before turning in, I confirmed my gratitude for her efforts. "Thanks again Shirley, for coming such a long distance."

She interrupted me, "Pendar, you don't have to keep on thanking me. It'll be my pleasure to look after you once we're back home."

She kept calling it 'home,' which I found strange yet reassuring. For a moment I thought of my *real* home in Tehran with Maman and Baba and my siblings, and how much I was going to miss them.

It was difficult to fall asleep, and I spent much of the night tossing in my sheets and staring at the ceiling, daunted by the roaring thoughts of another rejection at the embassy.

SEVENTEEN
U-TURN

FRANKFURT, GERMANY, DECEMBER 19, 1986.

I awoke to Shirley, her eyeglasses atop her head, pulling open the curtains to let the morning sun flood our room. The light was blinding and caused me to spring out of bed with urgency.

Once dressed, Shirley sprayed herself with that soothing, addictive, and flowery perfume. She had a calming influence over me and a certain inner warmth that she exuded. We headed to the hotel restaurant just off the lobby for breakfast. In no time flat, there was a freshly brewed pot of coffee on the table, followed by cakes, pastries, a cheese platter and a bowl of freshly-cut fruit. Shirley was optimistic and reassured me that success awaited us.

We approached the consulate, the compound was encircled by a tall, black wrought iron fence, America's red, white, and blue flag atop a towering steel flagpole marked its entrance. The taxi dropped us off directly in front of the gate and we proceeded toward the guard shack, where two armed soldiers were posted. One of them asked to see our identification, I found myself tensing up. Shirley flashed her American passport, and the guard instantly welcomed her with a smile. Before allowing us to enter, he politely inquired about my business at the consulate.

Shirley proclaimed proudly, "We're here to get Pendar a visa to America!" She spoke in an assertive tone, further boosting my confidence.

The tall gates opened, and we entered the building within a matter of minutes – something that seemed impossible only a few weeks earlier. The process of entry was the same: we walked through the metal detectors, presented our documents, then waited to interview with an American consul.

Shirley regarded this waiting period as an opportunity to communicate, but I was a jittery mess, as my appointment inched closer. I took a deep breath and tried to drive the negativity out of my head, but it was difficult.

To distract myself, I told Shirley about my friend Mohammad, and how we played soccer in the schoolyard. It made me feel better talking about him and reminiscing about our friendship calmed my nerves.

Shirley smiled. "Pendar, there are so many children in our neighborhood and at the local school, you're going to make lots of friends, I'm sure of it."

We'd been waiting nearly an hour when I heard my name called. Apprehensive, I grabbed Shirley's hand, and together we walked up to the window.

The consul was a middle-aged woman and she was professionally dressed in a peach, button-down top and dark-colored skirt. Her golden blonde hair was pulled back in a ponytail, and I grew increasingly nervous when she fixated her piercing, hazel eyes on me.

"Hello," she said politely, while inspecting my documents. "Do you need a translator?"

I smiled my warmest, fake smile at her.

"His English is amazing," Shirley quickly answered before I had a chance to respond.

"He needs to answer the questions, please, not you Ma'am," the consul said firmly.

"I speak English and don't need a translator," I said confidently.

"Can you tell me about your home? Your schooling?" She started with the typical questions.

I answered each one.

"What are your plans after graduation?" she posed, "when school is finished in America." There it was, the question Baba had prepared me for; the one that could seal my fate.

"I'll be returning home to Iran, just like I promised my family," I said. I felt bad for lying, but my guilty feelings were overshadowed by my desire to obtain a visa.

We waited as the Consul flipped through my documents, her eyes periodically shifting from me to Shirley and then back to me. Time slowed down. I could hear the isolated sound of my heartbeat palpitating inside my chest and felt it pulsating in my neck. I gulped, anxiously glancing at Shirley, who wore a big smile on her face, optimistic as ever.

The consul excused herself and stepped away from the window for a few moments.

Her walking cane in one hand, Shirley squeezed my hand tight with the other and said, "See, I told you we're gettin' you a visa today, didn't I?"

I perked up with excitement. I knew Baba was right all along. *Why did I ever doubt him?* All my prayers were being answered. Having Shirley with me had sealed the deal; they were finally going to issue me a student visa to America.

Still, each passing second felt like an eternity. As soon as I spotted the consul walking back toward the window, I straightened my posture and squeezed Shirley's hand. I tried to read her expression, but her face revealed nothing. I held my breath and focused on her lips, eager to hear that my application had been approved.

"I apologize for the wait," she began. "But we cannot issue you a student visa at this time."

Wait, what?

"There's a high probability that children in your age group will not leave America at the conclusion of their studies, therefore your visa application is denied."

Shirley's walking cane slowly tumbled out of her hand and fell to the ground, in slow motion. The high-pitched sound of the wooden handle striking the tile floor startled me.

That's when it happened; Shirley snapped out of her joyful mood and transformed into a fire-breathing dragon. It was a side of her I hadn't seen, like a second face, this one lurking just beneath the surface, ready to explode. She was furious and started to argue.

I quickly bent over, picked up her cane and placed it back in her hand.

"What? Oh no! There must be some kinda' mistake, this can't be right!" she railed. Her boisterous indignation echoed through the embassy, startling everyone. Her protective side was bursting out; she was not going to take no for an answer.

I put my head down in disappointment and tears started to pool in my eyes. I was ready to give up, go back home, but Shirley was a fighter, just like Baba.

"I flew a long way to make sure Pendar gets his visa; that's the only reason I'm in this country," she continued with annoyance. "He's going back with me, you hear me?"

I stood silent, watching her interact with the consul in a manner that I deemed inappropriate. Still, I was in awe of her insolence. Immigrants regarded the American consul with the utmost respect. For Shirley it was different, she argued with the woman showing a total disregard of her position or title. But her spirited debate didn't influence the outcome, the consul was extremely firm on her decision. "Let me speak to a supervisor at once!" she demanded, her voice growing louder.

The consul acknowledged Shirley's growing irritation and reluctantly agreed to summon her supervisor. Moments later, a man in a dark suit, presumably the woman's superior, approached the window and was immediately left speechless. He was no match for the sheer ferocity of Shirley's relentless verbal assault.

Tears flooded my eyes, in disbelief of her sheer audacity to speak to the supervisor in that tone. She demanded he approve my application at once, but his answer was a firm no.

"Ma'am, there's nothing I can do," he informed her. He then leaned in close to the window and in a firm voice, he issued a warning, "I'm afraid that if you don't stop the disruption, I'll be forced to have security escort you out." He then stepped away in frustration, only to return a few minutes later with my documents.

I had received another stamp in my passport, but not the one I was hoping for. I peeked inside, only to find another dreaded "APPLICATION RECEIVED" stamped in red ink. My heart sank. I felt a lump rising in my throat, and it became harder to breathe.

By now, Shirley was visibly distraught. Finally, she capitulated, and defeated, we walked out of the embassy together.

A terrible overwhelming wave of sadness came over me and I started sobbing out of control.

Shirley embraced me with empathy.

I buried my face in the warmth of her chest, weeping until my tears dried, until the shaking stopped. She was sympathetic, but I was inconsolable. My dream of going to America had crashed around me, again. I was not meant to get on that plane with Shirley. I was devastated and heartbroken, my prayers and frantic pleas had gone unanswered.

Shirley tried to comfort me. "Shhh," she said, wrapping her arms around my shaking body, rocking back and forth, she could feel me convulsing with each sob. "Shhh. It'll be alright, Pendar," she whispered softly. I held up my head and said through gooselike snorts, "I'm- I'm fine."

"Oh Shirley, what will happen now?" I asked, my voice muffled against her chest. My second attempt at the consulate had been a complete disaster and had run aground, and my self-esteem had crashed right along with it.

For the first time, Shirley was speechless. She sat beside me in the back of the taxi and clung onto me while I wept. I rested my head on the window, staring blankly at the passing traffic lights and rows of pollarded trees, my hot breath fogging up the glass. She struggled to console me, offering to take me back to McDonald's for dinner.

I nodded silently in agreement. Strangely, food was the only comfort I could count on to soothe my frazzled nerves. A delectable meal always remedied the unwanted feelings of despair.

Back at our hotel, we walked a few blocks to the restaurant holding hands in silence. The meal improved my mood, but it was only a temporary respite. This was the end of the line, the conclusion of my journey.

Back in our hotel room, I called home and told Baba the devastating news. I could hear and sense the heartache in his voice. When we hung up, Shirley called Texas to alert Kiya that despite her efforts, our visit to the consul had been unsuccessful.

For the rest of the evening, we watched television and tried to forget about the day's events. I was exhausted and fell asleep while watching TV.

In the morning, I called Baba to discuss my next steps.

He had already contacted Karim to tell him about our predicament. Once again, Karim agreed to drive back to Frankfurt to pick us up.

Shirley was scheduled to be on a plane back to America, the same flight I was supposed to be on. He would drop off Shirley at the airport, then bring me back to Munich with him. I would stay with his family while Baba arranged for my travel back to Iran.

I cherished my final days in Frankfurt with Shirley; It was bittersweet. All that would remain from this trip was fond memories and the reality that we might never see each other again. *Maybe it wasn't my destiny to live with Shirley in Arlington?*

The following morning, December 22, I sadly said goodbye to our fancy room. Shirley and I ate one last breakfast together in the hotel restaurant, then waited in the lobby for Karim to arrive. I was in a somber mood; my feelings were the opposite of those I had experienced on the day Shirley had first arrived.

She, too, looked visibly upset. I had grown close to her in this brief time, and it hurt deeply to let her go.

The emotional farewell at the airport was depressing. I held Shirley tightly for a few moments, taking a long last whiff of her perfume. These heartbreaking airport goodbyes were taking their toll on me.

Shirley kissed me gently on the forehead and said, "You're a brave boy, Pendar, I hope to see you someday soon."

Tears rolled down our cheeks, but it was time to let go. Shirley was on her way back to America, and I was headed to Karim's apartment in Munich and then home to Iran.

A few days later was Christmas and my thirteenth birthday, and for the first time I was in a strange land, far from my family and even further from my American dream.

Karim's wife, Mina, thoughtfully made me a cupcake with a single candle as an improvised birthday cake. I appreciated the gesture, but memories of my parents' spectacular birthday parties consumed me.

I thought about the pile of presents, my humongous birthday cake, and the countless guests. I reminisced about Maman's cooking and our family gatherings.

This is the saddest and loneliest day of my life, I thought.

It was the worst birthday celebration ever. I was supposed to be celebrating my birthday and Christmas in America. I couldn't wait for the trip to be over and to be back in Tehran, reunited with my family and friends.

I cried myself to sleep that night, feeling depressed and unwanted. The tumult of the day slackened eventually, and I realized that all my problems were because of my sole desire to go to America so badly. My life was not so bad, though.

Images of running on the black asphalt and kicking the soccer ball with Mohammad appeared in my dreams. Knowing we'd be playing together again soon heartened me. I couldn't wait to go back to my normal life, even if it meant returning to life in an Islamic state and a war-torn country.

EIGHTEEN
REST IN PEACE

TEHRAN, IRAN, DECEMBER 28TH, 1986

arrived home, greeted by my parents and a handful of family members at Mehrabad International Airport. I rushed towards Maman, falling into her loving embrace. I'd never been away from her for so long. She locked her arms around my neck, and I drew a deep breath, delighting in her familiar scent. It made me realize how much I'd deeply missed her, and the feeling was obviously mutual. Tears of happiness poured from our eyes. Her presence calmed and soothed me; everything was now just as it should be.

Baba stood by patiently, an endearing smile and a welcoming twinkle in his eyes. He lovingly caressed my face and said, "I heard you got in trouble with the German police in Munich. I know that must've been hard; but I'm proud of you, son."

I blushed. "Oh, Baba, I was crying the whole time. I wish you were there with me."

"It's okay, Pendar Jan. You're home now." he comforted me.

I felt an overwhelming sense of security, safety, and closeness in the embrace of my parents. I was anxious to get back to my home and school. During the car ride home, Maman rested her head on the passenger side window, but said little.

"Baba, I want to see Mohammad," I said. "When can I go back to school?"

My father looked at Maman with a wary gaze, "Yeah, sure azizam, we'll talk about it tomorrow."

"You'll be back in school soon," Maman reassured me. "For now, try not to think about the last few weeks." I sensed something wasn't right, but my apprehension was overshadowed by the euphoria of being back with my parents.

Stepping onto the elevator for the ride up to the twentieth floor, I was instantly at peace; I was finally home. Donya and Amin ran to greet me the minute I stepped through the apartment door. Our family was reunited at last.

Maman knew I missed her cooking and had lovingly prepared my favorite foods, Baghali Polo, 'rice with finely chopped dill weed and fava beans' topped with fall-off-the-bone, succulent lamb shank. Devouring supper felt satisfying while surrounded by my family again. The anticipation of getting back to my room and sleeping in my own bed had me rushing through dinner. I thanked Maman, then excused myself and raced to my room. It was spotless, just as I'd left it.

My *Adventures of Tintin* books neatly stacked across my bookshelf. Luke Skywalker, Han Solo and Zorro, amongst my favorite action figures, left exactly where I had placed them in my toy box next to the Ford Gran Torino from my favorite American television show, *Starsky & Hutch*. I was elated to be back in my room again. I couldn't wait to play with my toys, watch my favorite movies and catch up on TV shows. I also yearned to be reunited with Mohammad and my other school-mates. I said goodnight to my family and crawled into my comfy bed. I was exhausted, totally spent, and glad to be back in my own bed, but I couldn't sleep.

Thoughts of my failed trip kept creeping into my head, and insomnia ensued. It was a clear night, and the ashy rays of the full moon peeked in between my window blinds. After tossing and turning for several hours, I got out of bed to use the bathroom. As I stepped into the hallway, I heard Baba and Maman speaking in the kitchen and I quietly tip-toed over, put my back against the kitchen wall and began to eavesdrop. My parents had always tried to shield me from things, it seemed prudent for them to allow me to enjoy the blissful ignorance of childhood, at least for a while longer, but I may have expedited the inevitable.

Maman sounded concerned. "How are we going to explain this to him, Nader?"

"Well, I sure as hell can't give up now," my father replied. "I won't allow him to be sacrificed for a cause we don't believe in. There's no way he can stay here."

I wasn't sure what they were talking about, but curiously kept listening.

Baba's tone was filled with worry. "Well, we certainly can't let him go back to school until I figure this out," he said.

"When are you going to tell him about Mohammad?" Maman asked. "You know he wants to see him."

What had happened to Mohammad? I couldn't stay silent any longer and strode into the kitchen, startling both my parents. "What are you talking about? What happened to Mohammad? Why am I not allowed to go back to school? Baba, please tell me!"

"Pendar, please sit down," my father said, directing me to the chair next to his at the kitchen table. "What I'm going to tell you won't be easy for you to hear, but eventually you will need to know."

I gulped, then held my breath.

"While you were in Germany, Mohammad's father came to my photo lab with a request. He wanted to order photos and posters for a funeral procession. I offered my condolences and asked who had passed. He shared the terrible news that the funeral was for his son, your friend Mohammad."

The grief on Baba's face spread to mine.

"Mohammad volunteered himself to the Basij," Baba continued.

The Basij was a branch of the Islamic Revolutionary Guard Corps, a voluntary youth militia group established in 1980 by Ayatollah Khomeini. During the Iran-Iraq War, hundreds of thousands of Iranians volunteered to serve, including children as young as twelve.

I sat dumbfounded, my mouth agape, as Baba explained that Mohammad's regiment had been deployed directly to the front lines, and Mohammad's father had verified that his son proudly martyred himself.

My lips started to quiver, and my eyes filled with tears. My voice shaking, I begged my father, "You're joking, tell me this is a joke, right, Baba?"

"Pendar Jan, we're so sorry to give you the bad news. We wanted to find the right time to explain it to you, certainly not like this."

I buried my head in Maman's chest with great sadness and broke into sobs, thinking of my best friend, who I would never get to see again. "I never even got to say goodbye to him," I said. "Is this why I can't go back to school?"

Maman gently stroked my head. "Yes, honey, that's one reason," she said. "Please understand, we just want what is best for you, we were looking for the right time to tell you."

"We'll talk more tomorrow, I promise. Now go back to bed and try to get some sleep, son."

"Why did Mohammad volunteer for the war?" I asked.

"We'll talk tomorrow, Pendar," Maman said, shooing me towards my bedroom. "C'mon, time to go back to bed."

Baba rose from his chair and led me back down the hallway.

I let him tuck me into bed.

He stood in the doorway for a moment, the hall light illuminated behind him, with melancholy in his voice, "I'm sorry Pendar Jan, I hope it's your last loss. I love you, and I'll see you in the morning, azizam," he said lovingly before closing my bedroom door.

A sorrow as black as the night invaded me, and I felt my throat clamping like someone was choking me. Exhausted from the emotional reaction to Mohammad's passing and stricken with grief, I rolled from side to side for a long while before falling into a deep slumber.

That night, I dreamt I was lost in the middle of the desert. The wind was blowing viciously, howling past my ears, thrusting stinging sheets of sand into my eyes. I wobble through the gusts, calling for him. "Mohammad? Where are you?" I scream. But my calls are drowned out by the sound of the wind. Endlessly hiking through the barren desert, I fall to my knees onto the sand, panting, lost, and confused.

I could really use Mohammad's help right now. I look back and see the fierce winds have erased my fresh footprints. My hope is fading rapidly, but Mohammad's words echo loudly in my ears. "Don't give up, Pendar."

I cry out for my friend again, and this time there is a muffled response. I hear his voice in the distance, "Pendar, come with me!" Mohammad is calling out to me.

I shield my eyes from the sand and follow his voice. Out of the blowing sand, I catch a glimpse of something moving in the distance. A familiar shape materializes out of the shadows and takes me by the hand.

It is Mohammad. He is dressed in his green army uniform, an oversized jacket, and a red headband. He rushes me to the side of a building that has been ripped to shreds by bombs and rockets; it is riddled with bullet holes.

We hide out of sight. I squeamishly peek around the corner and see the street is filled with rubble. Destroyed military trucks lay across the road, tires still in flames, emitting black smoke. Loose newspapers tumble across the boulevard, stopped only by the remains of charred human bodies.

Mohammad commands me. "Stay here, you'll be safe, Pendar."

"Don't go out there, Mohammad, it's too dangerous." I plead.

"Don't be afraid, I volunteered to defend my country, it's an honor," he responds courageously.

The ground starts to rumble beneath my feet. The thunderous humming of a loud engine inches closer to our location. Around the corner, an Iraqi tank enters the street, heading straight for us. The enormous tracks crushed any debris in its path.

Mohammad looks at me and says, "My time has come."

I hold his arm tightly, "Don't go out there Mohammad, PLEASE!"

He stands there beaming under the dull gray sky, the chilly wind blowing in his hair. With the pad of his thumb, he gently wipes the tears streaming down my face. I clutch his arm tightly.

He looks into my eyes, gently removes my hand from his forearm and says, "Don't move, I'll take care of this."

I watch as he casually strolls out into the road, heading towards the tank. He removes his jacket and reveals that he's wearing a suicide vest, loaded with C-4 explosives front and back.

Eyes wide, I am frozen in my tracks; I can't move a muscle, I am disabled from the fear.

He confidently marches on, pausing for a moment to look back over his shoulder at me. He winks and gives me a loving smile.

I wave back, but I am spotted by the tank. The tank slows in front of the half-destroyed building where I am now hiding. The massive turret of the tank slowly turns towards me, making a loud screeching sound, the sound of metal, the sound of death. My mouth drops, frozen in horror as I prepare to die.

I spot Mohammad, crawling on his stomach within inches of the tank. He gives me a compassionate look of reassurance, deliberately pulls his hand out of his pocket, revealing a shiny silver detonator and a protruding red blinking button.

The tank turret stops and loads the ammunition getting ready to shoot. Mohammad tilts his head up to the sky, "Bismillah-ir-Rahman-ir-Rahim (In the name of God, the merciful and compassionate)," he recites. He then pushes down on the red blinking detonator, causing a humongous blast and a blinding light.

I instantly spring awake to a seated position; my shirt drenched in sweat from the night terror. I much preferred the euphoric dreams of living with Shirley in America.

I awakened the next morning to the scent of a savory breakfast. At first, I was in disbelief. *Was I still dreaming? Am I back home with my family? Was Mohammad gone forever?* Lying in bed, I watched a pigeon peck at some breadcrumbs outside my window, but my thoughts kept flashing back to Mohammad.

Dragging myself from the covers, I went to the kitchen. I didn't have an appetite for breakfast, I just picked at my food, pushing it around on my plate from one side to the other.

I was anxious to get back to school, regardless of Mohammad's passing. I was behind on my homework and didn't want another visit from Mr. Hakimi. I rushed into the living room and asked Baba, "When can I go back to school?"

"Not yet Pendar, It's too dangerous right now."

I didn't understand his answer, "What do you mean dangerous? Is there something else that I need to know?"

"Pendar, it's hard to explain, but I want you to listen to me very carefully. There are recruitment efforts at every school in Iran. Children as young as twelve are being taken to the front lines of the war. Some volunteer to the Basij, without permission or notifying their parents," he explained.

"Is that what happened to Mohammad?" I asked with concern.

"I think so, but I'm not letting anything happen to you. It's not about religion, God, or country, you're too young to go to war, and for what? Just to get slaughtered?"

I listened to my father in horror. I felt numb. It was difficult to fathom this turn of events. "What do you mean slaughtered?" I asked.

"Pendar, they're taking young soldiers to the front lines of the war, do you know what that means? They're marched out into battle, untrained and unprepared, only to be killed by landmines, enemy fire, or to walk in front of tanks as human shields," he explained.

"WHAT?" I exclaimed in disbelief.

Suddenly, I felt extremely apprehensive and doubtful about my return to school.

Maman walked in just then, "Nader, have you told him about your other plans yet?" My mother looked dejected.

"What other plans?" I demanded, feeling crazy with apprehension. "What now? More bad news?" *What else could they throw at me on my first day back?*

Baba instructed me to calm down and listen. "I've made plans for us to travel, to try again, to get you to America."

Here we go again. "No, I don't want to go to America anymore. The last trip was too hard," I loudly proclaimed. "I want to stay here with you."

"Pendar, that's not an option azizam," Baba said in a calm voice. "I have to get you out of here. If you stay, your life would be in danger as long as the war is raging on."

"What if I say no? What if I don't want to go?"

Maman started to weep, "He should stay here with us, his family.

That's where he belongs."

"He can't Ziba, it's not safe here!" Baba told her, before turning his attention back to me. "Pendar, you don't want to end up like Mohammad, do you?"

Maman's cries intensified. I felt disturbed and frustrated at the uncertainty I now faced and the rejection I felt from my own family.

Back in November, at the start of our journey, I was excited. I couldn't wait to get to America. But now, I felt differently. Leaving again wouldn't be so easy. But the rumors surrounding the child soldiers were terrifying and true.

Despite my indignation, Baba was unwilling to let up on me. "Children are being sent to the front lines without weapons," he said. "Some realize they've made a grave mistake, but it's too late at that point. The child soldiers are bound by ropes to prevent desertion. For them, there is no escape from certain death."

Maman was now weeping uncontrollably. "Isn't there any other option, Nader?"

My father was resolute. "No Ziba, we've got to get him out of Iran."

Tears began rolling down my cheeks; through quivering lips, I pleaded with my father. "Baba, I want to stay with you and Maman. PLEASE!"

"NO PENDAR! YOU CAN'T!" Baba shouted fiercely, slamming his hand on the table. For my father, there was only one option.

Deep down I felt conflicted. It was an awful lot to take in after my first day back from the arduous journey. Now talk of going back spun my mind in a whirlpool of speculation. My parents argued in the past like any married couple, but for the first time, I could detect a rift forming between them, whereas before they seemed very harmonious in all their decisions.

Out of fear of the government's recruitment efforts, my parents chose not to send me back to school. Instead, they explored alternative options. With my safety in question, staying in Iran was not possible. Every night, I witnessed the frustration they felt at this difficult cross-road. It was a big decision, leaving Maman heartbroken. Nightly, I heard her soft, quiet sobs coming from her bedroom.

Baba had a short window of opportunity to get me to safety. But the thought of leaving my family again sent chills down my spine. *What country would we travel to next? What strange city or hotel would we stay in? How was our luck going to change after two unsuccessful attempts?* The prospect of the unknown was unsettling, but certainly not alien to me.

While they both wished to keep our family together, my well-being and safety now took precedence. My parents were faced with a painful decision—to keep me in the country with the looming danger of being drafted by the Iranian army or the possibility of moving far away to a distant, strange country.

There was urgency in our situation and much had changed in a brief period. It was difficult to witness the agony of my parents as they tried to protect me in their own, unusual way.

Many nights Baba was on the phone speaking to Amoo Hafez or other friends about our situation, desperately evaluating alternative options. Often, he hung up disheartened by their responses. Most were not supportive of his decision to leave Iran again, and if anything, they were discouraging. They thought Baba was crazy to apply a third time for a student visa. Although he always told them, "Ta se nashe, bazi nashe!" Third time's the charm.

Most viewed it as nothing more than a waste of additional time and money. But my father ignored their warnings. He continued his relentless phone calls, contacting multiple travel agencies and immigration services until he found a solution.

Meanwhile, I was plagued by nightmares about the war, tossing and turning all night. Visions of children exploding into pieces in a minefield consumed my dreams. I saw child soldiers tied together with ropes who were proudly walking in front of a tank, then suddenly, 'KABOOM' they were blown to bits by a land mine exploding beneath their feet. I often woke up in a cold sweat, unable to fall back to sleep.

In my nightmares, Mohammad was always there, waving at me with a calm smile just before he was blown to Kingdom Come. Often, imagining my new life in America helped me escape the night terrors.

Baba continued his methodical planning, like a calculated game of chess, measuring every move with extreme caution. After two weeks of intense, investigative labor, he announced, "I just got off the phone with Mageed, our travel agent. He says Syria is our best bet, the American Embassy in the city of Damascus."

According to Mageed, the embassy in Damascus was rumored to be more lenient towards Iranians and other Middle Easterners. "We'll restart the visa process there," Baba said.

Despite Baba's optimism, I remained skeptical and tempered my expectations. Having just lost my best friend and no longer attending school, I was secretly eager to get back on the road with my father.

Our flight to Damascus was scheduled for the last week of January in 1987. After spending just four weeks back home in Iran, I prepared to say goodbye to my family all over again. With a few days remaining, my anxiety grew and became visible to everyone.

Baba reassured me nightly, sitting by my bedside in the evenings and offering me words of optimism. "Be patient, son, fate has other plans for you," he'd say. "You'll see for yourself."

Our failed attempts had only motivated him further. Baba's unspoken pledge, 'never give up' was provoked further by his fatherly instinct. The stakes were too high, with my life hanging in the balance.

On the day of our departure, only a small group of family members accompanied us to the airport, unlike the first time. Even Papa Jahan chose to remain at home that morning. After saying goodbye to him and Mama Goli at their apartment, he assumed his position at the kitchen window and lovingly waved me off as he'd done on many mornings. I watched out the car's rear window as his image grew smaller and finally disappeared. Sadly, it was the last time I ever saw my grandfather alive.

I imagined he and the others expected I'd be back home again soon, doubtful our visit to the embassy in Damascus would end in success. Frankly, at times, I felt that same way.

At the airport, Maman and I again shed many tears during our emotional goodbye. Maman's eyes were puffy and red, and she looked as heartbroken as I felt seeing her in that state. We were inches from one another, but already the distance felt immeasurable. The airport seemed to go silent as everyone stared directly at us. I collapsed into her embrace one final time, pressing my face tightly into her chest as my entire life flashed before me.

I recalled sitting snugly in her lap as we watched *Jaws* at the movie theater, her laughter, the addictive aroma of her perfume, the birth of my siblings. I even remembered the tough times, like running up and down the stairs, escaping from bombs. How desperately I wished this were all a dream. I held her tight, but my thoughts were interrupted by the intercom announcement, it was time to board our plane.

I wiped the tears from her jawline with the pad of my thumb. Meanwhile, fresh tears squeezed out between her eyelids. My face was full of tears, too, nose running. I couldn't catch my breath from the intense emotional hysteria. I planted a final kiss on her forehead, then her hand. Baba and Maman were cold and distant in their parting moments, maybe she felt angry and resentful towards him at that very moment.

Baba began to pull me towards the line, but Maman was not letting go. She held my hand so tight that my fingers turned purple. Her love and adoration for me was more obvious than ever before, both in her sturdy grip and in her unwillingness to let go. I know now that this was a better solution than going to war, but at that moment, I was not convinced, and neither was Maman.

NINETEEN
NEW ADVENTURE

DAMASCUS, SYRIA, JANUARY 26TH, 1987.

Damascus airport was crawling with passengers. Baba and I gradually claimed our luggage, headed for the terminal exit, and hailed a taxi to the hotel.

The streets of Damascus were congested with cars, motorcycles, and throngs of pedestrians. Parts of the city smelled like mold or grime, unpleasantly tickling my nose. We arrived at another second-rate hotel that was much like the one in Ankara.

We checked in, were shown to our room, this time relieved to find an attached bathroom and a phone on the nightstand. Baba began his customary calls, starting with one to Maman.

On the flight over from Tehran, I had been given another model Boeing 747 airplane and resumed playing with it, my arms extended like airplane wings, making flight sounds with my mouth as I soared to the four corners of our room.

When Baba was done on the phone, we decided to explore the city, another adventure to find dinner. That night in Damascus, Baba decided to venture out, seemingly craving something out of the ordinary.

"Why are we walking this far?" I asked, breathing heavily. "Where are we going?"

Baba sniffed the air like a hound dog following a scent, "Do you smell that, Pendar?"

"Smell what, Baba?" Suddenly, my nose picked up a distinct odor, "Do you mean the smell of charcoal?"

Baba smiled and nodded his head 'YES'.

"Tonight, we're going to follow our noses to the spot," he announced. "Just be patient, you'll find out soon enough."

Strolling along the sidewalk, we reached an offbeat alley lined with street vendors, each cart containing a flat top grille and a variety of meats on display. I expected to stop, but Baba continued walking past several food carts to an adjacent alley, featuring a new set of vendors. The smell of charcoal permeated stronger in the air.

Baba motioned for me to keep up, finally stopping at the manghal of a vendor preparing *delojigar*, the fresh internal organs of a sheep. We're eating dinner here tonight," he said.

He pointed to the liver, hearts, kidney, and a variety of delectable meats we were accustomed to eating back home, including the testicles. The vendor shouted instructions in Arabic at his assistant, and the young man promptly darted up the alley.

He pulled out his razor-sharp knife from the holster like a gun slinger, grinded it against the sharpening stone, then sliced the selected meats into evenly chopped, bite size pieces. He meticulously speared the meats using the 'Siekh' thin metal skewers. Then laid the skewers filled with meat on the manghal for a couple of minutes, flipping them over halfway through. Ahead of our order being ready, the assistant came running back with freshly baked, steaming hot flat bread. After the meat was cooked, the 'Siekh' was placed in the middle of the flat bread, and the vendor gripped the meat tightly. Then he'd remove the 'Siekh' with one fluid motion, leaving only the meat and bread behind like a wrap. Reminiscent of when Baba prepared the internal organs on his 'manghal' at our villa in Seaside.

We dug in at the makeshift table adjacent to the Manghal on the side of the alley. Baba ate quickly, hot steam escaping his mouth with every breath. We gobbled up multiple wraps, washing it down with soda. It was a delectable meal, and an even better bonding experience in the most unlikely of places – a memorable meal unlike any other. The supper included an important lesson: not all superior experiences in life must be expensive. I realized there was more satisfaction and enjoyment in an inexpensive roadside meal, rather than an extravagant restaurant. It was special and a treat to spend alone time with Baba, having him all to myself, bringing us closer than ever before.

I had a much deeper respect, love, and adoration for my father. Realizing the burden of responsibility, weighing heavily on his shoulders to keep me safe. I often thought our journey hadn't been easy on Maman or my siblings either. They were left alone, abandoned for weeks, they must feel isolated, the way I felt without Baba by my side.

The following morning, a taxi took us to the American Embassy. Baba had been told this embassy was more lenient, and the visa process could be easier for us, leaving me feeling optimistic about our chances. The embassy looked much like the others we'd visited, and a lengthy line of applicants, most of whom appeared Middle Eastern, Pakistani, Syrian and Saudi Arabian, amongst others.

Several hours passed and Baba had not spotted any Iranians in the cue. It wasn't for a lack of trying, he was anxious to strike up a conversation, to gather information. Slowly we crept forward. Later we observed applicants exiting the embassy and as they got closer, Baba overheard them speaking Farsi. "Wait in place," he instructed. Then left the line to catch up with them. When he returned, he looked frustrated.

"What's wrong Baba? What'd they say?" I asked.

"They said there are too many Iranian immigrants who are applying in Damascus; the embassy is not accepting applications from any Iranian citizens right now."

He insisted we stay in line, to confirm for ourselves. After hours of waiting, the armed guards at the gate verified what my father had been told and we were turned away without a chance of setting up an appointment.

Our ride back to the hotel was tense, Baba didn't speak, he just stared out the window. The minute we got back to the room, he was on the phone with the travel agent who had recommended Damascus.

Not wanting to get in his way, I busied myself with my model airplane, taking off, flying over the bed, but eventually the ill-fated toy went crashing into the wall. The force of the collision sent plastic airplane parts scattering across the floor. An ironic symbolism; like my dreams of going to America. I was putting the airplane back together when my father connected with Mageed.

"WHY DID YOU SEND US TO DAMASCUS?" he yelled into the receiver. "THEY'RE NOT LETTING ANY IRANIANS IN! THAT'S NOT WHAT YOU TOLD ME LAST WEEK BEFORE I BOUGHT THE TICKETS!"

My father hardly lost his temper or raised his voice in anger. But he was wailing at Mageed. He had become unhinged, certainly from the immense pressure.

"What? Where? You've got to be kidding me? Are you serious?" he asked skeptically. I watched as he grabbed a piece of paper and a pen from the desk and started writing. He was now pacing slowly, deliberately, until the telephone cord reached its end, and he got yanked back, his face contorting into a mask of unadulterated fury.

When he hung up, I inquired about what he'd learned.

"Pendar, we could be heading to China!" he exclaimed.

"WHAT!?" I asked in amazement.

"Mageed says they'll accept our application at the embassy in Beijing, but he's going to verify the information before he books our flight."

China? I couldn't believe what I was hearing.

I awakened the following morning to the sound of Baba on the phone. The desperation in his voice was concerning, but he was laser focused.

For hours he struggled to find answers about the embassy in Beijing. Later that day, he spoke with the travel agent again.

Mageed was unsure, telling him he'd call us back the following day. The next day became two, then three, with Baba desperately attempting to contact him on the phone.

Three days had passed before we reached him.

"Mageed, what happened?!" Baba shouted into the phone. "You were supposed to call me back, days ago. Do you have any updates?"

Mageed claimed that he had just this minute verified that Iranian citizens were being permitted to apply in Beijing. "I found out less than an hour ago," he said. "But the information is confirmed, I promise you."

"Are you sure, I don't want to drag my son to China and have the same thing happen!" Baba raised his concern about the dead end in Damascus.

"I'm telling you it's for sure. I had someone personally check out the embassy. That's why it took so long for me to get back to you. Should I book your tickets?"

"Yes, Mageed, book it!" Baba instructed him.

And just like that, we were going to China.

Chinese movies were amongst my favorite films-- I had seen every Bruce Lee movie and was a huge fan. I was anxiously looking forward to this next leg of our journey.

Mageed booked us on a flight, departing Damascus on February 1st, for Beijing. Baba phoned Maman to keep her informed of our plans.

"How can you trust Mageed?" I asked my father.

Baba smiled. "He's assured me we're not going to run into any issues in Beijing, Pendar! If we do, I'm going to skin him alive when I get back to Tehran."

Ever the optimist, my father told me, "Pendare nik, goftare nik, kerdare nik (Good thoughts, good words, good deeds)."

TWENTY
THIRD TIME'S A CHARM?

BEIJING, CHINA, FEBRUARY 1ST, 1987.

We arrived at Beijing airport following an exhausting 12-hour flight. At the terminal, I spotted a sea of Chinese people, as far as my eyes could see. To my inexperienced eyes, the people looked much the same. I was conflicted, ashamed about stereotyping, but for the first time, Baba and I were the minority in the airport.

The strange signs, people, even our surroundings made it troublesome to navigate towards the exit.

Baba used makeshift sign language skills to communicate with the Chinese as we struggled to exit the crowded airport.

Once outside, Baba flagged down the first taxi he spotted. He spoke to the driver through the passenger window, "hotel for businessman," he said in broken English, but the driver looked annoyed, pulling away while shouting at Baba in Chinese with outrage.

Baba turned his head to me, shrugged and said, "What the hell?" The communication was certainly going to be challenging.

We hailed another taxi with the same unfortunate result. Baba raised the palm of his hand and yelled, "Ta se nashe, bazi nashe." He stepped in front of the next cab like a police officer confiscating someone's vehicle. Third time lucky! The taxi driver nodded and understood Baba, agreeing to drive us to a hotel suited for a businessman.

Baba carried his shiny Samsonite briefcase with him everywhere we went, an attempt to look the part of a world traveling businessman.

On the way, I glanced out the window and witnessed a vast land, dry and absent of color. There were no trees, flowers or greenery spotted within miles. It was dismal, dark brown terrain, I thought China was indeed a strange land, different from other cities we had visited.

It was a quiet ride, except for the voice of the Chinese radio jockey coming through the speakers. Baba and I were in culture shock, staring out into the gloomy haze. We soon entered the city, greeted by the roaring tones of the crowd ahead. Screeching tires and deafening car horns overwhelmed my senses and echoed in my ears. Suddenly, our taxi was engulfed in a wave of traffic. There were bicycles, cars, motorbikes, and vans that intermingled with the crowd like thousands of ants.

The taxi driver meticulously maneuvered his car to avoid crashing into pedestrians or the bicyclists that flooded the streets. At one juncture in the road, there were more people, bicycles, and motorbikes than cars on the street. We sat quietly and rode in amazement.

After navigating the intense crowds, we were finally dropped off in front of our hotel. At first glance, it looked more like a hospital that was converted to a hotel. We stood out front, looking left to right trying to spot the entrance to the lobby.

We located the entryway on the side of the building. Inside, we found a long empty corridor with a small wooden desk at the far end. It was extremely quiet in the lobby; the only noise was my sneakers squeaking on the shiny vinyl floor.

We were greeted by a short, timid, dark-haired young woman, peacefully sitting at the reception desk.

"Hello, we are here to check-in," I politely said while Baba presented our passports.

Without many words spoken, we successfully checked in. She pointed to the stairway just past the elevator, which was roped off by yellow tape, indicating it was 'out of service'.

We hauled our luggage to the second floor, facing another long, shiny, vinyl corridor, with rooms along one side. Towards the end, an empty rusted wheelchair, and a few rollaway hospital beds with broken wheels, confirming my suspicions that this had once been a hospital. We opened the door to our room with trepidation, finding beds possibly left over from the last patient who had stayed here.

The room had cream-colored walls, chipped, cracked, dark moldings, and a gray glazed ceiling that was once white. The white sheet covering the bed spilled over the side brushing the grimly checkered tiles on the floor. The mattresses were harsh and lacked adequate cushioning.

I pressed my head against the glass window of our room, over-looking the parking lot, fogging up the glass with each breath. I drew the words USA on the window with my index finger, Baba snickering out of the corner of his mouth, "Soon Pendar, soon we'll be there!" Within seconds, the words were gone. Symbolic of chasing the American dream, dissipating each time, just like the letters I drew on our window.

The one amenity Baba was grateful for, the phone on the nightstand. Though in Beijing, he made fewer phone calls than before -- the language barrier presented a huge obstacle. He called Maman to let her know we made it safely to Beijing, then his trusted travel agent, Mageed. He confirmed again that the American embassy was open and accepting applications, regardless of nationality. The great news was followed by another dinner adventure in Beijing.

Our routine search for our next meal had become customary in every city we had visited thus far. While strolling outside our hotel, we walked by a nearby alley humming with activity, unaware of the bizarre fate about to befall us. We wandered in and made our way towards the food vendors. Suddenly, the pungent, disgusting odor of rotten fish hit me like a brick wall. "What's that smell?" I asked.

It was so strong it made my eyes water. It was a rancid stench unlike anything I'd ever smelled! I looked at Baba and his face explained it all, he had the same appalled expression. We were both overwhelmed by the vile foulness surrounding us! We continued into the musty-smelling alley in hopes of finding normal food. A few more steps, and the alley narrowed, putting us closer to the epicenter of the horrific stench. What we witnessed next was out of *Indiana Jones and the Temple of Doom*—the dinner scene at India's Pankot Palace. The vendors were serving a cacophony of nauseating concoctions. They were steaming, grilling, roasting and frying a variety of unfamiliar sustenance such as bats, rats, snakes, frogs, insects, lizards, and other bizarre creatures.

I was squeamish to crush an insect under my shoe, but to consider putting one inside my mouth made my skin crawl and violated every sense. Disgust oozed off the food like pus, I felt like vomit was going to projectile out of my mouth like Linda Blair in *The Exorcist*.

Yes, we were guilty of eating unusual animal parts in Iran, but these were distasteful critters, worthy of a creepy nightmare. One man's disgust was another's delicacy, or so I thought.

Feeling out of place like obvious foreigners, we strode briskly past the vendors, holding our collective breath and pinching our noses to avoid the unpleasant smells and the horrifying sights. I felt judgmental, but I couldn't help it -- this was entirely too strange for my palate, I may as well have been on another planet from *Star Wars*.

We finally entered an area of brick-and-mortar restaurants. In Beijing, finding normal sustenance was like obtaining an American Visa, illusive and a rare commodity. We observed the patrons sitting at tables inside one of the establishments and tried to read the menu posted outside. This was going to be even more challenging than we expected, the menu was in Chinese. *How were we going to order food?*

With few options, we nonchalantly walked past the first restaurant window hoping to catch a glimpse of what the patrons were eating. But we couldn't see inside due to the reflection, so we passed by a second time, looking through the window from a different angle. We spotted a young couple sharing a large bowl of soup. It was filled to the rim with steamy liquid, but the contents within were unclear. The couple was busy mixing, slurping, eating, as we leaned closer, trying to get a peek at what was inside the soup. My eyes scanned the spoon, which was slowly lifted, then accidentally locked eyes with the couple. An uncomfortable, awkward moment passed, we stared at each other with wonder.

Baba nudged me out of their view and towards the next restaurant, where a family sitting next to the window was served a large platter; a generous, appetizing, steamy pile of rice, fried with vegetables, various meats, and spices.

"Baba, the rice looks normal, should we try it?" I asked. "Yeah, let's try. Hope nothing weird is hiding in that rice!" he exclaimed. Baba put his arm around my shoulder, we bravely strolled in. Inside the restaurant, the whole place came to a standstill. There was pin-drop silence as everyone's eyes suddenly fixated on us, standing at the door. We casually walked to the counter, but the employees spoke only Chinese. After much miming and makeshift sign language, we decisively pointed to the fried rice on the family's table and asked to order the same. We took our seats and patiently waited for our meal to be prepared.

It was brought to our table; in addition, we were given two wooden sticks for silverware. I looked around the restaurant and observed the other patrons, utilizing the unusually strange wooden utensils to eat.

"They're called chopsticks, Pendar." Baba told me.

I remembered seeing the wooden sticks in the movies but had no idea how to manipulate or use them. For that matter, neither did Baba.

I gripped the chopsticks and attempted eating, but the food kept falling in between the two sticks back on the plate or on my lap before making it to my mouth. Baba mimed to the waiter, holding an imaginary fork and knife, bringing it up to his gaping mouth, pretending to shuffle food.

They eventually understood what Baba was signaling for. We cautiously dug into the rice, inspecting it, making certain there were no snakes or insects crawling in it. Once Baba verified the meat was chicken and beef, we attacked the pile of rice. The fried rice had spices, flavors, aromas that were new to my palate, savory and enticing. While eating, I sensed the restaurant patrons staring at us like amused children, looking at the animals in the local zoo. They must have been wondering; what are the two foreigners doing in our city? I wondered that myself, as our travels took us halfway around the world. Beijing made me feel like an outsider, not capable of hiding or blending in. I wondered what it would be like in America—*will I fit in or feel as alienated as I did in Beijing? Would I stand out like an obvious foreigner as I did in that restaurant?* The thought of never fitting in made me shudder. Even though my belly was full, I still felt the discomfort of my uncertain future.

Our stay in Beijing had left a mark, and I learned another important lesson – no matter which part of the world we lived in, what we ate, the language we spoke, or strange clothing we wore, we were all human beings who deserved not to be judged by cultural differences or religious beliefs. We were certain to walk a different route back to our hotel and avoid the alley of horror, filled with foods worthy of a nightmare.

I heard the distinct sound of a ping pong ball bouncing on a table, the noise it made when struck with a wooden racket, followed by applauding children. Closer, I spotted a few kids near the entrance of our hotel who were gathered around an old, scratched-up table.

I loved playing ping pong back home and was eager to join them. I was intimidated by the language barrier, but the desire to play overcame my hesitation. "Baba, can I play with the kids please?" I asked.

"No Pendar, it's almost dark outside, it's not safe," he told me.

With my head down in disappointment, we headed back to our room, Baba ready to get back on the phone. I stared out the room's window, looking at the kids below playing, wishing I were playing with them.

Without any other source of entertainment, I rolled up my socks into a ball, kicking them around like a soccer ball outside our room in the long corridor. I had energy to exert and time to waste -- my routine for the next few hours before retiring to bed.

All tucked in, I spoke to God again, just like other nights leading up to our visits to the embassy. I wished for the usual, closing my eyes, with thoughts of boarding a flight to America.

Morning time, Baba's bed was next to the window, the lower half lit by the early morning sunlight streaming through the square panels. He rubbed his sleep-clogged eyes and stretched before getting out of bed. We got dressed and headed for the lobby.

The young woman at the reception called a taxi and communicated the embassy address to our driver. Parts of the city boasted murals of political leaders, and many tall buildings displaying hundreds of Chinese flags, dancing in the wind. After an hour, we were dropped off in front of the embassy.

There were about thirty applicants in line, mostly Chinese or Asian, our chances for an appointment looked promising.

Baba had secretly—and discreetly—covered up the second "APPLICATION RECEIVED" stamp placed in my passport from Frankfurt. I knew that was wrong; my feelings were torn. Baba couldn't be blamed when my life was hanging in the balance. After a couple of hours of waiting, we arrived at the security shack, met by the armed guards.

The sight of the machine gun and soldiers in uniform immediately made me think about Mohammad. I imagined him fighting the enemy, or senselessly walking on the minefields, my regular recurring nightmare. My thoughts consumed with the gore, blood, violence, and senseless killing of children who didn't belong in war.

The guards verified our documents and asked, "The next availability to speak with a consul would be in four days, does that work for you?"

We quickly accepted the appointment. On the way back to the hotel, Baba asked the driver to drop us off at a large multi-level complex, a shopping center. We window-shopped for a while, luckily finding a food court on the top level, serving "normal" as in "familiar" foods.

As we approached the hotel, I spotted the kids playing ping pong again, wistful thoughts of my friends and family flooded my head. "Baba, since it's not dark out yet, can I play with the kids today?" I asked. I craved the camaraderie of kids my own age, eager to feel normal. My father reluctantly agreed, and I jumped at the chance, heading over to the table.

I was shy, only watching the kids at first. They were engrossed in playing, not even noticing me standing close by. Their skills, style of play and how they held the ping pong paddle was vastly different from what I was used to. It was like they possessed a Black Belt in Ping Pong.

I stood there intimidated, not sure how to introduce myself or how to ask for a turn. I couldn't understand what they were saying when suddenly the ball flew in my direction. I threw it back quickly.

They shouted a few phrases in Chinese, and I answered back in English. Quickly recognizing the language barrier, one of them approached me, offered me his paddle, and pointed to his own spot at the table.

Nervously, I agreed to play. My opponent stared me down, measuring me up from the opposite side of the table with a keen eye. He was the best in the group, hitting every ball with a purpose and technique I'd only seen in the Olympics.

He spun the ball with his paddle to which I had no response. I couldn't return his complicated serves across the table to save my life. The ball would hit the table or my racquet, then uncontrollably fly in the opposite direction. I was convinced the table was flawed as I struggled to keep up with 'Bruce Lee' of ping pong.

We were exuberant playing singles, doubles, and our own tournament well into the night, hardly noticing the sun had dropped behind the hills. Baba eventually came downstairs and forced me back to our room. We said our goodbyes and the kids invited me to play again tomorrow, in sign language, of course.

Children playing - ping pong, soccer, or even in the snow - have their own special language that only they can relate to.

I played with the children every chance I got for a few more days, leading up to our appointment. When the day finally arrived, we took a taxi and arrived an hour early for good measure. We successfully passed the security checkpoint with ease. Inside the building, we were greeted by a beautiful, blue-eyed blonde-haired woman, her bangs laying just above her eyebrows. Sitting at the front desk, she wore a power suit paired with a crisp button-down blouse with big shoulder pads. The embassy was not crowded like we had expected.

Baba scanned every corner of the room but failed to spot any other Iranians or Middle Eastern applicants. I felt like a regular at the embassy. After all, this was my third time applying for a visa, but my low self-esteem and lack of confidence left me feeling incompetent and inadequate. I thought of Baba's favorite phrase.

"Ta se nashe, bazi nashe! Third time's the charm!" I said jokingly.

His frustrated frown turned into an endearing smile, "Ta se nashe bazi nashe!", 'Third time's the charm," he said back to me. A thread of optimism was the only thing we were hanging onto. The pretty blonde-haired receptionist showed us to the next room.

We were seated and patiently waited for my name to be called. This could be the last time I visited an American embassy; it was perhaps my final attempt. My heart started racing, my palms were clammy, and I felt nervous anticipating the dreaded interview again. Seconds plodded by each separated from the next by an eternity. Finally, my name was called by a loud booming voice.

I hesitantly walked to the window, Baba only steps behind me. He cocked his head to the side, smiled at me, then put his arm around my shoulder and squeezed, as if to say, "Come on son, you've got this!"

The counsel was an older man who had a deep voice that could be heard from down the hall. He was wearing a burgundy suit, a thick silk tie and had the worst toupee this side of the Great Wall of China. He commenced with the customary questions. I already knew the routine, calmly answering him.

The inquiry about my plans post-graduation came up. My answers remained the same about going back home to Iran after graduating, but he didn't look satisfied. "You're telling me that you're going to go back to Iran once you graduate? Is that right?" He shrugged, squinting his eyes at me while tilting his head to one side. His abrasive personality started to appear, apparently, he wasn't believing a word of it.

"Yes, of course I plan on going back, I promised my mother!" I was sure to mention.

"Pendar," he retorted, "we don't typically see children growing up in America, completing their education, and then suddenly returning back home to their country because you made a promise to dear old mom."

He paused and then continued, "I don't believe we're going to be able to proceed with your student visa at this…"

"SIR!" I interrupted him before he could finish. During my last two interviews, Baba and Shirley put up a valiant fight, but this was my chance to convince the consul. "Sir, I'm only thirteen years old, and kids my age are being sent to war in Iran. My friend Mohammad has already died, and I don't want to be next. Please, I'm afraid and don't want to go to war," I continued. "If you deny my application, I'll have to return to Iran, and I'll be killed! Please!" I pleaded with him.

He looked entirely unfazed and only kept staring at my documents, flipping through the pages one by one, giving me a small glimmer of hope.

My fingers intertwined with Baba's, who looked with uncertainty from me to the consul.

Did I say enough, or was I convincing enough to overturn his decision? I was tense, grabbing onto the last loose thread of hope that remained.

After a few uncomfortable moments of silence, the man looked directly into my eyes, "I'm sorry to hear about that," he said icily. The way he looked at me, we might as well have been talking about something else.

"But sir, let me expla..." he cut me off before I could make my point.

"That will not be sufficient to overturn the decision. Unfortunately, we cannot grant you a student visa to America. The risk of you entering and not returning home is too great," he said with a tone that was nonchalant and entirely unsympathetic. A serious stare ensued that could have burned a hole in the back of my head.

I put my forehead against the bulletproof glass, deep erratic breaths started to fog it up. Soon tears were rolling down my cheeks, realizing my dreams of escaping the war and going to America were shattered. I couldn't find the inspiration to fight or argue about returning home after graduation. A high pitch noise filled my ears, all I heard was a loud ringing sound, buzzing in my head. I silently screamed with frustration.

A lump began to impede my breathing and I turned numb from the shock; how could this have happened a third time?

Baba shouted my name several times before I snapped out of it and tried to argue with the consul, but the answer remained the same.

"PLEASE," said Baba, but the consul walked away, and the interview was over.

I'll never forget the way my father said "please" in English, the pain in his plea, the fear in his eyes about the unknown future.

My third application for an American visa was denied, a cloud of despair began rising to my brain stem. The shadow of a deep disappointment settled over me, astonished and feeling helpless, I sobbed out of control. I looked to Baba for comfort, but he was distraught and inconsolable.

We walked away from the embassy with a familiar feeling of failure. Despair set in, we'd hit our final roadblock in Beijing and maybe now, Baba was convinced to make plans on returning home. He turned to me, hugged me tightly and wiped the tears streaking down my cheeks with his thumb.

The future was a dark, unknown highway, and we were blindly traveling on it. No headlights or signs for guidance, no plans for our next steps. I couldn't find the words to express how disoriented I felt. I was beyond devastated, but already the wheels of fortune were spinning in Baba's head. I had come to know him well during our journey, his body language or demeanor was not of someone who was ready to give up.

To an outsider, Baba didn't look scared, but his face was imprinted in my earliest memories, and I knew all its subtle nuances, knowing each twitch or flicker that rippled across it. I knew he was scared plenty, just as I was but you couldn't tell by looking at him. On the way back to the hotel, Baba and I hardly exchanged a word. Once back, the sight of kids playing ping pong made me cheery.

I didn't have to ask Baba for permission – he was already nodding his head in a "yes" and told me, "I'll be up in the room, making phone calls."

I wiped away the tears, tried looking normal before joining the kids. I didn't want them to know I'd been sobbing moments earlier.

No matter, I played for the rest of the afternoon before returning to our room. Surprisingly, Baba was still on the phone with his trusted travel agent, asking more questions about embassies in other Asian countries and exploring other options.

He was still on the phone when I went to sleep that night. I was physically and mentally exhausted from the day's events.

In the morning, the sound of Baba on the phone woke me up early. He had awakened well before me to make more calls, desperately searching for another solution. The image of the telephone receiver wedged between his cheek and collarbone was a sight I'd become accustomed to.

I politely waited for him to finish his last call. "Good morning, Baba," I said politely.

"Good morning Pendar Jan, how did you sleep son? Did I keep you up?" he asked, still focused elsewhere.

"Maybe a little, but that's okay, are we going back to Tehran?" I finally asked him.

Immediately he shook his head, "No, Mageed is calling me back with some options. You're not ready to give up yet, are you?" He asked.

Deep down, I was fed up with the journey after my third rejection, ready to admit defeat. It would be much easier to fly back home and deal with the consequences. But Baba's unwillingness to give up against all odds was truly inspiring.

"No Baba, I'm not giving up. Let's continue, where to next?" I eagerly asked.

"Mageed recommended we continue in Asian countries – shorter waiting periods at the embassy. What do you think about going to Tokyo?" he asked.

"TOKYO?"

"It's the capital of Japan, and I've already told Mageed to book our flights," he told me, winking.

"Okay Baba, YOU GO, WE GO!" I smiled at him. The shock value of "where to next" was dwindling though, nothing Baba did surprised me anymore.

I put my trust in Baba, asking God to lead us on the righteous path. I didn't know what possessed my father to continue, but I suddenly remembered the old psychic lady and the story of the panther climbing the mountain, painted inside the coffee mug.

Just like the psychic convincingly said, "There is nothing that will stop the panther from reaching the top of the mountain." To me, Baba had become the panther, facing an enormous mountain, impossible to climb. But no matter how difficult, or how unattainable, he never gave up, only working harder to reach the peak after each defeat.

TWENTY-ONE
AN EXPENSIVE STOP

TOKYO, JAPAN, FEBRUARY 9, 1987

Upon landing in Tokyo, we were greeted by the high-tech atmosphere of Narita International Airport. I was dazed by its glossy floors; the overall cleanliness was impressive. The terminal smelled brand-new like it was recently constructed and looked extremely modern. Overflowing with vibrant, colorful neon billboards, and advertising signs that hung at its every corner. Most in Japanese, but few advertised well-known brands such as Coca Cola and Marlboro.

We cabbed it to the hotel, on the way I was struck by the elegance of the city's architecture, modern and sophisticated. I marveled at how there wasn't so much as a speck of garbage on the streets or a brush-stroke of graffiti on the walls or buildings.

Baba had booked a lower-ranked hotel near the airport, but the nightly prices were outrageous, far more than what we had become accustomed to in the previous cities we'd visited. Baba looked at the invoice with a mix of shock and confusion, but soon realized that finding cheaper, alternate accommodations would be a lengthy process, and he hesitantly agreed to pay in exchange for the keys.

We didn't eat adequately during our flight on Japan Airlines. Foods served on the flight smelled fishy, including the strange green tea.

We were hungry and decided to venture out for dinner after Baba made his customary phone call to Maman. The first restaurant we arrived at was a small shack serving charbroiled burgers.

At the counter, I ordered two basic cheeseburger meals, but Baba did a double take once he received the receipt. He thought a mistake was made on our order.

The cashier checked and told us the amount was correct. With patrons waiting behind us, Baba reluctantly paid. He was concerned, rolling his neck slowly in a great circle as he calculated our budget. He quickly realized staying in Tokyo was going to be very expensive, calculating the cost of hotel, food, taxi trips to the embassy and incidentals.

In the morning, Baba was in a hurry to call Mageed. My suspicions were confirmed when he told him, "We can't stay in Tokyo, Mageed. You've got to book us on the next flight out of here. I'll run out of money fast," he told him in a panic.

In Tokyo, everything cost four to five times more than any other city we'd been to, and the length of our stay was unknown prior to visiting the embassy.

"We can't continue to eat six-dollar hamburgers," Baba continued. He looked stressed and frustrated.

Thus far Baba had not mentioned money, the financial weight of the traveling, however, and the burden of obtaining a visa was undoubtedly substantial. Visiting many countries, staying in various hotels, and paying for Shirley's entire expenses in Frankfurt amounted to a small fortune. But he purposely kept his concern from me, likely to protect me. He didn't want to burden me with the same worrying thoughts. I already had enough to be concerned with. Still, I felt guilty, but I never questioned him about it.

Upon hanging up with the travel agent, Baba called Maman, informing her about our short stay in Tokyo. When I sensed he was winding down the call, I asked for the phone.

Hearing Maman's soothing voice was comforting. She was busy in the kitchen, preparing dinner. In the background, the familiar hissing sound of her pressure cooker made it hard to hear her. "I love you Maman, we'll talk soon!" I told her.

"I love you too azizam. Be safe, kiss Baba for me," she said.

For the rest of the evening, the intense hissing of the pressure cooker lingered in my head, which in comparison was exactly how I felt.

Mageed booked us on the next available flight departing Tokyo and on to Seoul, Korea on the 13th of February. That was in three days! It was disappointing not to explore the city of Tokyo as we had in other cities. I never expected this journey to take us halfway around the world. I was content to let Baba plan our next stop but my hope for success kept dwindling.

We spent the next two days mostly in our hotel room, Baba on the phone, ensuring that we strike better luck in Korea. He verified the rate of exchange in Seoul and found it reasonable. We should have no financial trouble, considering food, accommodations, and enough to visit the embassy, one more time.

TWENTY-TWO
CHOCOLATE-COVERED STRAWBERRIES

SEOUL, KOREA, FEBRUARY 13, 1987

Seoul presented another extraordinary tale to our wild roller coaster ride. In fact, some of my best memories from the journey were made there, where I lost something precious. Baba had brought along his 35-millimeter camera to record our experiences; the same one we'd taken to Turkey with my uncles.

Upon parting Iran for a second time, Baba documented our visits in Damascus, Beijing, Tokyo and now Seoul. His Canon camera could take up to 36 pictures, but he used it sparingly, snapping only a few photos in each city. He'd saved just enough to document our triumphant moment of entering America.

Once on the ground, we battled the airport rush and collected our luggage. Like in Tokyo, I noticed that many Koreans spoke English, including our taxi driver.

In broken English Baba told him, "Hotel for businessman."

The driver quickly nodded and took us to a hotel in the center of the city. The giant lobby was humming with activity. There was an American Express service desk, a travel agency, a rental car company, a money exchange kiosk, and other business-related services available to hotel guests.

Many of the hotel guests were dressed in business attire, suit jackets, neatly pressed slacks, and colorful silk ties. While waiting to check in, Baba overheard two men behind us speaking in Farsi. Hearing someone speaking our language turned my father into a great white shark that had just detected a drop of blood in the water from a mile away, sending him into a frenzy.

I saw his eyes widen and watched as he turned to look over his shoulder. Within seconds, he identified where the voices were coming from and left me holding our spot in line. He met Vahid and Kamran, who operated an import/export business back in Iran and regularly sent crates and containers around the world.

Baba regretfully told them about our failed visa attempts in Ankara, Frankfurt, and Beijing. Sympathetic, they invited us to join them for dinner that night. Baba politely declined the invitation. Time was running out on his visitor's visa to America, less than three weeks left until it expired. Baba wanted to use every second of our trip in Soul to further our goal.

I wore a brave face, but deep inside, I was discouraged and disillusioned. My hopes of a visa and dreams of going to America had evaporated right in front of me after three unsuccessful attempts. I couldn't help but think our visit to the embassy in Seoul would be a fourth and final failure. The weight of Baba's financial troubles made things worse. We were running out of money, options, and time.

I snapped out of my musings as Baba finished the check-in process. The rest was routine, we got to the room, unpacked, and I entertained myself as Baba made phone calls. The room was full of amenities, including a television set. Excited, I flipped through the many channels; all the programming was in Korean.

Once Baba had checked in with Maman, it was time for dinner. He suggested we grab food and bring it back to our room. We walked to a mini market just outside our hotel. Baba settled on hotdogs out of the refrigerator, packaged in a sealed bag, a loaf of white bread, condiments, and a bottle of soda.

"How are we going to cook the hotdogs back in the room Baba?" I asked.

"Patience my son. You'll have to wait and see for yourself."

Back in our room, Baba went into the bathroom and turned on the hot water in the sink. In a few seconds, the water pouring out of the faucet was scalding, hot enough to steam up the tiny room. He closed the door and told me to wait. Soon, like a scene out of a horror movie, steam began seeping out through the small gap below the door.

Baba rushed into the bathroom, disappearing into the hot mist like a firefighter entering a smoke-filled building. When he entered, a wall of condensation poured into the room. Baba plugged the sink, carefully placing four hot dogs into the steaming hot water.

We waited with bread and condiments in hand, ready for the inventive dinner. After five minutes, the hot dogs were steamed, we sat at the edge of our beds eating. Oddly, eating hotdogs out of the sink was gratifying.

I felt safe in Baba's presence, no fancy food was needed for that. I soaked up every second with him, learning new lessons along the way. If my destiny were to die in war, at least I felt better knowing I shared incredible, one-of-a-kind, once—in-a-lifetime-moments with Baba. That was priceless, and nobody could ever take that away from me.

The following Monday on February 16, as we set off for the American Embassy, I was grappling with mixed feelings. I was exhausted from running around the world only to have my dreams crushed every time. The excitement was gone, I wasn't even praying anymore—it hadn't helped yet! I was secretly hoping we didn't get another interview, desperate to avoid yet another rejection. At times, going back to Iran sounded better; I was ready for this journey to end one way or another.

When we first left Iran for Turkey, I couldn't wait to arrive in America, but now I couldn't wait to get back home. Only a small glimmer of hope remained, but I couldn't let Baba know how I felt.

I contemplated surrendering, but that never entered Baba's mind. I thought; *How long could he hold out? How much longer can he continue?* Financially, he was at the end of the line.

I snapped out of my thoughts as the cab came to a stop in front of the white, multi-story embassy with the American flag marking its entrance. We exited and immediately noticed there was no line, and for a moment I felt a spark of hope. Looking to the left, then to the right, we realized in addition to the lack of applicants, there were no military personnel inside the familiar guard shack.

We walked closer, it looked like the facility was completely abandoned. No signs, no posted operating hours, and not a notice in sight to explain when they'd reopen. We stood there, facing the black wrought iron fence, watching the American flag dancing atop the flagpole, listening to it, flapping in the wind.

The fight had gone out of Baba. Deflated, I felt sad, yet relieved; like a weight had been lifted off my shoulders.

Something was lost between Baba and I after leaving the embassy. Landing in Seoul, a flicker of hope had returned to his eyes, but now the light was gone. I wondered when or if it would return. *How long before he endearingly smiled at me again? How would he overcome this latest obstacle?*

"What are we going to do now Baba?" I asked.

He didn't answer, only shrugged his shoulders, shook his head, and stared out of the cab window at an abandoned, fenced-in sandbox and swing set by the side of the road. They may as well drive me home to Iran in a hearse, I thought, because I had an eerie feeling that I was heading back to my own funeral.

We returned to the hotel in silence, only to run into Vahid and Kamran, the Iranian businessmen we had met the previous day, in the lobby. Immediately, they detected that we were down and out, our long faces an obvious giveaway.

Baba told them of our disappointment, and they genuinely felt our despair and heartache. They insisted we go out with them for a night out on the town. "Nader agha, you should come with us tonight to the nightclub, what do you say?" Vahid offered Baba.

"Thank you, gentlemen, but I can't leave my son alone in the hotel, he just turned thirteen."

"Your son can come, too. There is no age limit here in Seoul," Kamran said with a chuckle.

Baba tapped me on the shoulder. "Pendar? Do you want to go to a club tonight?"

"What do you think?" I asked eagerly. "Can I join the grown-ups Baba?"

Baba had not been to a nightclub following the Revolution, after the prohibition of alcohol, music, and any form of public dancing. Reluctantly, he agreed, and we fixed a time to meet up later in the lobby. Afterall, a bit of excitement was a welcome respite from this morning's complication.

I was excited to tag along. On our way to the nightclub, I spotted a restaurant called Wendy's, a block from our drop off point. The picture on the sign looked like Pippi Longstocking, a fictional character in a series of children's books written by a Swedish author that I had read in Iran. Pippi Longstocking was a nine-year old girl, with bright red hair, tied in pigtails and a freckled face just like the girl on the Wendy's sign.

"Is that a restaurant? What kind of food do they have?" I curiously asked Vahid.

"Wendy's is an American restaurant chain, they serve hamburgers and French fries, kind of like McDonald's," he said.

DING! He said the magic word, my eyes lit up, I started emphatically begging Baba, "Can we eat at Wendy's please, Baba, PLEEEEEASE?"

Everyone agreed, and we ate dinner at Wendy's prior to entering the night club. With full stomachs, we headed towards the entrance, confronted by a chunky bodybuilding sumo wrestler-type, the security guard at the door. The boom of the bass could be heard blasting out of the club.

The man waved us in with the open palm of his hand, nodding his head to welcome us.

Walking into the club, the roaring sound intensified with every step. Inside felt magical: the loud bass thrumming through my body, the dark ambiance, the colorful strobe lights, and lasers were blinding. People of all ethnicities danced to the melodic beats. Beautiful, barely-clad waitresses were serving drinks. The four of us sat at a table, Baba ordered adult drinks for the gents and a Coca Cola for me.

While sipping on my beverage, I stared at the dance floor in wonder, the beautiful women catching my eye. Korean pop music, heavy on bass, shook my seat with every beat; it felt like a sensory overload!

Hypnotized by the dance floor, out of the corner of my eye, I noticed a pair of attractive Korean girls walking towards our table. They looked to be in their early twenties, the taller girl was wearing a skimpy, short skirt, a glittery, low-cut top barely covering her midsection, and fishnet stockings stuffed in high heel pumps. Their suggestive stride and undulating hips were irresistible to my eyes.

I locked eyes with the taller girl, my heart started beating faster, and I consciously reminded myself not to drool while my jaw hung open. I gulped as they sauntered right up to our table, she never broke eye contact with me.

"Dance?" she asked.

I was shocked, embarrassed, and dumbfounded barely managing to shake my head "no."

She persisted, motioning to me with her right hand raised, and fingers waving inward, as if to say, "Come with me!"

I didn't know how to act in this scenario, looking to Baba and his friends for guidance. They were encouraging me to dance, waving me forward. I felt nervous and out of place. I thought about how silly I would look, dancing with a girl who was clearly older. I refused again; but felt a pang of regret after the two women slowly walked away from our table.

Baba lightly smacked me on the back of my neck. "What's wrong with you?" he asked.

"What? What did I do wrong? I don't feel like dancing, I'm tired," I said.

"Pendar Jan, it's rude to turn away a pretty girl who's asking for a dance," Vahid said.

I nervously turned around, spotting the girls sitting at a table across the dance floor. The tall girl threw me a wink, waving me over while giggling with her friend.

"Come on, go and dance with her," Kamran encouraged me. Baba in the background, giving me the unfriendly frown and motioning me with his eyebrows and chin as if to say, *step up, be a man.*

Finally, I mustered the courage to ask her for a dance. I walked towards them with a confident gait, imitating John Travolta, strolling smoothly like in the movie *Saturday Night Fever*, but my knees were shaking, and I was choked up from my wracking nerves.

Feeling shy, I slowly raised my head to meet her overpowering gaze. I locked eyes with her pretty hazel eyes, and by the way she was looking at me, I might as well have been the owner of the club.

I flashed her a devilish smile, to which she grinned broadly, my signal to proceed. I went for it and asked her to dance. She looked at me and shook her head side to side as if to say "no".

I was confused, she was just at our table and wanted to dance with me! I put my head down in disappointment and turned around to walk away. She quickly stood up, grabbed me by the hand, and forcefully pulled me onto the dance floor.

Vahid showed up shortly to dance with her short friend.

Soon I was lost in the middle of the dance floor moving to the hypnotic, roaring beats. I had only seen this in movies, but there I was, dancing the night away in a nightclub surrounded by gorgeous women. It was the perfect escape, considering the unknown future which was a heavy burden to bear at times.

At the end of the evening, we said goodbye to the girls and headed back to our hotel. I crashed in my bed, exhausted from the dancing, ears still ringing from the blaring music.

The following morning, I was jolted out of bed by the sound of rapid knocking on our door. This was abnormal, I sprung out of bed flabbergasted, like a wanted criminal.

"Go answer the door, Pendar," Baba instructed me.

To my astonishment and delight, I opened the door to find the two Korean girls from the night club standing in the hallway.

"Who's at the door?" Baba asked.

"It's the girls we met at the club last night, the same ones I was dancing with," I told him.

"What are you waiting for? Let them in!" he shouted.

The shorter girl carried a bouquet of red roses, the taller girl held a box full of chocolate covered strawberries. An unexpected visit, I thought; *What in the world is going on?* My mind was flooded with confusion.

I motioned them into the room, the shorter girl walked past me over to Baba's bed. She laid down on top of the sheets separated from him, facing the wall. Baba quickly turned his back to us, and nonchalantly closed his eyes. The tall girl gestured to my bed. She was wearing a beige raincoat with perfectly matched high heel shoes.

With her knees slightly bent, I let my eyes run down the full length of her legs which went on forever. She crawled into my bed while I stood there in awe, speechless, looking at her with a wild-eyed gaze. I pinched myself and thought, *this must be a dream.*

She slowly unbuttoned her raincoat, revealing a sexy, lacey, red lingerie exposed underneath. She had a thick mane of dark hair, fair white skin, and a tight little body. My heart was racing, and my eyes were wide as saucers. I struggled to gulp, mouth dry and unable to swallow. She motioned me to get in bed with her by tapping the palm of her hand on the mattress beside her.

My palms got sweaty, I felt like a nervous wreck. I took a hesitant step forward, before I could take another, she yanked my hand pulling me into the bed with her. I laid next to her on my back, besides her warm body, nervously looking up at the ceiling with a blank expression on my face. I tried making polite conversation, but she put a forefinger to my lips and said, "Shhhhhh!" I breathed in her marvelous scent, feeling her body, and sensing the warmth of her heavenly legs while her satin smooth ankles rubbed against mine.

Her soft hands were stroking my face, my chest, and moving down-wards. She peppered me with luscious juicy kisses. The hair on my arms and the back of my neck were standing up, body tingling with a million goosebumps. I never felt like this before. I caressed her supple skin to which she didn't object.

Her skin was buttery smooth and utterly flawless. Feeling a woman lying in my bed was a new, yet heavenly experience. I felt a pleasant tingling sensation shoot through my upper body and directly into my loins. I couldn't believe this was happening, hoping it wasn't a wet dream! The surreal moment kept getting better. I hadn't woken up yet, but I was expecting to at any second.

She directed my hands to help remove her lingerie. Caught up in the moment, I forgot about Baba and her friend laying in the bed, only feet from us. I looked over to check, and they were both facing the wall, apparently sleeping. I had slept in bed next to my uncles, and mostly men all my life. That morning, I discovered the warmth and tenderness of a woman, lying next to me.

All at once a warm feeling came rising up my brain stem, as a pleasant tingling sensation went ricocheting through every molecule of my body. Goose pimples took over and I was seductively deflowered in Seoul by a girl I had barely met.

Indeed, I lost something precious in Seoul that morning, my virginity which took only a few seconds, but it also felt like a rite of passage. It was as if I had officially become a man.

I used the bathroom to wash up, when I walked back into the room, everyone was up, acting like nothing had happened. "Good morning, Baba," I smiled; feeling a mixture of pride and embarrassment, I was now a man, or so I thought.

Baba acted normal, casually looking over unimportant paperwork. The taller girl now wearing her raincoat, grabbed the chocolate covered strawberries and started feeding them to me in bed, treating me like a king, making me feel even more special. She was attentive and friendly.

When the girls left, Baba eagerly got back on the phone. I sat across the room and watched television while he disappointedly made one call after another. When each call ended, he put his head down for a moment, inhaled a deep breath, and started dialing again.

To be nosy, I eavesdropped on his calls, but none of them were regarding plans to go back to Iran. With no good news on the horizon, and Mageed the trusted travel agent all out of options, Baba looked for answers in the most unlikely of places. He dialed the room number for Vahid and Kamran, the businessmen.

"Can I come up to your room?" he asked. "I have an important question to ask you."

"Sure, come on up, see you in a minute." Vahid told him.

What is Baba up to now? I thought.

After a half an hour, Baba returned with a glimmer of hope back in his eyes. A bright shining light of renewed optimism was emanating from his face. Clutched in his hand, was a small piece of paper, information scribbled on both sides like a newfound inspiration. I thought; Oh boy, here we go again.

"Aren't we headed back to Iran, Baba?" I asked him directly.

"No, Pendar. With the help of Vahid and Kamran, I'm considering other plans," he said.

"Looks like we'll be heading to Mexico next. But there is still a catch," he informed me.

"What is it Baba?" I wondered.

"We would need a visa to enter Mexico and will have to go to the Mexican embassy here in Seoul."

"Where is Mexico, Baba?" I asked in confusion.

"It's a country that borders America to the south," he said. "This may be another way for us to enter the United States."

"Do we still need to get a visa to enter America?" I asked.

"The route that we're taking to America, won't require a visa," he said confidently.

"Why are we going to Mexico then?"

"The plan is for Kiya and Shirley to drive down from Texas to a town called Nuevo Laredo in Mexico. It's located just south of the American border. Once we meet up with them, they'll drive you back across the border, straight into America."

Baba then got on the phone with Maman.

"Ziba, I'm running out of cash, and I need you to call Hooshang." He was an acquaintance Baba knew from work. He paused for a second, then came the shocker. "I want you to let him know that I've decided to sell him my Cadillac."

My jaw dropped, the Cadillac was Baba's favorite car, his pride and joy, a prized possession that had taken him years to acquire. He loved his Cadillac; I couldn't believe he was willing to consider the unthinkable, just to continue our never-ending journey.

Our world travels had put him in a precarious position. With dismal funds remaining, he made a difficult decision. "Tell Hooshang I'm in a bind and if he wants to buy it, he's got to come over now with the cash," he instructed her.

Hooshang had long admired Baba's Cadillac and was always offering to buy it from him, although I'm sure he never expected that my father would agree to sell it.

Maman called back shortly and informed my father that Hooshang had dropped what he was doing and was on his way.

He hung up with Maman and said, "The Cadillac is sold, Maman is going to visit Western Union and will wire the money. It should arrive in a couple of days. We can pick it up at the local branch."

I felt remorseful. His love, determination, and devotion to saving my life had never been so obvious. Our desperate quest had driven him to do illegal acts, not concerned with the consequences or fear of getting caught, and now he was selling his favorite car, to help realize our dream at any cost.

The following day, Vahid had scheduled an appointment for Baba and me at the Mexican Embassy. Before our visit, Baba made a detour to the Western Union office, picking up the cash Maman had wired. The taxi dropped us off in front of the Mexican Embassy, or so we thought. We faced a four-story narrow red brick office building, located in the busy, rundown street.

I had been to six American embassies, but this didn't resemble any of them. No armed guards, no tall wrought iron fences, and no Mexican flags waving in the wind like expected. The building was aged, decrepit, and run-down. The awful whiff of mold awaited us on the bottom floor as we entered. The lobby was small and noisy. We thought we were dropped off at the wrong address. At the information desk, we were told the office of the Mexican embassy was located on the third floor.

We rode the rickety elevator, exiting to find a long, dim, and musty corridor leading to the embassy door. I felt saddened by the austere surroundings. We arrived at the door that read, "Embassy of Mexico." There were no chairs, no armed security, metal detectors, nor anyone to greet us.

We entered slowly and walked up to the small, rectangular window. I announced, "Hello, anybody here?"

The window slid open; I spotted a middle-aged woman with a puffy beehive hairstyle in business attire. Looking through the window, I saw a tiny Mexican flag, about four inches tall, sitting on her desk. "How may I help you?" she asked politely.

I told her that we had an appointment with Mr. Garcia, one of the consuls at the embassy. That's who Vahid instructed us to ask for.

She took hold of our documents, then looked around her shoulder conspiratorially, as if she were about to pass on a piece of top-secret information. She opened the waiting room door, inside a handful of chairs and another door, leading to the next office.

Within minutes the next office door opened; we were greeted by Mr. Garcia, the Mexican consul. He was wearing a cashmere business suit, had a thick mustache and smelled of cheap cologne. He had olive skin and dark brown hair, slicked back tight on his head. He was very cordial, even greeted us with a personal handshake, rather than introducing himself behind the bulletproof glass. This was vastly different from my previous experiences at the American Embassy.

"Can you come with me please?" he asked Baba, making a hand gesture to follow him to the next office.

Out of habit, I immediately stood up to follow along, but Baba and

the consul simultaneously insisted that I stay in the waiting room. Baba
was jabbing his index finger on my chair as if to say, *Sit back down!*

"Baba, you don't need me to come with you. And translate?" I asked
with concern.

"Pendar, what Mr. Garcia and I are about to do, doesn't require any
talking. All I have to do is hand him an envelope and we should be on
our way," he told me before he disappeared behind the door.

I tried processing the information, looking for answers, Baba's confidence had certainly caught my attention. I sat quietly and thought of a
movie I'd seen in Iran called *Bring Me the Head of Alfredo Garcia*, a man's
journey through the Mexican underworld with a mission to collect the
bounty on a gigolo's head.

Before long, the two men came walking out of the office. Mr. Garcia
handed Baba back the paperwork and passports which now contained a
large colorful stamp and a visitor's visa to the country of Mexico.
"Congratulations!" said Mr. Garcia with a big smile.

Finally, the words that I had been dying to hear. After so much rejection, a "yes" felt so good! I wanted to celebrate with another Wendy's
burger, but our limited budget meant hot dogs out of the sink for the
next few days while Baba made travel arrangements to Mexico. Our
desperate scenario had driven Baba to act erratically and out of character. It was strange for me to witness a side of him I never knew before
and the extent to which he was willing to go to achieve success. I recognized that when Baba's mind was set, he could work through any problem, no matter how insurmountable it might seem. Another hurdle with
my father was that he refused to accept that failure had gotten the better
of him.

It had cost my father $1500 to obtain our visas to Mexico. The price
of a bribe. But I would pay the ultimate price in our quest for success.

TWENTY-THREE
POINT OF NO RETURN

MEXICO CITY, MEXICO, FEBRUARY 21, 1987

During the flight from Seoul to Mexico City, I watched an American movie called *Jumping Jack Flash*, along with several others. On the flight I must have eaten something that didn't agree with my stomach. Subsequently, I spent the remainder of the trip in the fetal position with intense stomach pains and cramps.

I was woken up by the unmistakable screech of landing gear being lowered from the enormous belly of the jumbo Boeing 747 airliner. Slowly regaining consciousness, I looked at Baba, sitting next to me with concern written all over his face. Although my eyes were open, my chin was still tucked between my collarbone in sleep mode. Landing in Mexico City that evening, I was hunched over from the pain.

My stomach was in knots like something was doing backflips in there. It felt like a mutant creature was getting ready to pop out of my belly just like in the movie '*Alien*'.

I could barely think or see straight while making our way through customs and passport control. I kept drifting in and out of consciousness, but between the moments of struggling to keep my eyes open, I noticed Baba was being questioned by the airport police. My head felt scorching hot, I pressed my knees together, and held my bladder. My stomach was throbbing, and I'd broken out in a drenching sweat.

He kept pointing at me as I laid in the fetal position on chairs nearby. I was gasping for air, my heart hammering in my ears, and struggling not to vomit.

Baba kept repeating, "My son sick, my son sick, please!"

I struggled to keep my eyes open, eyelids feeling heavy before succumbing to a complete blackout. I woke up the next day in a hotel room in Mexico City, hardly remembering how I had gotten there.

I slowly started to rise, but my mouth felt dry as the desert, my tongue felt like sandpaper, and my eyes were glued shut from the mucus accumulated overnight. I struggled to open them and saw a blurry Baba. He was holding a white bath towel, which he'd dampened with cold water, and was wiping the sweat off my forehead. My eyelids were drooping in the way, but Baba at first sight was an immediate sign of relief.

"Good morning sunshine! How did you sleep son? Are you feeling better?" he asked with concern.

"Good morning, Baba. I must have blacked out and feel much better now. I don't know what I ate that made me feel this way," I slurred.

"Well, let me tell you something; it was a blessing in disguise," he said, surprisingly.

"What do you mean?" I wondered.

"At passport control, the airport police were asking too many questions. Luckily, I didn't understand them, and you were too sick to translate. But that worked to our advantage," he continued.

"How's that Baba?" I asked.

"They detained us for some time, asking questions about the missing U.S. visa in your passport. They noticed my passport had a valid American visa, expiring in a short time, but yours did not." he explained.

Who would have thought; becoming deathly ill from food poisoning was perceived as a blessing. But during those times, every advance made was considered a small victory.

I washed up, brushed my teeth after my twelve-hour slumber, and felt hungry.

I ordered reasonably priced room service, a delicious hamburger with fries and a drink which was delivered directly to our room. I was excited to spot a TV set, with multiple channels. While eating, I watched an American movie called *Fright Night*. Some words I heard were unfamiliar or pronounced differently just like my English teacher had taught me about.

It already felt like I was closer to America.

Meanwhile, Baba was on the phone, but he didn't call Maman. That was unusual, because he routinely called her every time with updates of our safe arrival in a new city, but not in Mexico City.

"Aren't you going to call Maman, to tell her we've made it?" I asked.

"No, and I'm not going to." He exclaimed.

"But why not Baba?" I asked.

"She would worry to death and have a heart attack if she knew we were in Mexico. Look, parts of this country aren't considered safe, and I think it's best that we don't tell her. For now, what she doesn't know, won't hurt her."

"So, Maman thinks we're still in Korea?" I asked.

"Yes, I'll call her when the time is right, son. Don't worry about that right now, we still have a long distance to go," he told me.

Finishing my meal, I heard Baba on the phone with Kiya in Texas. Once he hung up, he turned to me with a serious stare. "Pendar, I need to talk to you about something," he said.

I listened very carefully. "Shirley and Kiya are driving to the city of Nuevo Laredo to meet us at the border city. The plan is to put you in the trunk of Shirley's car and drive you across the border, right into America," he said, his tone dead serious.

"What do you mean, 'in the trunk'? Why can't I ride in the car like a normal passenger?" I asked.

"The border they're driving you through is heavily guarded," he said. "The border patrol and immigration police make sure nobody is illegally crossing.

"At this checkpoint, they search all vehicles, passengers, and check everyone's passports. Eventually they'll see that you don't have a visa."

"So, what we're doing is illegal?"

"Yes son, but it's our last resort to get you into America. You'll be safe in the trunk, no more than ten or fifteen minutes," he told me. "You'll have to stay quiet because not only you, but Kiya and Shirley would be in a heap of trouble if you're caught."

The word illegal and images of me, Kiya and Shirley in handcuffs was enough to send a shiver down my spine. The mere thought of us being arrested sent my spirits plunging to a downward spiral.

His words raised the stakes for me, realizing the importance of the next step in our journey.

"After all, they wouldn't think or expect a sweet old lady would do anything like this," Baba continued.

Now I realized why he didn't want Maman to hear about the very insanity and uncertainty that lay ahead. I was speechless but nodded my head in agreement, to confirm that I comprehended the gravity of our situation. Without a proper visa in my passport, no entry was permitted or worse, being arrested and sent back.

Kiya and Shirley were driving to our rescue but taking a big gamble and putting themselves at risk.

They had sworn to fight tooth and nail to the bitter end, regardless of the precarious course we were undertaking.

Baba had discovered that there were no direct flights to Nuevo Laredo from Mexico City. We would have to take the bus or the train to arrive at our next destination.

Racing against time, we checked out of the hotel and made our way to the nearby train station. We purchased reasonably priced tickets on a train, destined for Nuevo Laredo. In broken English, they told us that our tickets were first class accommodations aboard the train which was leaving promptly.

We walked to the designated track, clueless about the unexpected shock that awaited us. After our comfortable train ride in Turkey, we were assuming similar accommodations on this train. Instead, we spotted an old locomotive, like the ones in old Western movies. We noticed passengers boarding towards the back of the train.

We walked past the first train cars, which were a sad carcass of rusted metal and quickly realized this train was utilized to transport livestock and other goods. The putrid smell of barn animals in the air unpleasantly tickled my nose. We walked further back, hoping the upscale passenger car "first class" was at the rear of the train where others were boarding. To our disappointment, we found nothing but twelve rows of wooden benches in the passenger car. *Was this our "first class" accommodation for the next twelve hours?*

With tickets in hand and time running out, seconds echoed away in my ears like a swinging pendulum. Baba was hesitant to exit the train. "Can you handle being on this train for the next twelve hours? That means we'll be stuck on these wooden benches," he asked me.

Deep down, I didn't want to stay on that train and would rather find alternate transportation to Nuevo Laredo. But I knew staying on the train was the fastest way to get to the U.S. border.

"Sure, I can handle it Baba," I told him confidently. Mentally, I prepared myself for the long ride.

The seats were hard with no padding, just long planks of wood screwed together. I could squeeze my fingers right through the gaps.

But then other, more pressing concerns made themselves known. There was no food car on the train, and we had no refreshments. Then there was the public bathroom, a stinky and disgusting stall at the end of the passenger train that hadn't been cleaned in weeks!

The train left the station and slowly started to pick up speed. The train was old, jerky, and prone to making loud squeaking noises with every small imperfection on the track. The constant bumpy motion of the train swaying back and forth was difficult to get used to.

And if that was not bad enough, the stench of live animals and manure from the train cars ahead of us, carried to the back of the train, entering the passenger cart through open windows. There was no escaping the putrid smell or getting a break from it.

After a couple of hours, the train came to a slow rolling stop.

I spotted a few passengers getting off, among them a father and son. While stopped, various vendors boarded the train carrying large trays, held by a strap wrapped around their neck and shoulder. On the trays, strange-looking food items and snacks for sale.

Baba bought me an orange-colored candy on a stick. The candy was seasoned in a sweet and sour rub, but spicy, setting my lips, tongue, and mouth on fire. The stop lasted less than ten minutes and prior to departing, I spotted the father and son coming back on board. They had meals on a paper plate, filled with hot savory food. It smelled delicious!

Baba and I decided to get off at the next stop and explore our food options. Afterall, food adventures with Baba had become customary on our journey!

At the next stop, Baba grabbed my hand, and we exited the train. There was a horde of people bustling about. Local merchants seizing supplies off the train, including some of the livestock. Vendors selling food or souvenirs, and the passengers who bought them. Shuffling through the dense crow, I got separated from Baba. Though it was only for a moment, I froze in terror.

Panicked, he found me in the dense mob, "Pendar, next time you need to hold my hand, do you understand? You can't wander off out here?" Baba scolded me.

I complied without a fuss; I nearly had a heart attack in the minutes that we separated. Unfortunately, not enough time remained on our stop to get food. Back on the bumpy, smelly, and crowded train we went.

In boredom, my mind wandered about the unknown future. I thought of my unconventional method of traveling across the border, in the trunk of Shirley's car. How many more strange cities, unusual food or people, and bizarre encounters could I expect on the remainder of our journey?

The beaming orange glow of the sun started fading behind the hills, shadows rising from the ground as we witnessed the magnificent sunset. With dusk upon us, Baba recognized the urgency to buy food at the next stop, or risk going hungry. Luckily, the next stop wasn't crowded, and we quickly grabbed two plates of steak, rice, beans, and two pieces of round flatbread before jumping back on the train. We ate on the harsh wooden benches, drawing comfort from a hot meal in the most uncomfortable of places.

On the next stop, we exited to stretch, hoping we would be at our destination soon. We ran into a train employee who spoke broken English.

"How much longer to Nuevo Laredo?" I asked him.

"Twelve hours more," he said.

I was sure to confirm, but we were shocked to discover; We were stuck on the train, through the night! Another misunderstanding when Baba purchased the tickets. Instead of arriving in a few hours, we'd be in Nuevo Laredo early the following morning.

The thought of spending more time on the arduous train nearly killed my spirits. We left the station; I went back to gazing out the windows and watching the ever-changing terrain pass by. The notion of sleeping on the wooden benches had me shuddering.

The night air was chilly, and we had no pillows, no blankets, nothing but the benches or the floor to sleep on. I snuggled up against Baba but kept waking up with every bump, unable to find a comfortable position. This was the worst sleeping arrangement we had experienced thus far.

"Baba, everything should be easier after we get off this train, right?" I hoped.

He tsk'ed his tongue and sucked in a big sigh of relief, "We're getting closer, that's what's important," he said optimistically, while looking helplessly at the horizon.

In the morning, my neck, back and shoulders were stiff, consequences of the sleepless night. Dozing on the train was nearly impossible -- The extremely uncomfortable train ride made me feel broken inside.

Baba rotated his head, first pushing his chin close to his chest, then spinning up to look at the sky and so on. I heard the numerous cracking of his neck, making a crunching sound.

Time had passed slowly, each second feeling like an eternity, but we had finally arrived. Before the passengers were permitted to disembark, two armed police officers in uniform boarded our train. They made an announcement to the few passengers in Spanish.

The only word I comprehended was "passport." Soon passengers were digging out their passports and showing them to the officers.

The couple a few benches in front of us had American passports. I recognized the eagle on the cover. They inspected everyone's passport, permitting each person off the train one at a time. Everyone ahead of us checked out, but when the police officer took our passports, he did a double take.

Looking at Baba, then back at me. He was more astonished to see we were from Iran, even our passports looked alien to him -- he opened it from the left side and flipped through its empty pages.

He soon realized that he had it backwards, starting again to flip the pages from right to left. He spotted the American visitor's visa in Baba's passport and was satisfied, but upon inspecting my passport, he started asking questions in Spanish.

I asked him to speak English, but he only knew Spanish. He waved us to follow him outside the train and held on to both of our passports.

Baba asked for our passports back, but the officer refused. Outside the train, they escorted us to an older model truck and motioned for us to get into the back seat.

NUEVO LAREDO, MEXICO, FEBRUARY 23RD, 1987

We were driven from the train, directly to the local police station in town. I saw the eyes of the police officer in his rearview mirror, skipping from Baba to me, back and forth, back and forth. Arriving at a small one-story building, we noticed the armed officers who were guarding the police station.

Multiple police vehicles were lined up against the side of the building. I slid out of the truck, stretched, then took a deep breath before they marched us into the police station like a couple of wanted criminals.

The guard sat us down in an empty office, then put up the palm of his hand as to say, 'stay here.' The office was dimly lit, personal items were scattered on the desk.

I spotted a name plaque holder that read, 'A. HERNANDEZ, Capitan de Policia.' We were sitting in the office of the police captain, which was startling. It was early in the morning, and the captain had not yet arrived.

Baba's sixth sense kicked in, he knew we were going to be interrogated, the fight or flight instinct immediately took over. He leaned over to me, lowered his voice conspiratorially to a whisper and said, "When the captain gets here, he's going to ask questions about our passports and paperwork. I need you tell him exactly what I'm about to say and translate everything word by word, do you understand?" he asked.

I nodded my head in agreement. I started to tense up, flashbacks of the interrogation I had endured in Germany consumed my thoughts.

"Tell him we're tourists and have come to the city for a visit to sightsee and buy souvenirs. Once our visit is over, I plan on visiting

Texas for business, while you go back to Iran. You need to convince him; like a secret agent, a spy just like in the movies," he continued.

"You mean like James Bond?" I asked.

"Yes, Pendar, exactly like James Bond. You're on a secret mission, and you have to get past the police captain." He encouraged me to lighten the mood and raised his eyebrow three times in rapid succession.

Baba sat next to me, breathing rapidly through his nose. He spoke so flatly, I strained to hear the apparent fear, hiding beneath his calm voice. I attempted to keep calm and collected, but feeling the pressure sent my anxiety through the roof. I had never struggled with my nerves this way or felt the strong yearning to control myself. The outcome of this interrogation clearly depended on my performance. I was perplexed, lying in the face of the police captain.

Growing up, Baba taught me to be truthful and to never lie. Now he was telling me to do the exact opposite.

He kept nervously looking over his shoulder, out into the parking lot, where he spotted the truck, and our luggage still sitting in the back. Thus far, I had witnessed him tell harmless lies to the American consul, he then secretly concealed the "Application Received" stamps in my passport, he overlooked the girl in Seoul who stole my virginity, and lastly, he bribed a Mexican official. His instructions to lie spun my mind in a whirlpool of skepticism. The thought of outsmarting the police captain was exhilarating and dreadfully frightening. Suddenly, the slamming sound of the front door against the wall startled everyone in the station.

Everyone was at a standstill, all commotion stopped, and a pin drop silence ensued. At the door, an older, scruffy, heavy set Mexican man, wearing a worn-out gray suit about two sizes too small, stained thick burgundy polyester tie hanging loosely from his neck, and a white dress shirt that couldn't be buttoned up all the way, because of his noticeable double chin.

The two officers at the front desk quickly stood up, clicked their heels intently, and respectfully saluted him. One handed our passports over while they conversed in Spanish.

"Think happy thoughts, "Baba said in my ear, while his hand clamped down on my thigh like a hidden signal that my performance was about to start.

The captain walked in, threw his almost empty pack of cigarettes and matches onto the desk. He sat across from us and for a few moments, he said nothing, just sat there, staring at us with a suspicious look. The repetitive second hand of the clock, hanging on the wall, was the only noticeable sound that echoed in the room. He slowly drew a cigarette from the pack and started twirling it between his fingers in one hand, drumming on the desk with the other. The three of us exchanged glances but still not a word. After all, what was there to say to him, we had to let this play out. He wasn't getting the truth out of me no matter what.

Finally, after a few tense moments, he struck a match to light his cigarette, then took an enormous pull from his Marlboro red death stick and expanded his mighty chest to twice its normal size. Baba was nervously watching me like a hawk, I had no choice but to start my performance soon.

"Hola Senor, how are you doing today?" My name is Captain Hernandez," he said in English with a raspy voice and a heavy scuffled accent. "My officers told me; you speak English? Is that right?" he continued, looking directly at Baba with a smile and a slight hint of annoyance in his voice.

"No, my son," Baba replied.

"Yes sir, I speak English and will translate for my father." I nodded, feeling the pulsating beat of my heart throbbing in my neck while looking directly into his dark, intense eyes.

He started taking huge puffs, filling the small, congested room with smoke. He meticulously flipped through our passports one by one, before asking more questions. I noticed he had a scar above his right eye, which was cutting a crooked path through his bushy eyebrow and onto his stubby cheeks.

Our situation was dire, we couldn't afford to be turned away or to face another hurdle. In the next few moments, I needed to calmly collect my nerves, take a deep breath, and contrive my lies convincingly.

I had only told white lies to my parents or friends in the past, nothing of this magnitude considering my own life hung in the balance. My nerves were frayed, lying to the police captain took being deceitful to a whole other level. With plenty on the line, the silence only heightened the level of tension in his office. I didn't feel safe, even with Baba sitting by my side. I was petrified of what would happen next. Nobody knew we were at the police station. I thought about movies and how criminals often got tortured, imprisoned, or sometimes murdered after the unscrupulous police captain interrogated them.

"What language do you and your father speak then?" He wondered as I snapped back to reality.

"We speak Farsi, but I learned English in Iran, before traveling with my father," I proudly proclaimed.

"Really? Is that it, Farsi, ha?" He said, while his eyes lingered on Baba.

"You may know, we don't often get a lot of 'Farsi' or visitors from Iran around here." Without missing a beat, he distinctively sucked huge puffs of the cigarette with each breath, while it rested in the corner of his lips. The cigarette never left his mouth, with no pause in between puffs as he commenced with the ritualistic interrogation.

"Why are you here? And what business do you have in my town?" His tone was calm yet menacing. He did this amazing trick with the smoke-letting a dense cloud of it escape his mouth, then sucking it up through his nose and mouth in twin thick columns. Clouds of his cigarette smoke were hovering over the desk, ascending to the half lit fluorescent lights overhead.

I manned up, put on a brave face, took a deep breath, and hid what a nervous wreck I was on the inside. I turned to Baba and translated it for him.

Baba systematically started to tell the tale about why we are in Nuevo Laredo. He stopped frequently, giving me an opportunity to translate from Farsi to English and continued to explain his improvised story. As Baba continued, I found myself mesmerized by his ability to tie so many lies together and make each sentence so convincing. There was a cunning and manipulative side to my father that I'd never witnessed.

The captain was shaking his head up and down in confirmation, lips in an upside-down frown, one eyebrow raised, meticulously listening to my every word.

"What about all these unusual stamps inside your passport?" he asked me, leaning back in his chair, and lacing his fingers behind his head.

It was a question I had not prepared or rehearsed for. I translated for Baba and waited for him to feed me the answer. He nodded sagely, as if he was measuring the appropriate fictitious response. Baba was a cool character when he had to be, a smooth operator, even now, under the direst circumstances, he was calm as a cucumber.

"Tell him that we've been on a business trip, traveling through multiple countries. The stamps in your passport are like a souvenir, a keepsake from the countries we visited."

I took a deep breath, then plowed on translating for the captain while I nodded my head with conviction, wondering if what I'd just explained made even the slightest bit of sense.

The conversation continued as I watched the ashes from his cigarette growing bigger and bigger, but he didn't bother to touch it, like he forgot it was ever there. Some of the ashes fell on his shirt, which went unnoticed by him. He kept examining both our passports and inquisitively asked the next question which was direct and to the point.

"Why does your father's passport have an American visa that expires in less than ten days, but you don't have one at all?" he continued in his heavy accent, "but somehow you managed to get a visa to Mexico," he cocked his head to the side, the way a person would after they've just been told something that completely defies logic. "I wonder how that happened?" he continued in a sinister tone ripe with disbelief.

"My father will continue on his business trip to America, and I'll be going back to Iran," I said, trying not to tremble with every lie.

Again, I was met by his silence. The blank, cold glance on his face suggested that he wasn't believing a word. He slowly rocked back in his chair as it squeaked. He began repeating the same questions over and over to see if there were variations to my answers. He was skeptical, not buying into the made-up story as easily as we might have expected.

He finally took another puff on his cigarette and put it out in the ashtray. He started to get aggravated and inconvenienced. He gave me a dismissive look, this one with a hint of barely suppressed animosity before lighting another cigarette.

Once lit, he placed it back in the same spot in the corner of his lips. The loud heavy puffs and the sizzling of the tobacco burning bright orange at the end of his cigarette rang in my ear with every passing second. "Let me see if I understand this correctly," he said sarcastically. "You are tourists? Are you doing some sightseeing or shopping? You've come all the way here to our small city to pick up a few souvenirs, is that right?" he asked, fingers tapping on his desk.

I took his sarcasm in stride, paused for a moment to confirm my made up story and said, "Yes, sir, that's right." lying through my teeth.

He was not convinced and got more agitated with every answer I gave him. There was no empathy in his eyes. "Let me ask you one more time. You are tourists, visiting our town, and doing some shopping?" his eyes darted between Baba and me again.

"Yes, that's correct sir," I repeated insistently.

I thought I heard him chuckle at that.

"Well, let me show you something!" He calmly and slowly stood up out of his chair and took a few steps to the back wall of his office. I sensed an unease in him, saw it in the way his eyes began to flick from side to side. He pointed to a tiny map hanging on the wall in a wooden frame. "Do you see this map?" he asked us, pointing to a small line in the middle of the map. Baba and I nodded up and down in unison.

"Do you see this tiny little line here? Can you guess what that is?" he asked.

I shrugged my shoulders and shook my head side to side. *What was he talking about?*

"The small line on this very tiny map represents the city of Nuevo Laredo. This line is the main street that travels from the north, all the way to the south ending in downtown." He turned his head sideways and looked at me like he'd busted me for my dishonesty. After a few more smoke rings and a bit more heavy, nasal inhaling, the captain said, "You see, Muchacho, Nuevo Laredo is not a tourist town. Some would even say it's an unsafe area, filled with dangerous people. Certainly not where you would take your son on vacation, ha?" Shaking his head at Baba, the way a person does when they're running out of patience. He wasn't even convinced that Baba didn't speak English.

The captain took a deep breath, walked over to the side of the desk, and sat on the edge, arms crossed beneath his chest in a gesture of frustration. His face began to harden, his eyes narrowed in contempt, gazing straight into my eyes, looking for any hint, or clue, waiting for me to flinch. Through exhaled smoke, he flashed me a conspirator's smile, and said,

"I'm having difficulty understanding," after a couple of more huge puffs on his cigarette, he sat back in his chair, tilted back and continued, "For the last time, Senior, what are you two doing in my town?"

A poisonous silence now filled the room; I couldn't wait for the madness to end. He stared into my eyes with an intimidating demeanor. From the look on his face, he wanted to squash me beneath his shoe, like an annoying insect who accidentally crawled into his office. I was frightened and nervous, but never faltered. I started repeating my story, but midway, the captain was waving his hand in small circles, as if to say, "Speed it up!" since I was repeating myself like a broken record player.

Although I was attempting to lie with confidence, a bead of sweat started to slowly drip down my forehead. I wiped it off quickly before the captain spotted it.

He leaned back into his chair and crossed his legs, exposing the enormous revolver holstered around his waist. He abruptly said, "You know what? You want to visit our city? You want to go shopping? And do sightseeing? I approve. I want you to enjoy your stay here. You're free to go! Welcome to Nuevo Laredo," he said with an exaggerated enthusiastic voice and an ominous smirk forming on his face.

Not quite trusting of him, we calmly stood up to exit the office. Looking at Baba, I noticed an uncomfortable look in his eyes. He turned to me, "Pendar, ask him for our passports."

Baba motioned to the captain with his right hand raised, then began waving his fingers inward, as if to say, "Hand them over!"

"Sir, can we have our passports back please?" I asked him.

The captain's grin grew wider. We stood there for a few uncomfortable moments, curiously staring at each other, wondering why he was smirking at us, laughter lurking just beneath the surface. He slowly raised his arm, then swayed his index finger back and forth like a pendulum in the air as if to say 'no' then said, "You can shop, act as tourists, and visit my town. But your passports will stay here, in my desk drawer. After your visit is over, you can come back to my office, and I'll return them to you. Until then, enjoy your time in Nuevo Laredo. Bienvenidos!" He almost laughed in our faces, dismissing us with a flap of the back of his hand.

I translated for Baba and his worst fears were confirmed, our passports were being held hostage by the police captain.

"Pendar, ask him if I can pick up both passports on the day that we're leaving, even if you're not here with me."

I started to translate, but the captain interrupted me.

"And I will need to see *both* of you in my office before releasing your passports!" he said, favoring Baba with an ill-natured wink.

We walked out of the police station and removed our luggage from the back of the truck. "I knew that bastard wasn't going to let us off that easily. I could tell by the shit-eating grin on his face!" Baba said in anger.

I was numb inside, defeated and exhausted from our prolonged train ride in first class accommodations, we headed to the nearest hotel. An uncomfortable silence was upon us after receiving the devastating news from the police captain.

Baba was outraged, squeezing his fist tight with irritation. We checked into the only crummy hotel in the small town and found uncomfortable spring mattresses in our room. After barely sleeping on wooden benches, in a bumpy livestock train, Baba and I found comfort in the most unlikely of places.

Baba quickly called Kiya and Shirley to give them an update. "You don't need to drive to Nuevo Laredo yet, we ran into a roadblock," he continued, "the police captain kept our passports, now we have to act like tourists for a couple of days. But we're sticking to the plan. Once I get our passports back, we'll meet up," Baba told them.

We passed out almost immediately, taking a nap to recover from a sleepless night on the train. We woke up in the late afternoon, refreshed and hungry for sustenance. We stuck to Baba's plan and ventured out into the city to act like tourists. Baba suggested we stay in Nuevo Laredo for a few nights to make our act look convincing.

As usual, we scouted for food and were soon chowing down on local Mexican cuisine. Food was a balm to our anxious souls and made the terrible feelings of despair temporarily fade away, at least for a while.

That night we walked the streets and did some window shopping before going back to the hotel. We crashed early and slept through the night like a couple of logs, recovering from the unrest. The following day, we headed back into the center of town.

Baba reasoned with me, "If we buy local Mexican souvenirs, it'll be more convincing once we're back at the police station."

Baba planned on visiting the downtown areas on our last day. He was convinced that the police captain had us followed, therefore he wanted to act the part of a typical tourist.

He had brought along the 35 mm camera to snap a memorable photo in town, in hopes of appearing more touristy. I couldn't wait to have the film developed, to relive the adventure through the rare photos taken from cities around the world; it was like history in the making.

The small town was filled with bicycle riders, mule-drawn carts swerving in traffic and piles of debris. I snapped a nice pic of Baba standing next to a statue in the middle of town.

We took a taxi back to our hotel, where I placed the camera next to me in the back seat. It wasn't until we got inside the hotel that I realized I no longer had the camera with me. The taxi had long driven away, and I was devastated, wanting to crawl under a rock and die.

I was grieved and hurt over the loss of the camera and so was Baba. "I know I shouldn't have trusted you with the camera. Your head is playing with your ass!" Baba said in anger and frustration.

I felt terrible and couldn't believe what I had just done. The camera had so many priceless memories and they were all gone! How clumsy and careless did I have to be to make such a regretful mistake! I thought Mexico must be cursed. Nothing went right from the moment we arrived. Worse part, I couldn't look to Baba for comfort, he was already furious at me.

I crawled under the covers of my bed, hid from the cruel world, and cried myself to sleep. The next morning, I thought I would get an earful from Baba, but he didn't mention anything more about the camera. He must have heard me whimpering during the night and realized how awful I felt. He acted like it never happened, like the morning in Seoul, and he turned the other cheek.

It was important for him to get back on track, and losing the camera was not going to hinder or slow him down. He was up early and anxious to head for the police station, determined to get our passports back.

We arrived at the police station, carrying local shopping bags to show our legitimacy as typical tourists. "We're here to see the police captain," I told the officer at the door.

We were escorted to meet the captain, who was calmly leaning back in his office chair, legs up on the desk with a cigarette resting firmly in the corner of his lips.

"Welcome back," he said. "And how was your stay in our town?" he asked enthusiastically.

"It was great, we shopped at most of the stores, did some sightseeing, and ate at a few of the restaurants in town," I told him honestly this time.

He leaned back in his squeaky chair and listened carefully, nodding with a smirk. "I'm happy you had a wonderful stay in our city. My officers will now gladly give you a ride to the bus station," he said.

"Thank you, but that won't be necessary," I told him, knowing we just needed to retrieve our passports.

"But I think it's very necessary," he continued.

I translated for Baba, but he was not satisfied. "Pendar, tell him we're fine, and we'll find a way out of town ourselves." Baba replied and I translated.

"Not a chance, in fact I wasn't asking, I must INSIST!" the captain said, nodding his head.

Baba knew what that meant. He turned to the captain, put out his hand, and asked, "passports?"

The captain politely smiled back, "The officer has your passports, and he'll return them to you once you arrive at the bus station," he said firmly.

During our short ride to the bus station, Baba asked the officer for our passports again. The officer waved his finger and shook his head, "no." He parked, then waved us to follow him to a particular bus.

Before we arrived at our designated bus, Baba kept insisting on the return of our passports, but the officer paid him no attention. We arrived at a bus nearly filled with passengers which was ready to depart. I spotted the sign on top of the windshield, on a bus headed to "Monterrey."

The officer waved us to get on the bus, Baba still asking for our passports. He then vigorously dragged us on the bus and waited until we were securely on board, then relayed a message to the bus driver in Spanish before stepping off the bus.

Baba desperately begged for our passports and followed the officer to the bus door. Only before the bus doors shut closed, the officer slipped Baba both passports through a small gap. With the doors closed, the bus driver pointed us to the back of the bus. After we had gotten far enough outside of town, Baba made one last attempt to communicate with the driver, asking him to stop the bus for us. The bus driver ignored him, only to shoo him away and back to his seat.

Thus far, Nuevo Laredo might have been our closest chance to enter America, but all hope was gone. It felt like we got close enough to touch America, yet we were still so far and now getting even further. We were back on the dark highway without guidance, helpless and traveling in the opposite direction. The feeling of the uncertain future and being lost in the middle of a strange country had never felt this strong. *What was going to happen to us? Where were we going next?*

I looked to Baba for guidance and comfort, only to see he felt lost and disoriented just like me. We didn't know what other surprises lay ahead of us in the next city, or how we were going to find our way to America with this new setback. "What will happen next Baba?" I asked worriedly.

"Be patient Pendar, I'll think of something," Baba continued, "We've come too far to get turned away like this. I promise you; I'll find a way!" he said convincingly, even in our most desperate hour.

My father's persistence and unwillingness to give up left an ever-lasting impression on me, but the out-of-control roller coaster that paralleled my life plunged ahead and I felt powerless to stop it. Our downward spiral continued further, now we were heading away from America, and onto another unknown city, in the middle of Mexico.

TWENTY-FOUR
LOST

MONTERREY CITY, MEXICO, FEBRUARY 27, 1987

We were finally permitted to exit the bus at the Monterrey bus station following a three-hour ride. Meanwhile, Baba was pulling out his hair, searching deep to find an alternate route. We landed at a nearby hotel more desperate than ever.

In the room, he disappointingly called Kiya and Shirley, "I just don't know what to do, Kiya," I heard him say in defeat, while scratching his head and nervously tussling his dark mane.

Kiya had no solutions but offered to help in any way possible. It felt like we were stuck between a rock and a hard place. Even though I assumed we'd reached the end of our journey; Baba nervously paced back and forth in the room, unwilling to entertain our inevitable return to Iran, even if it seemed our only option.

"Do you want to call Maman and let her know where we are?" I asked, hoping he would check in with her, then make plans for us to return home.

"Maman thinks we're still in Korea, waiting for our interview. I don't want her to know we're lost in the middle of Mexico right now." he replied.

Baba laid on the bed, scraped the palm of his hands against his forehead and wiped all the way down his face in frustration. He was hyperventilating and breathing erratically before passing out in a deep slumber.

I admired him lying there, and even though he was napping out of exhaustion, I whispered to him, "Baba, I love you no matter what, and I'll always know that you did your best." No response. He just laid there with his head back and his mouth open, a gob of drool glistening in the afternoon sunlight.

He slept peacefully for an hour, before violently waking up, like he'd had a nightmare. He sat up and said, "I just thought of someone."

I was confused and thought he might still be dreaming. "Who are you going to call, Baba?"

"Maman's uncle 'Dayi Omid' who lives in America. Do you remember Dayi Omid?" he asked.

"Kind of, is he the loud uncle, full of stories with all gray hair? I think we saw him last year at Mama Goli's apartment."

"That's right, Dayi Omid is your grandmother's brother. He moved to America after the revolution and when he visited Iran last, he gave me his number in Los Angeles and told me to call him anytime," he said, digging out a black address book from his briefcase. "He's our last hope, I pray he can help us."

Flipping through the pages in search of the phone number, Baba grew increasingly frantic. "I know I wrote it here somewhere. Oh, here it is!" he yelled with excitement.

Immediately, he grabbed the receiver and dialed Dayi Omid's number in Los Angeles. Baba perked up, giddy to make contact on the first try.

I curiously leaned in to eavesdrop on their conversation. Dayi Omid had heard about our trip. "Did you make it to America yet, are you in Texas?" he asked my father upon answering the call.

"No Dayi, we haven't made it yet. That's why I'm calling you."

"I thought you left Tehran weeks ago, where have you been this whole time?" Maman's uncle asked.

Baba gave him the quick rundown of our dire situation, the different cities we had visited and the various rejections.

"Where are you now? Dayi Omid asked.

"We're somewhere in Mexico, a city called 'Monterrey'," Baba regretfully told him.

Dayi Omid was shocked to hear of our misfortune, but mostly he was concerned about our whereabouts in Mexico. "My God, what the hell are you doing in Mexico? It's dangerous over there, you have to be very careful," he yelled into the receiver.

"Dayi, we're safe in a hotel right now, but my visa expires in a few days, you're my only hope to get Pendar into America. Is there anything you can do, or anyone you know that can help?"

"Listen, I own a car wash in Van Nuys and many of my workers are from Mexico. They travel back and forth all the time, bringing liquor, medicine, and have even helped their family and friends cross the border. Give me a couple of hours, I'm going to call someone I know to see if he can help."

We agreed to contact him later that evening for an update. Baba was determined to change the course of my life, to alter my destiny. Hope fluttered in my chest once again.

After two hours, Baba picked up the receiver and again dialed Dayi Omid's number. I stayed away, too nervous to hear the outcome, I was on pins and needles. It seemed like everything Baba had done up to this point was hinging on this phone call.

My heart was in my throat when Baba first began the call, but I started to feel encouraged when I saw a smile slowly spread across his face.

"Baba, what is he saying?" I asked.

He abruptly cut me off, asking for a pen and paper. He furiously began to write, his eyes filling with hope, like he had just received a message from the heavens. "Dayi, I have another favor to ask, can you cover the costs and the fees? I'm running short on funds, but I will make good on my debt as soon as I get back to Iran," he said.

Once the call ended, I demanded to know what had transpired. "What happened? What did he say?"

"He knows a guy named 'Pedro' who has agreed to help us. But we can't stay in Monterrey, we have to get to Tijuana," he exclaimed.

"Where's that?" I wondered.

"It's another Mexican city that borders America, just south of California."

Now we had another dilemma. Tijuana was on the west coast of Mexico, almost 1500 miles from Monterrey and clear across the country. Driving, taking a bus or train was not an option, time was running out on Baba's visa. We rushed to the lobby, where Baba purchased airline tickets from Monterrey to Tijuana.

Flying around the world, staying in multiple hotels, being interrogated by the police, sleeping on wooden benches, eating strange foods, spending my nights on unanswered prayers to God; I was about to blow an emotional gasket, my exhausted heart and mind couldn't bear much more. I'd also witnessed my father sell his beloved Cadillac, bribe a Mexican official and resort to lying to a police captain. My view of life, my family, and the world had forever changed. With multiple windows of opportunity shattered in Baba's face, he was now ready to unleash his relentless wrath with complete impunity and disregard for any local or international laws.

———

The flight from Monterrey to Tijuana took nearly five hours. We arrived in the border city with just three days remaining on Baba's visitor's visa to America. We disembarked from the plane, collected our luggage, and headed down the long, narrow corridor toward the airport exit. The sun shone in through the large floor to ceiling windows, and as we neared the door, Baba suddenly hesitated at the sight of an airport police officer. I watched as the color drained from his face, and his eyes widened.

The police officer was stationed at the exit gate and was inspecting everyone's passports before they were permitted to exit. My heart immediately dropped to my stomach, and I started assuming the worst. Baba pulled on my hand and said, "Pendar, let's separate, you go ahead in line, and I'll be about ten spots right behind you. We may have a better chance of getting through security separately."

I nervously continued ahead, my stomach in knots, my palms sweaty. As I neared the exit, I turned back to look at Baba. He was on edge and appeared frightened, but he flashed me a nervous grin and motioned for me to proceed. "Ta se nashe, bazi nashe! Third time's the charm!"

Our encounter with the police captain in Nuevo Laredo had been an unexpected roadblock. Now, faced with the prospect of a repeat scenario, he was apprehensive, although he never once betrayed just how terrified he felt at that moment.

When I reached the front of the line, I presented the officer with my passport, said a prayer under my breath, and waited for his response. He was dressed in a beige uniform, had a big belly and a full mustache. I held my breath as he started flipping through the pages, not once, but twice, before asking me to step aside and exit the line.

Immediately, I looked back and saw the expression on Baba's face. He was distraught and shaken. He approached the exit, pulled his passport from his briefcase, and handed it to the officer, who quickly homed in on the page he was searching for, verifying that Baba had a valid American visa, and allowed him to exit.

Baba approached me, but the officer stopped him. "My son, my son!" he told the officer. Only then was he allowed to join me.

"Stay calm, Pendar," he whispered, "Just like in Nuevo Laredo, we stick to the same story."

The officer allowed the last passenger in line to pass before returning to the waiting area where Baba and I were now seated. "Do you have a visa to enter the United States?" he asked me in broken English.

With practice and rehearsal under my belt from lying to the police captain in Nuevo Laredo, I spun my tale, telling him what I hoped would be the last in a long line of shameful lies. I'd gotten so absorbed in the glory of our falsified story that I stopped sweating. In fact, I was completely at ease now. The words gushed out of my mouth, without the slightest bit of conscious effort, pouring out from force of habit.

"My father is a businessman and we have traveled throughout many different countries," I said. "We've been to Turkey, Syria, China and so on," I continued.

Baba was confidently shaking his head up and down as if he understood, agreeing with everything I had just told the officer. Despite my nerves, I stayed on script, and in character while the police officer attentively listened to my whole saga. I was unsure how much of it he understood, as he watched my lips with a blank expression. When I was done, he refused to let us exit. Instead, he held onto our passports and instructed us to remain seated. "Wait here," he said before disappearing behind a secured door.

The waiting area was adjacent to the airport exit. We had a clear view of the street just beyond the sliding glass doors where a row of taxis lined the curb.

"What if we are held up again?" I asked.

"Stay positive, Pendar." Even as it was becoming clear our journey was nearing its completion with another failed attempt, Baba remained optimistic. We were sitting in green plastic chairs in the waiting area, leaning against each other, hanging on by a loose thread of hope.

With every passing second, I grew more concerned. *Will I have to speak to his supervisor or worse, another chief of police? Are we going to be interrogated? Tricked? Sent back to Monterrey? Stuck on another bus to nowhere? Will we be jailed?* The waiting was unbearable. Although the officer returned after ten minutes, it felt like hours. He looked at us, held up our passports and said, "Welcome to Tijuana!"

In disbelief, Baba quickly grabbed them from his hand and said, "Thank you!" before hot footing out of there. He hailed the first taxi in sight. "Take us to the Hotel Fiesta Americana, please?" I said.

As the taxi pulled away from the curb, Baba kept looking over his shoulder and didn't exhale until the airport was a blur behind us. Pulling me into his embrace, he said, "We're getting closer to the finish line!"

Being allowed to enter Tijuana felt like a huge victory, and we were elated. Soon, we were in front of a fancy hotel, where I spotted a uniformed door attendant making his way to us. He cordially opened the taxi door, grabbed our suitcases from the trunk and led us to the lobby.

The lobby was elegant, with shiny marble floors and expensive-looking art covering every wall. A live band was performing classical music in the adjacent lounge.

Our stay at the Hotel Fiesta Americana would be far more expensive than the previous hotels. Cost was a big concern for Baba. He needed to ensure our funds lasted for the remainder of the journey.

We had chosen this hotel because Dayi Omid told us it was the pickup point for my adventure across the border. What he failed to mention was how expensive it would be.

Baba instructed me to call Dayi Omid collect. I dialed zero, once connected, "I'd like to make a collect call to the United States," I said, my lips puckered, and cheeks slightly compressed, which really brought out my best American accent.

I provided the phone number and was heartened when Dayi Omid happily accepted the charges. Baba quickly grabbed the receiver from my hand and started to ask questions about our meeting with Pedro later that night.

He provided Dayi Omid with our room number, which is where Pedro was scheduled to be at 10 p.m. that evening. Before hanging up, Dayi Omid warned Baba not to venture out from the hotel, Tijuana was a dangerous city, and to avoid unpopulated areas.

Baba found reasonably priced hamburgers on the room service menu and ordered two hot meals to be brought to our room. We spent the rest of the afternoon watching television. I got dressed and was ready to go at 9:45 p.m.

Baba nervously paced the room. Ten p.m. came and went with no sign of Pedro. Then Eleven p.m. rolled around and still no sign. At the stroke of midnight, it was apparent that he wasn't going to show up.

Baba shook his head in frustration. He felt it was too late to contact Dayi Omid; we waited until the morning to call.

It was now March 2, 1987; Baba's visitor's visa to the states was expiring in two days. I got on the phone with the operator first thing, "I want to make a collect call to the United States," I pronounced.

Baba liked to poke fun at my American accent, but always in a loving way. Perhaps to lighten the mood, he proceeded to mock me while I was on the phone with the operator. Dayi Omid answered on the first ring and once again agreed to accept the charges.

"What happened Dayi? I went crazy last night waiting for Pedro. Have you heard from him?"

Curious, I pressed my ear on the receiver next to Baba's.

"Nader Jan, I don't know what happened, I'll call him right now to find out," Dayi Omid said. "I'm sorry, he's always been reliable. I'm not sure what to say. I'll call you back shortly with an update."

Baba was angry and disappointed but, with no options, he patiently waited by the phone for Dayi Omid to call us back and nearly tripped over himself to answer when it began ringing an hour later. "Aha, aha, aha, that's fine," he said into the receiver, "we'll be here waiting for him again tonight, Dayi. But please make sure he knows the right room number."

One more day of hanging around the hotel, eating from room service and waiting for 10 p.m. to arrive.

Just before 10 p.m., there was a knock at our door. Baba excitedly opened it and was greeted by a hotel employee in uniform. "Pedro?" he asked.

"No, my name is Jose, and I have your bill."

Baba accepted the invoice and disappointedly closed the door. We waited another few hours until 1 a.m. without a sign from Pedro. Baba was going insane; I couldn't stay awake any longer and went to bed in my regular clothes.

The following morning, I woke up to find Baba lying in bed, staring at the ceiling. He was stressed out, tense, and from the black circles under his eyes, I presumed he hadn't slept a wink.

As soon as he spotted me awake, he sprung out of bed and directed me to call the hotel operator.

"Good morning," I said. "I want to make a collect call to the United States." The phone rang but no one answered.

Worried, Baba had me order breakfast to the room. After an hour, we tried him again, still with no luck. "My visa expires tomorrow," he said. "This can't be the end, it just can't."

We assumed that Dayi Omid's plan had failed, and that Pedro was not going to show up. We skipped lunch, neither of us hungry. For the next several hours, we called Dayi Omid repeatedly, but the phone rang endlessly without an answer. In the late afternoon, we finally got a call back. Startled, yet hopeful, we took a moment to regard the phone, looking at it with sinking hearts. At that moment, it felt like my pulse was quickening with each ring until Baba finally answered it.

"Dayi, we waited all night again for Pedro," Baba said, "he never showed up. I have just one day left before my visa expires. Does Pedro even exist?"

I watched Baba chew on his lips and pull at his hair while listening to Dayi Omid. "As a matter of fact, my contact just spoke to Pedro. He says he came to your hotel the last two nights but hasn't been able to get inside."

"What do you mean? We were here the entire time, in our room, waiting for him. We're out of time and options. What do we do now?" He was gripping the receiver so tight his knuckles had turned white.

"I promise you, it's for sure tonight, trust me. Don't even wait in the room. Go outside the hotel and walk one hundred steps to the left at the first streetlight. That's where you should wait for Pedro to pick up Pendar."

"This is our last shot, Dayi. We can't have anything go wrong. Please make sure he's there tonight at ten o'clock. We'll meet him underneath the streetlight."

Baba had one final question before hanging up. "How am I going to recognize Pedro?"

"Insert a pen in the corner of your mouth, that's how Pedro will know it's you."

Baba hung up and sat down on the edge of the bed in a state of disbelief. His level of stress was at an all-time high and starting to show. We were scheduled for the third night to meet Pedro at 10 p.m., but this time down the street from our hotel.

Would Baba's favorite saying become a reality? Ta se nashe, bazi nashe, third time's the charm. We could only hope.

Baba's visa expired at midnight on the 4th of March, but even then, questions lingered about my fate. *Was I going to make it across the border safely?*

We stayed in our hotel room for most of the day, in anticipation of the twin evil sisters, 'Fate & Destiny' to play out another cruel joke on us.

We watched television to pass time, what laid ahead weighed heavily on my mind.

"Pendar, we're all set," he said. "I'll drop you off with Pedro tonight. Dayi Omid says he can be trusted and will take you the rest of the way."

"How will Pedro get me to America?" I asked.

"Most likely in the trunk of his car, then drive you over the border. The same way Kiya and Shirley had planned."

"Don't worry, it should be easy. I'll wait here to confirm you've made it before buying an airline ticket to Los Angeles." he said with a smile.

We were so close once again. "There won't be any more trouble, and nothing is going to stop us, you watch," he confidently assured me. At this point, there was no Plan B. The consequences of failure became so dire and so unthinkable that my father had no choice but to do what-ever was necessary to succeed.

We restlessly waited until 9:30 p.m. before getting dressed to meet Pedro at the designated pick-up location.

Baba wore his favorite loafers; he planned on handing me off to Pedro in a few minutes for the final leg of the journey. We went downstairs early to ensure there was no chance of missing Pedro's arrival. We exited the hotel, and walked one hundred steps to the left as instructed.

There was a bright streetlight, the only one illuminating this part of the block. Baba took out a hotel pen and placed it in the corner of his mouth. I watched him intently chewing on the pen, his head cocked in an attitude of intense concentration. I wondered if he was thinking what I was thinking, which was: Is Pedro ever going to show up?

We stood there in the dead of night, and a few minutes past ten o'clock, we heard a vehicle driving towards us from a distance. It was a dilapidated van, and it came to a slow stop right in front of us. It was in horrid condition, not only did it look old and decrepit, but it was clearly on its last leg based on the clanking sounds coming from the engine. Once at the curb, the driver turned off the ignition and for a moment, there was silence. We noticed the silhouettes of three men inside the vehicle, the one in the front passenger seat was intently looking us up and down. Once he confirmed that Baba had a pen in his mouth, he opened the squeaky door and stepped out of the darkness.

The man now standing before us looked like a homeless person. His jet-black hair was in disarray, his clothes were ripped and dirty, his hands and fingernails were blackened. Baba moved closer to me and whispered," This might be the wrong person."

I sensed Baba hesitating, caught between suspicion, fear, and hope. The man inched closer, and Baba asked, "Pedro?"

To our wide-eyed astonishment, the man nodded his head and confirmed it was him. His appearance was off-putting, and I suddenly felt afraid. He had dark intense eyes, one that wandered elsewhere, thick fleshy features, a face full of acne scars and was even missing a few teeth. He was wearing a wrinkled navy jacket, which hung on his thin frame like a cheap car cover, a ripped gray T-shirt, torn up shoes, and mud-caked Levi's jeans that looked like he had slept in the dirt.

Baba looked at me and in a faint voice said, "Now I know why they didn't let him up to our room."

Fiesta Americana was a five-star hotel, there was no way Pedro would have made it into the lobby, much less past the door attendant. Now it all made sense, he even looked sketchy standing here in the street.

My heart was pulsating out of my chest when he slid open the side door of the van and waved me in. I unconsciously took a step back and looked at Baba. Getting inside that crummy van, especially with intimidating strangers, was a scary proposition. Above all else, I was suddenly filled with dread at having to say goodbye to Baba.

I didn't want to disappoint him, but I was reluctant to get in. I examined the two creepy-looking men already in the vehicle. In my mind, I had anticipated they would look like guardian angels, but I was faced with characters who looked more like hardened criminals.

Although he didn't say it, I sensed that Baba shared my concern as his grip on my hand grew tighter. He had many questions for Pedro, but the language barrier made it impossible to communicate. He wanted me to ask where and how they were taking me to America.

I asked Pedro, but he spoke little English, and my attempts only drew a blank expression. He was clearly in a rush and kept gesturing for me to climb into the van.

"Pendar, ask him how long it's going to take?" Baba instructed.

"How long, how long Pedro?" I tapped on my wrist repeatedly.

He looked straight at Baba and said, "One hour."

That seemed reasonable, but Baba was apprehensive to let go of my hand. Meanwhile, the driver's head was on a swivel; he kept nervously looking behind his shoulder.

Baba noticed the driver's eagerness to leave, and after contemplating our other options which were nonexistent, he hesitantly let go of my hand and instructed me to get inside the van. I gave him a quick hug and climbed into the empty middle row. As I turned around to wave goodbye, Baba climbed in after me, and firmly sat beside me.

Pedro was furious and started arguing with my father in Spanish, clearly ordering him to exit the vehicle. He threw up his index finger, indicating that he was only supposed to pick up one person, but Baba didn't budge, extending his palms towards Pedro and shaking his head emphatically, as if to say, "NO WAY JOSE!"

They argued extensively, but Baba wasn't willing to let me go alone. The faint sound of the ding-ding-ding signal of the open door only added to the tension.

Baba's face was flushed red, his lips pulled back in a snarl. "I'm going with you, whether Pedro likes it or not! He can't stop me! I'm coming," he sneered.

Soon, Pedro came to the realization that my father was not getting out of the van. With a look of disgust, he slammed the sliding side door shut, and frustrated, he climbed back into the passenger seat.

Baba then grabbed my shoulders with both hands, looked me straight into my eyes, "I'm not letting you go anywhere by yourself, son! I'll be here every step of the way until I know you've made it."

"I thought you were going to wait behind. What happened?" I asked.

"I changed my mind! You go, we go." he told me.

We drove away from the lights of the city and started heading up a dirt road without street lights. The busted headlights of the van barely illuminated the road. I couldn't help but notice the irony of our situation.

Many times, when we hit a roadblock in the past, I'd compared our circumstances to traveling on a dark road, with no signs, barely enough light to see ahead, and not the slightest clue where we were going. In fact, that's exactly how I felt, it was a very fitting scenario at that very moment.

Whether it was the vibrations from the engine, or the bumps in the dirt road, the tension Baba and I felt couldn't be more apparent. It was imperative that we succeeded this time. The following day was March 4th and the visa in Baba's passport would expire; we were quickly running out of time and options.

Everyone stayed quiet, but the beat-up old van was making a racket. The upholstery was worn out, ripped and tattered, the carpets were moldy and smelly, and the knobs were missing for the rolled-down windows. I hoped this was not the vehicle that they planned on driving across the border with!

After a few minutes, the dirt road ended and the cracked headlights of the van were pointed straight up a hill, now the only source of light in quite a distance. It was the beginning of a trail, it looked as if we needed to cross a ridge to arrive at our next checkpoint. The driver killed the engine and we sat for a moment, listening to the tink, tink of the engine cooling off, neither Baba nor I said a word.

The driver nervously dangled the keys, still hanging from the ignition switch. We were ordered to exit the van, Baba, me and the other male passenger, apparently another one of Pedro's customers hoping to cross the border. He was of Mexican descent and hardly spoke. He was dressed in dark clothing, a black hoodie and carried a small backpack. Pedro grabbed Baba by the forearm and attempted to force him back inside the van with the driver. But my father refused, shaking him off like an annoying fly.

"NO!" he roared.

Everyone flinched, including me when his loud, booming voice echoed in the valley.

In Farsi he said, "I'm coming with my son!"

Pedro argued further; he clearly disapproved of Baba's plan to accompany us. This may not have been a part of the original arrangement, but Baba wasn't having it any other way. Finally, Pedro agreed but his reluctance and unfriendly demeanor was evident.

The four of us began walking up the hill to reach the top of the ridge. The clanky engine struggled to turn over, but finally the van started. The headlights came on and cut twin funnels of light in the dirt we had kicked up, floating in midair. The van drove away, as we witnessed the blinking red lights slowly fade away in the dimming moonlight.

The hill was covered with bushes and trees on both sides. Soon, we were in complete darkness, only the ashy rays of the moonlight illuminated the hillside. After climbing several hills, we were surrounded by mountains and heavy foliage, no visible lights in the near distance. Slowly I lost track of time, but it seemed like we had been walking for over an hour.

I was starting to feel tired, cold, and was gasping for air with every breath. I was not accustomed to this type of exercise. My legs were getting sore, burning from the uphill trek.

Baba was struggling to balance in his loafers - they were not meant for this type of terrain. Although it was pitch black, Pedro knew exactly where he was headed and didn't slow down.

Baba asked him, "How long, how long?"

Pedro's answer, "One hour."

Baba was confused because we had already been walking for at least an hour or longer. He looked at me and out of breath he said, "The next checkpoint should be soon Pendar, keep walking."

Pedro kneeled to the ground, picking up a fist full of dirt, smelling it and then slowly letting it sift from the bottom of his closed palm, slowly releasing the tension in his fist. Then he ritualistically watched the sand and dirt with his lazy eye, as the wind shifted it in the air ever so gently, the breeze blowing it in different directions.

After a couple of hours of walking up the hills and climbing through tough terrain, Pedro suddenly came to a halt. Breathing heavily and struggling for breath he said, "Stop."

We froze in our tracks.

"Down!" he said next. We fell to the earth immediately and got on our bellies.

He put his index finger to his pursed lips and shushed us, not to make a peep. It was early hours of morning, and my eyelids were feeling rather heavy. At that moment I began to drift, resting on Baba's shoulder, my eyes closed shut for a few brief moments. Abruptly, I was startled by Pedro's voice, "LETS GO!"

I barely had a chance to rest. Baba stood up quickly, dragging my limp body up with him. I was in a daze, up on my feet and walking again. I was drowsy, groggy and should have been in bed or asleep, but we were slowly hiking through uncharted territory. I was parched, my mouth felt like a desert, and to make things worse, we hadn't brought any water. On that chilly, cold March morning, vigorous exercise was the only activity keeping us warm. It appeared that there was nothing but darkness for miles ahead.

I heard Baba hyperventilating while he followed just two steps behind me. After climbing another ridge, Pedro again said, "Stop, down!" waving us to the ground with his arm.

"Is there another car or are there other people that will help us cross the border?" I quietly whispered to Baba as I tried to catch my breath. I was looking for any excuse to end the misery. I was exhausted and confused about what we were doing in the middle of the mountains. I was certain, absolutely convinced, that we had taken a wrong turn somewhere, that another car was certainly waiting for us.

Baba must have seen my confused expression, "No, Pendar, there is no one else, or another car coming to our rescue. We've got to walk the rest of the way, we can't give up now," he told me. He then turned to Pedro and quietly asked, "How long? How long?" While pointing to his wristwatch.

Pedro replied, "One hour." Baba shook his head in confusion.

We had already been walking for hours, but Pedro's answer never changed. We had no choice but to trust Pedro and rely on his guidance and expertise to cross the border safely. Based on his appearance, Baba couldn't trust Pedro for a millisecond, but in the most unlikely of places, he was our only hope, and the one devoted ally that we could rely upon.

The degree of difficulty gradually became more intense with each passing step. I was drained and wished to lay down for a nap. Every time my pace slowed down, Baba was there, pushing me forward, placing his hands on my shoulder and encouraging me to continue walking. Neither of us were prepared for a night like this. This was testing the limits of our physical and mental endurance. That night, my eyelids were so heavy that I felt like I was sleepwalking.

This had to be a dream. It had to be, or a nightmare? I'll wake up in the morning, peek out the window, and we will already be in America. Looking back at Baba, I realized he was dressed in slacks, a button-down shirt, a light jacket, and his favorite loafers, all of which were covered in dirt or mud from laying on the ground multiple times. The look on his face said it all. He felt extremely out of control in our dire situation. He had overseen every minor detail of our travels, but now was forced to rely on a total stranger who would help us navigate through the worst of conditions, in almost complete darkness.

By the time we reached the top of the next craggy hill, each ragged breath felt like inhaling fire. Sweat trickled down my face as I heard Baba wheezing and saw him cramping on his side. As time passed, we took short breaks. I took the opportunity and leaned on Baba, closing my eyes, snoozing for a moment. Still catching my breath, I fell asleep instantaneously when my head hit the dirt floor.

The dreaded words of Pedro had become my alarm clock through the night. "LET'S GO!" he said again.

I struggled to walk while the torturous cramps in my calves and legs were starting to take a toll on my body. The worst part was not knowing how much further to go. Into the early hours of the morning, I kept hoping that the next hill or mountain top we crossed would be our last. *How much longer will the torture continue?* While my thoughts consumed me in the quietness of night, I heard Pedro say, "Stop, down!"

We dropped where we were standing and again, I leaned on Baba for comfort and heat.

I spotted Pedro lying down beside the other traveler who was also struggling to catch his breath. Pedro carefully picked up another fist full of dirt and let it drain from his palm, carefully observing the direction it flew in. Afterwards, he put his ear flush to the ground and listened meticulously. *Was this guy crazy? What was he listening for?* All of the sudden, he waved his arm, instructing us to get underneath the bushes nearby; he put his index finger to his lips, instructing us to stay quiet. We had already been through this exercise a few times through the night and patiently waited. This time we heard the distant roar of an engine, coming directly towards us.

Pedro waved both his arms in a panic, palms facing the ground, up and down, making sure that we stayed down and out of sight. The vehicle came to within fifty yards of where we were laying down behind the bushes and stopped. The engine was turned off, the door opened; we heard footsteps walking closer to our location. Dead leaves and branches from nearby trees were crushed under the boots, and the only sounds we heard in the silent night.

I was a nervous wreck, keeping still, not making a sound. I could hear my own heartbeat, jumping out of my chest. The footsteps stopped, the person drew something out of his holster and turned it on. It made a clicking, then beeping sound, and, in the distance, we heard the indistinctive sound of a man with a raspy voice. It sounded like he was reporting back on his walkie talkie, but I couldn't make out what he was saying. I was flustered and hoping we wouldn't get caught.

Eventually, after a few nerve-wracking moments, the person turned in the opposite direction, and we heard his footsteps getting further away. The door of the vehicle opened, he got inside, closed the door, then started the engine and drove away from our location.

To me, Pedro's façade had faltered, and he revealed a glimpse of the madness hiding behind those crazy looking eyes. We were relieved and understood that there was a method to his madness after all. "Let's go." he whispered, and we were back on the trail.

I hobbled along, spikes of pain battering my scraped-up knees. Baba patted the dust and dirt off his shirt and pants, but to no avail. Without drinking water, we were dehydrated. The dirt floor beneath me began to feel like a part of my body, and my breathing grew heavier and more deliberate. I wanted to sleep, shut my eyes, and lay my head down on the cold earth to drift off.

I was sluggish, but Baba kept up, motivating me to continue forward. At the next stop, I leaned over and put my hands on my kneecaps, exhaling to catch my breath. In the quiet wilderness, I hear a branch snapping, an owl hooting nearby, the wind whistling in my ears, clicking through tree branches, and stirring bushes on the nearby hills. I could hear the faint sound of water tumbling through the valley.

Baba wasn't going to allow me to give up, no matter what. We had come too far and were now past the point of no return.

"You have to continue, we're almost there," he said, panting heavily. "I can smell McDonald's," he said jokingly, while struggling for his next breath. His face illuminated by the silver shining of the moonlight. His words of wisdom about not giving up rang loudly in my ears more than ever before, but the end didn't arrive soon enough, as we continued hiking in the rigid terrain and frigid weather conditions.

I kept hoping that the suffering would soon be over. During the initial part of our walk, Pedro was rather relaxed, walking briskly in the darkness. He knew the exact direction without a map or compass. After a few hours of walking, we approached an area where he started to walk at a slower pace. He had become more alert and proceeded with caution in every step. He was gazing in every direction and sensed that we may not be alone.

I noticed his body language had changed as well -- he was now listening carefully for any sound and intently looking at the horizon ahead. I had completely lost track of time. Pedro intently told us, "Down! Down! Down!" with a clear panic present in his voice. He sensed that something was wrong.

After a few tense moments of hiding beneath the thick foliage, a vehicle passed by and continued to drive away. Pedro waited until it was completely out of view before instructing us, "Let's go!"

We obliged, knowing that he was more aware of our surroundings than we had originally thought. We plowed forward while I prayed for the pain in my legs to subside. Another agonizing hour went by, Pedro sensed that we may be in grave danger. "Stop, down! stop, down!" he instructed.

Quickly, he stuffed us into the thick foliage and gave us the quiet signal. My heart was throbbing, and I was out of breath. He then disappeared beneath the nearby bushes with the other traveler.

I was so weakened that I cupped my hands into a makeshift pillow and laid down to rest. The peaceful night offered some escape from my reality and to the lull of the crickets I fell into a deep sleep, dreaming about Shirley and my new life. Shirley and I were slowly walking in a park, hand-in-hand watching the beautiful afternoon sunset.

"BLEEP BLEEP!" The crackling of a walkie-talkie startled me awake.

I felt Baba's hand over mouth, his eyes telegraphed fear. My heart started racing, my breath erratic. I laid there nervously, listening to the muffled voice of the man talking into the radio. He was so close I could feel his footsteps on the other side of the bush. Suddenly, the beam of his flashlight illuminated the area just beside us.

I could hear the man clearly. "I don't see anything or any movement in this area," he radioed. "I'll keep searching and will report back."

The night was silent; we couldn't afford to make the minutest noise. Small insects, mice or perhaps a snake rattled the leaves close to where we lay. I was creeped out, but I didn't dare make a move. I held my breath as the officer walked within feet of our hiding place, then continued to inspect the surrounding area with his flashlight. My nerves were frayed, wishing for this moment to end.

"Nope, nothing sir," BLEEP, BLEEP.... I could hardly hear his voice over the booming of my heart, beating erratically out of my chest. We waited as the footsteps grew fainter, relieved when we heard his car start and the sound of his tires on the sandy ground. Still, no one moved.

Finally, Pedro and the other guy crawled out from the bushes and let out a sigh of relief. Pedro was quick to wave us forward.

Hiding that close to a border patrol officer had scared the sleep right out of me and the exact wake-up call necessary to push forward. An exhilarating rush of adrenaline took over; my heart was beating faster than a rabbit's, my blood pressure was higher than a stroke victim's and my mind was in overdrive. I had to keep it under control.

Baba and I soon realized that American authorities were thoroughly searching this area, but Pedro was vigilant, the perfect lookout, even with his lazy eye. Somehow, he always knew where the officers were and stayed one step ahead of them. He was much smarter than he looked.

I kept forcing the air into my lungs in big heaps, but it didn't help clear the clamping I felt in my chest. Struggling up the next hill, I thought about the movies I had watched in Iran. Some were about cops and robbers; I always imagined myself as one of the cops or one of the good guys. Now, we were hiding and avoiding the authorities like wanted criminals. The song *The Ecstasy of Gold* by Ennio Morricone boomed in my head from the finale of *The Good, The Bad, and The Ugly.*

At the end of the movie, the characters are searching for bags of gold buried inside a marked grave hidden in a giant cemetery. The buried gold was a perfect metaphor; my gold was entry to America and finishing this journey once and for all.

Baba and I had gained a new level of respect for Pedro and now considered him very capable. Though we hadn't trusted him at first glance, we were now following his every footstep without hesitation.

We had no idea how far we'd walked, or how much further we had to go. *Would we make it? Or would the border patrol track us down?* More determined than ever and hoping to put an end to the pain, I kept fighting and climbing ahead. Still, the point of exhaustion loomed closer, my mouth was as dry as the Sahara Desert, and I felt thoroughly battered by the unwelcoming hills and mountains we traversed.

As I struggled to climb yet another hill, Baba quickened his pace to catch up with me, then breathlessly whispered one of our favorite movie lines in my ear, "Don't worry son, I've got you." It was what Superman said to Lois Lane when he rescued her for the first time.

I replied as Lois had, "You, you've got me. Who's got you?"

Drawing a deep breath, Baba uttered a single word, maybe the only logical explanation as to how we'd made it this far. "GOD!" he exclaimed, huffing, and puffing with each step.

We eventually climbed another ridge. As we reached its peak, the shimmering lights of a giant city rose up in the distance. We stood on top of that ridge, resting for just a moment, gazing at the incredible scene, mesmerized by its dazzling beauty. Somewhere over the mountains ahead of us slept the city where we were heading. Somewhere over there, others were waiting for us. With that thought, my lips parted in a smile.

Under the glow of the moonlight, I sensed America humming beneath my feet. *How much longer did we have to walk? How much longer before we heard the wailing of a siren, or spotted the flashing lights of a border patrol? How much longer before we are handcuffed, and placed in the back of a police cruiser?* Well, the odds were certainly stacked against us.

I was suddenly overwhelmed with emotion. I silently asked God for forgiveness. *God, what have I done to deserve this?* It dawned on me that I was escaping the war, cheating death, and yet, perhaps it was my destiny to die all along. I didn't have any other way of comprehending what I was going through, it was surreal, like I was a character in a movie. My cousin Shahin had flown to America on an airplane, having obtained an American visa stamped in his passport. But this seemingly simple task had proved far more difficult than anyone in my family could have ever predicted.

Why did my case have to be so impossible? Did I do something wrong to justify my life's new direction? My legs, knees, feet, and back were weak, cramping like I'd never felt before. I didn't know if I had the physical capacity to continue. All I heard was the thumping of blood pounding in my head. If Baba was right and there was a God, then he'd let this be over.

I looked over at my father. He was exhausted, filthy dirty, still wearing his dress loafers, now blanketed in dust, and I was reminded of his perseverance. I knew I had no choice but to press forward, if not for myself, then for him. My renewed determination was instantly rewarded by the sight of a creek, running water, just ahead of us. I ran toward it and kneeled along its bank to collect a handful of water. I cupped my hands, filled them with water and raised them to my lips just as I was about to drink, I heard Pedro yell, "No! No clean! No clean!"

The water was not potable. Once again, it felt like the universe was teasing me; this creek might as well have been a mirage. There was no way to avoid getting our shoes wet, we had to cross through the shallow creek to continue. We emerged with muddy shoes and wet socks. The next uphill barrier came in the form of a sandy embankment that stretched for miles in every direction. Pedro effortlessly led the way up the hill, then crouched down on his stomach to crawl the last three or four feet, motioning us to do the same. Loose sand and gravel rushed past us like a river, when we finally reached the top, Pedro raised his head slowly to peek over it.

I braved a glance and saw a dirt road to the left, which led to a soaring guard tower, equipped with an enormous spotlight. It was manned, and through the night's grayish haze, I could see the silhouette of a uniformed officer holding a machine gun.

Pedro instructed the other traveler in Spanish, then turned to Baba and me, and in his best broken English, he whispered, "Let's go fast. Police shoot, yelling freeze, you no stop. Only run! Very fast, okay?"

We understood that no matter what, we were to run as fast as possible across the road and down the embankment. Even if the guard spotted us, shouted at us to stop, or even shot at us, we were to keep going, to run fast!

In the pale moonlight, I could see the terror on Baba's face. He looked as if he'd seen a ghost and was starting to hyperventilate when Pedro gave the command, "LET'S GO! LET'S GO!"

In unison, we sprang to our feet and raced across the road. In the darkness, and in a hurry to cross, I hadn't noticed the steep drop on the other side. The ground dropped from under my feet as I fell. I felt myself tumbling, doing somersaults in the sand, and then...BOOM! I was lying flat on my back, in a state of semi consciousness, staring up at the bright stars that filled the cloudless sky.

Pedro, Baba and the other traveler slid down the embankment on their butts and came to a smooth landing at the bottom.

Pedro shushed us, making sure we didn't make a sound. He also put both palms out and motioned for us to stay down. I laid there, catching my breath, wondering when this madness would finally end. We had been walking for what felt like days. This part of the journey was evoking emotions I didn't even know existed. I was tired, worn down, I wanted it all to stop.

As soon as Pedro rose to his feet, Baba rushed to my aid, and thankfully I was fine. I stood up on my own, no broken bones, just a broken ego. As I brushed the sand and dirt from my clothes, I noticed that Pedro was sweating. Despite our initial doubts about this man, there was no denying he was smart as a whip, cunning as a fox, slippery as a serpent, and above all else, loyal as a dog. If he had been honest about the conditions and the nine-hour journey that lay ahead, we may never have agreed to accompany him.

After another hour of walking, the pain vibrating down my legs was excruciating and ceaseless. My only relief was the short breaks we took, mostly to hide from the authorities. We finally arrived at a long chain link fence.

"Stop, down!" Pedro directed in a low voice.

A tangle of brush and foliage was growing along the fence. Pedro shoved us further into the brush, until we were completely out of view. I assumed this was another maneuver to avoid being detected. I was exhausted, leaning my head against the fence and quickly fell asleep.

TWENTY-FIVE
REACHING THE SUMMIT

MARCH 4, 1987, U.S. BORDER

t was just before 8 a.m. and the intense sound of a ringing school bell startled me awake. My vision was hazy and completely blocked by the thick foliage that enveloped me. I heard distant laughter, the distinct sounds of children playing. I rubbed my eyes open and looked around, blinded by the blazing light of early morning.

My heart felt like a jackhammer in my chest, blood thudding in my ears. This didn't seem right, had this all been a dream? I pressed my palms against the soft grass and slowly crawled out of the bushes on all fours. Turning my face up to the sky, squinting, drawing a deep breath, the smell of freshly-cut grass permeated in the air.

The sun shone brightly in a cloudless blue sky; I watched as a tiny jet in the upper atmosphere left twin white trails while passing overhead. I was staring out at a large, grassy field, several brick buildings, likely a school, standing at its edge. I could see children pouring into the yard. Confused, I watched them as they were divided into multiple single file lines.

Baba was right behind me. "I think we've made it," he said.

I couldn't believe it. I wanted to enjoy the rest of this euphoric dream, at least that's what it felt like, expecting to be startled awake at any moment by Pedro's raspy voice.

Turning to Pedro, Baba asked, "America?"

Pedro nodded in the affirmative, "YES!"

Baba and I embraced for an extended period, tears of happiness pooling in my eyes. This was an unbelievable moment; one we'd been longing for. I hopped up and down, laughed and wept. "We did it, Baba, we really did it!"

I imagined Baba as the panther who'd watched over me during this journey; he had been my guardian angel who finally reached the top of the mountain. The emotions I felt were stronger than any I had ever experienced in my life. I pressed my face into Baba's chest and hugged him firmly.

We looked terrible but floating on Cloud Nine, feeling an exaggerated sense of accomplishment.

Pedro interrupted our joyous moment, insisting we move away from the school. We followed him to the other side of the fence leading to an unpaved road. Suddenly, an old, black sedan appeared and drove directly towards us creating twin clouds of dust, sunlight reflecting off its hubcaps.

Baba and I panicked, thinking the authorities had finally caught up with us, but Pedro calmly walked up to the vehicle and waved to the driver.

Approaching the car, Baba pulled me close to him and glared into my eyes with an ominous stare and in a tone implying the utmost seriousness he said, "Pendar, I have to leave you right now and go back to Tijuana."

"I left my passport, briefcase and our clothes at the hotel last night. I need to make it back in time because my visa expires tonight. I've got to gather our things, purchase an airplane ticket, and make it to the airport in Los Angeles before midnight. I have to go," he continued.

The glorious moment of arriving in America was abruptly cut short by my father's pronouncement. A terrible sinking feeling overtook me when I realized he was leaving me with Pedro, the driver, and the man who had made it across the border with us. I broke down and started sobbing out of control. In a few minutes, tears of delight quickly turned to tears of heartbreak and sadness.

I was not ready for Baba to leave my side. He had been much more than just my father; he was my savior, companion, best friend, and protector. Thinking about proceeding without him made me ill to my stomach. I didn't feel safe. He was the one steady pillar of hope in my life for the past few months and I couldn't tear away from him. Nothing could remedy the discomfort or the agony I was feeling, I was crushed. I wondered where they were taking me.

Baba reassured me, "We'll be seeing each other later tonight in Los Angeles, I promise. You'll have to be brave and go the rest of the way without me."

"I don't want to go without you, Baba," I told him, gasping, holding back the hysteria. I would have walked many more miles or climbed mountains for days, only to keep Baba at my side. But he had no choice and was racing against the clock.

Tearful and reluctant, I climbed into the back seat of the car and stared at Baba through the back window as we pulled away. A cloud of dust, whipped up by the car, enveloped him. We locked eyes, and I kept him in my sight before fading away. The complex emotions I felt were difficult to comprehend. I'd made it to America, which had been my only goal, yet I felt lost.

Our driver was young, had dirty blond hair and light blue eyes. He looked American but spoke fluent Spanish with Pedro and the other traveler. "It's okay," he told me in perfect English. "You're going to be safe, don't worry."

The car ride was short; we drove through a residential neighborhood and into the driveway of one of the homes. I was still tearful at having been separated from my father.

An older, heavy-set Mexican woman stood at the front door, and when she spotted me, she quickly rushed to my aid. Clearly, she saw my distress and yanked me from the rear seat and into her embrace. In a thick Spanish accent, she said, "Everything is going to be alright, honey. You're in good hands now!"

She clutched me while shouting instructions to the other men in Spanish, then welcomed me into her home as the car with Pedro and the other two men backed out of the driveway. There were no goodbyes, and I never saw Pedro again.

The living room was spacious, with plush brown carpeting and a big leather sofa. A television set caught my eye. All my life, I yearned to watch American television. I perked up realizing I was in a family home and started to feel secure. The smell of fried food filled the air, an appetizing, irresistible aroma.

I was drained, famished, and thirsty enough to drink a river. She graciously brought me a large plastic cup filled to the rim with ice and water. I drank up in big gulps while it spilled over my dirt-stained shirt.

"Take it slow," she said. "You don't want to get a stomachache." It sounded like she cared about my wellbeing. "You must be starving, do you want chorizo and eggs?" she asked.

"I like eggs, but I'm not sure what chorizo is," I told her.

"You're going to love it," she smiled. "It's Mexican sausage. You never had it before?"

"No, I don't think I've ever eaten that."

"Why don't you wash your hands and face before eating?" She pointed out the bathroom at the end of the hallway.

I entered the bathroom and was taken back by my reflection in the mirror. My face was unrecognizable from the dirt, streaked where my tears had rolled down and dried, leaving a trail. My hair was a mess, tousled, tangled, and flecked with sand. I vigorously washed my hands and face, attempting to shake the dirt off my clothes. I exited the bathroom to the sound of a sizzling pan.

The woman invited me to sit down at the round table in her kitchen. She served me a plate of hot scrambled eggs, with the Mexican sausage 'chorizo', and the familiar round flatbread I had eaten all throughout Mexico.

"I've had the round flat bread before, what is it called?" I asked.

"Tortilla is the name of this bread. Chorizo, huevos, and tortilla," she said, pointing to the sausage, eggs, and bread.

My first meal in America! It was delicious, unusually spicy, and prepared by the stranger I had just met. I devoured everything on my plate and thought, "There is nothing like a full belly to make my troubles disappear." Still, I couldn't stop thinking about Baba, worried about where he had ended up, or how he would make it back to Tijuana in time.

After I ate, she instructed me to get back into the bathroom, to take a shower and wash off the sweat and grime. She asked me to remove my dirty clothes.

"I'll have a set of clothes waiting for you when you get out of the shower," she said.

I turned on the shower and stepped in, the hot steamy water felt amazing against my cold skin. I hadn't yet warmed up from our prolonged, unexpected overnight journey. I washed my hair and body with an apple-scented shampoo, dried myself with fresh linens that smelled like a flower field, and emerged from the bathroom feeling squeaky clean. I noticed a pair of pajamas were lying on a bed in the spare bedroom. While dressing, I was startled when the woman knocked on the door, before she entered.

"Get some rest, you need sleep," she said before tucking me into the comfortable bed.

Somehow, she knew about the overnight torture and how little I had slept. Although she was very cordial and motherly, I still felt shy and didn't know how to act in this awkward scenario.

Just before closing my eyes, I thanked God for finally answering my prayers, then I prayed for Baba's safe and on time flight to Los Angeles. I prayed we'd meet later that night just like he had promised.

I passed out rapidly and slept for a few hours. The revitalizing sleep felt great for my body, but when I woke up, my mind drifted back to Baba. *Where on earth could he be? What could he be doing right now?* Waking up in a stranger's home and not yet knowing the outcome of our reunion was unsettling. I emerged from the bedroom to find my host at the kitchen counter, cutting up an assortment of vegetables.

"Good afternoon, Mijo," she said enthusiastically.

"Good afternoon," I replied, although I presumed it was still morning.

"You have a couple of hours before you need to leave, would you like to watch television?"

I nodded enthusiastically, wishing she had asked sooner. I sank into the cozy leather couch and spread my arms on either side to watch a movie called *Teen Wolf*. This was my first movie in America. It was about a teenager, who had difficulty fitting in at school and in the community, because he happened to be a werewolf. I could never have imagined the irony of his story and how I would be confronted with similar challenges when starting school.

I was fascinated by the commercials that interrupted the movie every so often, I had never seen them before and was captivated by it. American products I'd always envied like Coca Cola and Corn Flakes, plus an introduction to Ronald McDonald, the spokesperson for McDonald's. I was in heaven, losing myself not only in the movie, but in the advertisements, which were just as entertaining. There was a certain respite from the day's madness when it came to watching American television.

Shortly after the movie ended, my host came into the living room with a change of clothes. "You're going to be driven from here to Los Angeles, and you need to start getting ready, Mijo," she said. "You need to change out of your pajamas and into these clothes."

I was unsure about the status of my previously worn foul-smelling, dirty clothes and happily returned to the bedroom to switch into the garments she had provided, a white tank top and a black football jersey with silver lettering that read, "Los Angeles Raiders." The jersey had tiny translucent holes, making the white tank top worn underneath visible. The pants were too short (or perhaps they were shorts that were too long?). They only covered my legs just below the knees. The long white socks stretched above my knees, I wasn't sure about this look, but I was relieved to have clean garments. Lastly, I slid on the white sneakers the woman had provided. I looked at myself in the closet mirror and was perplexed. The football jersey hung loosely over my bony, slumping shoulders, the shorts/pants were too long/short, and the socks pulled up over my knees looked ridiculous. I wondered about this style of clothing. Maybe it was the new trend, the latest fashion in America?

I came out of the bedroom to find the woman patiently waiting for me in the hall. She gazed at me from head to toe and inspected my appearance. She seemed satisfied and nodded her head up and down with approval, a small grin spreading across her face. "You look good, now sit on the couch and wait," she told me.

Just minutes after I assumed my position on the couch, the front door burst open and the blond-haired, blue-eyed driver appeared in the living room. I immediately tensed up. *Was he here to harm me? Or to take me back to Mexico?* But then he spoke.

"Your outfit looks good, you remember me?" he asked. He walked towards the couch, but frightened of him, I gulped and pressed my back into the cushions. Before he got any closer, my hostess entered the room and addressed him. "Hi Mijo, how are you?" What took you so long?" She gave him a bear hug and kissed him on the cheek.

"I had to fill up the gas tank." He told her, annoyed and embarrassed, the way I looked at my mother when she embarrassed me in front of my friends. She turned to me and said, "I see you've met my son. Don't be afraid, he's a good boy."

They both chuckled while she pinched his cheek.

"Nice to meet you," he said, then disappeared into the kitchen to pour himself a beverage. He then yelled out to me, "You ready to go?"

I nodded yes. I was eager to start the drive and couldn't wait to reunite with Baba.

SAN ISIDRO, CALIFORNIA, 5:00 P.M.

It was dusk when we left the house that evening. My hostess came outside to hug me one last time "Good luck, Mijo," she said, waving us off as her son pulled out of the driveway.

Once we exited the neighborhood, my driver asked if I was hungry. I hadn't eaten since breakfast and agreed.

"Good, because we have a three-hour drive ahead of us. We can get something to eat in the car on our way up. How about we go to a drive-through?"

"I've never been to that restaurant, what kind of food do they have, is it like McDonald's?" I asked.

"Wait. I'll show you," he said.

Within minutes, we pulled into a parking lot. Out front a sign on high stilts, a large square red box with white letters that read "Jack in the Box".

Confused, I asked, "Weren't we going to a place called Drive-Through?"

"We are, wait and see."

He drove around the side of the building and showed me a sign that read, Drive-Through.

I had never heard of such a thing. We entered a one lane road, then pulled up to a speaker box.

"What do you want to eat little man?" he asked me.

"Aren't we going to go inside?"

"No, that's why it's called a drive through, get it? Driiiiiivvveee thrrrrooouughhh?" he said, shaking his arm through the air in a wavy motion.

I soon got the concept. "A double cheeseburger, fries, and a Coke," I cheerfully said.

I was alarmed by a voice booming through the speaker box," Welcome to Jack in the Box, can I take your order?"

After ordering, we pulled up to a window, where my driver paid and was given several white paper bags containing our food.

We ate in the car as we started our drive towards Los Angeles. The cheeseburger was heavenly; drive through was now my new favorite thing about America. Baba would never let us eat in his Cadillac; he didn't want crumbs on the upholstery. Again, my thoughts returned to Baba, had he made it safely to Tijuana? I could only hope.

Soon we entered a highway. Unbeknownst to me, there was a secondary border patrol checkpoint on this highway. Hence the reason they had dressed me, to look like a cholo (Mexican street gang member), an attempt to fit in. I had to endure another uncomfortable, hair-raising, suspenseful moment with a border patrol officer as our vehicle came to a stop at the designated checkpoint. He peeked into our vehicle, and luckily he waved us to proceed forward and allowed us to pass without any complications.

Relieved, I stared out the window, admiring the passing scenery, palm trees, wide roads, and lots of American brand cars. It was now too dark to see the passing landscape. We were moving at a rapid clip and with the motion of the car, my eyelids grew heavy. With a belly full of fast food, I slept for the remainder of the ride to Los Angeles.

TWENTY-SIX
REUNITED

woke up in the car, descending down a big hill and was astonished by the million dazzling city lights in the valley just ahead of us. The view was breathtaking.

"Where are we?" I asked.

"Still north on the 405-Freeway, entering the valley," my driver told me.

"What city is that ahead of us?" I asked.

"It's called the San Fernando Valley. We should be arriving in fifteen minutes."

We exited the highway and pulled into a gas station off Reseda Boulevard. We arrived before eight o'clock. I saw Dayi Omid and his son Cyrus, waiting to greet me. I remembered his distinctive white hair from his last visit to Iran.

"You've finally made it," Dayi Omid said with elation, throwing his arms around me.

"I didn't recognize you," Cyrus told me. "You look different in those clothes."

I thanked the driver and waved him farewell. I climbed into the back seat of Dayi Omid's fancy Mercedes-Benz. It was a luxurious car with soft, cushy leather seats and many amenities. There were so many buttons, gadgets, and gauges on the dashboard that it felt like we were in a spaceship.

"Do you know where Baba is? Do you know if he's safe?" I asked my great uncle with concern.

"He made it back to Tijuana and will be on a flight to Los Angeles later tonight," Dayi Omid told me. "In fact, he told me it was the last flight of the night."

We arrived at Dayi Omid's upscale home in Reseda. We were greeted by his wife Mona, and their three older children. Cyrus was the youngest of the four.

While stepping inside, I was greeted by the scent of Persian cuisine. It smelled like home and reminded me of Maman's cooking. I was in good hands with Dayi Omid and his family and the anxiety I'd been feeling all day started to slowly dissipate.

Their beautiful home had marble floors throughout, an enormous kitchen and sliding glass doors that opened onto a gorgeous, vast resort-style backyard that boasted magnificent views. There was a swimming pool with an attached jacuzzi and a fire pit on the patio, it felt like paradise.

I wish Baba were here to see this. Still worried, I asked about his impending arrival.

"We're picking him up at the airport in a couple of hours," Dayi Omid's wife told me.

"I want to come to the airport with you."

"No Pendar Jan, you get some rest, we'll pick him up. Don't worry!" she reassured me.

I was worried and distrusting even towards my family. I still wanted to hold him in my arms and wished he were already here. Mona announced that dinner was ready, and asked me to join the family at the dining room table. The mouthwatering smell of the food was driving me insane; it had been weeks since I'd eaten Persian food.

Once we were all gathered, Mona began piling delicious rice, stew, and other delicacies onto our plates. I was in heaven, eating real food for a change instead of bathroom-sink steamed hot dogs or unidentifiable meats.

After dinner, I retired to the guest room, laid my head on the cozy pillow, and fell right to sleep. It was just after 2 a.m. when I was awakened by the sound of the door opening. I opened my eyes to Baba's silhouette in the doorway. I was elated. I sprang out of bed and into his embrace, tears of joy and happiness pouring from my eyes. My hero, my travel companion, my mentor, and my partner in crime was here in America with me!

For the first time in a long time, I felt like a big burden had finally been lifted from my shoulders. My ordeal was over once and for all, and now a new life could begin.

It was late and the rest of the family was already in bed. Baba quietly settled into the bed next to mine. I had a hard time falling back to sleep. I had so many questions for Baba about what had happened after we separated.

Waking up in my great uncle's guest room in America next to Baba was like a dream come true. The sun was shining brightly through the window, the sound of many birds chirping echoed throughout the quiet neighborhood. Looking out, I spotted two brown squirrels chasing each other up a tree. *Had we really made it across the border safely?*

I turned to Baba and in a sarcastic tone I asked, "Are we really in America right now?"

"We did it Pendar, we really did it!" flashing an ear-to-ear grin.

I smiled at him with adoration. Although many had doubted him, including me, he never gave up, no matter how dire the circumstances. He had delivered me safely to America, perhaps a secret vow he'd unknowingly made long ago, to reach the mountaintop, just like the panther in the coffee mug.

I told Baba about the Mexican woman who took me into her home, fed me eggs and strange sausage and gave me fresh clothes. I also bragged about my visit to Jack in the Box, my first drive-through experience.

"Now tell me how you got back to Tijuana, Baba?

My father's experience was far more stressful than mine. Baba recounted his long walk to the main road. He said he worried the entire time, fearful he would be caught and arrested because of the way he looked, mud-caked, exhausted, and desperate. "I was hungry, thirsty and had blisters on my feet thanks to my uncomfortable loafers. I would have worn comfortable shoes; had I known I'd be coming with you." he said.

It took him over an hour to reach the main road, where he found a diner. "I stood in front of it for a few minutes contemplating but eventually found the guts to walk in and ask the worker to call me a taxi," he recounted. "I was a nervous wreck, waiting for the taxi to arrive. My heart sank with each passing vehicle. I feared the worst, that one of the employees or customers would call the police because I looked out of place. It felt like everyone in the diner was staring at me, wondering what I was doing there.

"Finally, the taxi arrived and drove me to the border. The taxi could only drive me so far, and I had to walk the rest of the way, directly in the path of armed border patrol officers.

"I was terrified they'd stop me for questioning. That would have been a disaster; I had no passport or paperwork. Under surveillance, I slowly walked past them and pretended that I knew the way. Somehow, I miraculously made it across the border and back into Mexico, then hailed a cab back to our hotel.

"The door attendant at our hotel recognized me, but the look of shock and surprise on his face said it all. He had seen me with clean clothes, shiny shoes, and an overall presentable appearance, but now I looked like Pedro!

Once back in the room, I made my flight arrangements with barely enough cash left in my pocket, and luckily booked the last flight of the night to Los Angeles."

Baba had illegally entered America, then turned around and headed back to Tijuana. It was an unbelievable adventure, a journey of a life-time, a torturous feat to cross the border, one I may not have survived without my father's presence.

"Pendar, let's call Maman, and let her know we've made it. I'm sure she's worried sick about us; it's been nearly two weeks since we've called her."

With his mood lightened up and feeling relieved, Baba had Dayi Omid call Maman for an exceptional surprise.

"Hi Ziba Jan, it's Dayi Omid azizam, how are you?" he said when she answered the call.

"We're good, thank you," she replied. "Listen, have you heard from Nader or Pendar? Do you know where they are?"

I could hear the panic in her voice, and I felt sorry that we had caused her such alarm.

"Hold on," Dayi Omid told my mother. "There is someone here that wants to speak with you."

He passed me the receiver and I saluted Maman. "Salam Maman."

"Oh my God, Pendar, is that you? Is that your voice?"

"Yes Maman, it's me, how are you?" Tears pooled in my eyes hearing her voice.

"Where have you been? And what are you doing with Dayi Omid? Is he in Korea with you?" She was puzzled and was banging away with her rapid-fire questions.

"No Maman, we're not in Korea anymore. Baba and I are sitting in Dayi Omid and Mona's house in California. We've made it to America!" Tears rolling down my cheeks, a steady stream of drops repeatedly hitting my shirt.

"WHAT?! How did that happen? Why aren't you in Texas?"

"It's a long story, Maman, we just called to say we're safe, and to tell you that I love you and I miss you very much. Baba will explain the rest." I was choked up and elated as I passed the phone to my father.

Before hanging up, Baba informed her about our plans of traveling to Texas. That was my next stop, I was leaving for Dallas to live with Shirley.

Baba's next call was to his old pal Kiya. He was excited to share the good news with him and Shirley. We'd be staying in California for a couple of weeks before heading to Dallas——our final stop in the journey.

During our stay, Mona spoiled me with all types of treats. I had corn flakes and milk for the first time! I visited a McDonald's drive through, ate Shakey's Chicken and Pizza, watched American television, and accompanied by Baba, she took us to the "happiest place on earth" —— Disneyland.

Living in America seemed a breeze, everything was going as planned for a change. Baba purchased our plane tickets to Dallas where Kiya and Shirley happily awaited my arrival. I was eager to reunite with Shirley and looked forward to settling down in my new home in Texas.

Our flight left Los Angeles on time. Baba was assured that no documentation was required to travel domestically. This was the first time I became aware of my status as an "illegal alien" in America.

At the airport, I wondered how my life would be affected in the future by this burden, and how it would ever be resolved. I would soon discover that illegal aliens were frowned upon; disheartened to find out that Americans looked down on undocumented immigrants like me, which felt like an immediate disadvantage.

TWENTY-SEVEN
ENROLLMENT

DALLAS, TEXAS, MARCH 23, 1987

The reunion with Shirley at the airport in Dallas was a joyous occasion, just as I'd always imagined it. She embraced me, rocking me back and forth in her arms. I drew in a breath of her perfume, reminiscing about our first meeting in Frankfurt.

"Do you remember me?" Kiya asked me after embracing Baba. They had not seen each other for almost ten years, making it an emotional reunion for them.

"I'm sorry, I don't," I said politely. "I was young when I saw you last in Iran."

It was odd to think I'll be living with strangers I hardly knew. During the car ride to Shirley's house, Baba and Kiya caught up about old times. Shirley and I sat together in the back seat, and I regaled her with stories of our adventures in Syria, China, Japan, Korea, and Mexico, careful not to spill details about my extracurricular activities in Seoul.

Kiya drove us to Arlington, located west of Dallas airport. We entered a pristine, quiet suburban neighborhood. Gazing out the window, I admired the family-friendly area, anticipating our arrival at a permanent place I could finally call home. The mesmerizing orange glow of the sunset reflected against the puffy clouds, funnels of sunlight shining through the clouds in tall columns. The sun setting was symbolic of arriving in my new home. It was a magnificent scene, I considered it a signal from the heavens, secretly telling me, 'Everything is going to be alright'.

"This is our street," Shirley announced in her sweet southern accent.

The residential neighborhood was tranquil, well maintained, and far from the city and major highways. Turning onto her street, I observed many children playing outside in their front yards, some playing basketball in the driveway. A group throwing a football, and children riding bicycles up and down the street. It felt like I had hit the jackpot. I looked up to the sky and silently thanked God for answering my prayers. It was a difficult journey to get here, but now that I'd made it, the neighborhood resembled the American dream I had always imagined and dreamt about.

Children of all ages played in the sunset and through dusk. We pulled into the driveway of her lovely one-story home; Shirley was anxious to show me around.

"This is your room, Pendar," she said lovingly. She had been anticipating my arrival for weeks, she had considerately decorated my room with a bed, desk, and a nightstand. I hadn't had a permanent home for months. Living in uncertainty for so long, flying from city to city, living out of our suitcases and staying in various hotels. My feeling of contentment was enormous.

Next step was to register at a junior high school near Shirley's home. I left Iran in the middle of eighth grade, with intentions of continuing in the same grade.

That night, I crawled under the cozy sheets of my own bed. In the morning, Shirley drove us to the junior high school nearby. Baba carried his briefcase and in it, my passport, birth certificate, education records, and translated documents necessary for registration. Walking towards the office I noticed the sheer size of the school and how immaculately tidy it looked. Walking in, the loud school bell rang for a few seconds, giving me flashbacks of waking up in the bushes at the border. Students started to fill the hallways as we navigated to the admissions office.

Baba turned over my folder of paperwork to the cordial clerk, everything except my passport. "Aren't they going to need that for registration?" I asked.

"I hope not!" he answered.

"Have a seat, and we'll call your name shortly," the clerk said politely.

After ten minutes a school counselor emerged from one of the offices. "Pendar?" she said. She was a young woman, professionally attired in a beige skirt suit, nylon stockings and flat black shoes, her blonde hair cut in a shoulder-length bob.

Shirley and I walked into her office, while Baba stayed behind. On her clipboard was a checklist of the items required to register in school. Our interview was going well until she reached the section titled Immigration and Naturalization Services, or INS. "May I see your passport please?" she asked.

"It's back at the house. We didn't think we were going to need it." I was forced to lie again out of necessity. I knew she was looking for a student visa, which I didn't have, hence the reason Baba hadn't removed it from his briefcase.

"Well," she replied, "the school will either need to confirm your student visa or see documents from immigration to show your legal status in America."

And just like that she broke the bad news.

My jaw dropped. I stumbled to come up with an appropriate excuse, unable to get the words out.

"Is there anything that can be done?" Shirley inquired.

"A student visa or the required paperwork, Hun. I'm sorry there's nothing else I can do."

Unable to register, we left the school feeling disappointed, a cruel reminder of the rejection we'd faced at the many embassies along the way.

"Don't you worry, Pendar. There's another junior high just on the other side of the house," Shirley informed me. "Tomorrow morning, we'll go there and get you registered."

Unfortunately, the next day the exact same scenario played out. The counselor at the new school explained, "There ain't no gettin' round them rules for foreign students. A student visa, or other acceptable paperwork is required to complete his registration."

After our second failed attempt, it was clear we'd face the same grim outcome at all other schools in Texas. Yet another devastating blow.

Exiting the second school, I felt even more rejected, defeated. I had finally begun to feel secure about my new home, my legal guardian, and my future school, but now I felt like the safety net had been pulled out from under me. Another turndown, an unexpected slap in the face, a reality check.

The future looked unclear once more. Not able to register for school meant I couldn't live in Texas. I quietly wept in disappointment. The ground I was standing on was unstable, like sinking into a muck of quicksand. Soon we'll be back on the road again and possibly end up in another state, but where? And with who?

For a moment, it felt as though I was on the easy road to the American dream, but fate and destiny constantly kept me in check. Once back at Shirley's, I parked myself in front of the TV and zoned out.

In the background, I heard Baba speaking to someone familiar on the phone. It was Amoo Hafez, his eldest brother, and my beloved uncle.

During his stay in Istanbul, Amoo Hafez had successfully secured a visitor's visa to the United States. As luck would have it, he was scheduled to arrive in Los Angeles the following week. He was planning to rent a one-bedroom apartment for himself in Los Angeles.

Without hesitation, he agreed to take me in and consented to becoming my legal guardian. It looked as if we were going back to Los Angeles.

That night I dreamt I was stranded in the middle of the ocean. The bright rays of the sun illuminating the tranquil sea, yet I swam endlessly and could not make land. The sound of seagulls nearby and the constant clanging of the bell from the red buoy bobbing back and forth in the waves echoed in my ears.

Suddenly I see the fin of a giant shark breaking the surface, coming directly towards me. My heart starts beating out of control, terror takes over me. The fin slowly slices through the water, the gigantic fish lurking below the calm surface and inching closer. The fin slowly circles around me. I quickly swim towards the red buoy. I look back, and the fin is still following. I swim faster, but the fin keeps creeping closer. "BABAAA, BABAAAAA PLEASE HELP ME!" I scream, my voice echoing across the water.

I am pulled below the water by a great force as the shark clamps down on my leg. The thrashing and biting so intense, the water around me stirs with blood, turning the ocean red. I am in a full panic, hyperventilating, trying to escape the jaws of death. Suddenly, I woke up! Drenched in sweat, Baba was sitting at the edge on the bed, squeezing my legs to rouse me.

"I heard you calling for me, are you okay?" he asked with concern.

"Yeah, Baba, I'm fine. I was just having a bad dream," I told him.

The day came to say goodbye to Kiya, Shirley, and Texas. It was a gloomy morning having to leave the people who felt like family and the house I got to call home for only a week. Shirley insisted on sitting in the back seat with me for the ride to the airport.

Once there, She and Kiya escorted us to the gate. Tears started rolling down my face as Shirley embraced me for the last time.

"Keep in touch, Pendar. I wish you the best and good luck with everything in your life," she told me. Tears pooled in her eyes, "I know you have a bright future ahead of you, it just wasn't meant to be here with me."

My life had become a repetitive cycle of separations, goodbyes, let-downs, and disappointments. The future was becoming a dark highway once again.

When is the uncertainty, and the emotional roller coaster going to stop? I asked the cruel universe in frustration.

TWENTY-EIGHT
PARTING WAYS

SHERMAN OAKS, CA, SPRING OF 1987

O ur first few nights back in Los Angeles, Amoo Hafez, Baba, and I slept on the floor of a friend's flat in Glendale. While Amoo Hafez searched for a suitable apartment, Baba and I investigated the local schools.

We found one in Sherman Oaks and we arranged for the three of us to visit. Once at the admissions office, we didn't encounter any issues with my immigration status. This time it was Amoo Hafez's documents that were not acceptable to the school.

To become my legal guardian and register me for school, he had to be an American citizen or have permanent residency. He didn't have either; he had only arrived on a visitor's visa a few days earlier.

Once again, we spent the evening brainstorming a solution. Amoo Hafez suggested we contact Azad and Star. The same relatives who had helped Cousin Shahin when he first arrived in America, who'd also helped with Shahin's school registration. They now lived in an apartment in Sherman Oaks, close to where the junior high was located. Perhaps they would be willing to do the same for me?

"He can still live with me," Amoo Hafez said, "but we can work around the system?"

Baba quickly jumped on the phone with Azad and after a lengthy conversation, he and Star agreed to help us.

Star arranged to accompany me to school the following day, and with her assistance, I had no trouble registering and was enrolled to continue in the eighth-grade.

After my fourth attempt, I was ecstatic to finally be registered for school.

I was anxious to start my new life here in California. Azad also assisted Amoo Hafez in finding an apartment for us, a small one-bedroom right down the street from where they lived.

We had no furniture or belongings, just a few hand-me-downs given to us by various acquaintances. We didn't even have beds, just two folded up blankets on each corner of the floor.

I had successfully registered for school, and we were settling into our new apartment. Baba was anxious to call Mamam to share the joyous news.

"Yes Ziba Jan, it was always meant for Pendar to live with my big brother. Amoo Hafez was like a father to me and my siblings as well. I've already purchased an airplane ticket and will be flying home soon," I overheard him say. "I love you and miss you, too. Kiss the kids for me."

My heart sank once I heard he was leaving. I felt a lump swelling in my throat and bolted out of the room, blotting my tears with my sleeve. Unpleasant thoughts of separation and abandonment swept over me. By now, I was emotionally exhausted, tired of dealing with bitter feelings. I didn't want Baba to see me crying. I wanted him to perceive me as brave and strong, no matter how lonely and weak I felt deep down inside. But the reality of his departure was heart-wrenching.

I resolved to make every minute we had left together count, uncertain when I would see him again. He had stood by me with unwavering loyalty, unwilling to give up at any step of our arduous journey. We'd experienced the good, the bad, and the ugly; that's what had made our bond stronger. The unbreakable connection we had formed over the suffering we had endured together would last forever.

In Los Angeles, I was headed towards the unknown. Relying only on my uncle, Azad and Star to guide me. Still, I simply couldn't fathom life without Baba or my extended family. Saying goodbye to my father, and best friend was without a doubt going to be extremely hurtful. I couldn't bear the idea of another melancholy scene at the airport, or one more heartbreaking farewell.

Over the last several months, I'd fallen asleep and woken up in many strange cities beside my father, every breath, every meal, every adventure had been taken together. I'd heavily relied on him for love, advice, hope, companionship, and direction. I often prayed that our difficult journey would end soon. But now with our separation looming, I felt otherwise.

I knew Maman, my siblings, and the rest of our family back in Tehran missed my father dearly, he had no choice but to return. We had attained our goal, and it was now time for me to proceed on my own. I had to accept my destiny. I was torn and profoundly hurt that I would no longer be included as a part of our family, that I was somehow meant to live a lonely existence on the opposite side of the world, away from everyone I loved and everything I cared about.

I hid the turmoil and pushed aside the roaring thoughts of loneliness, savoring my last hours with my father. When the dreaded departure day finally arrived, Baba and Amoo Hafez urged me to go to school instead of accompanying my father to the airport. I was disappointed, yet strangely relieved. I loathed the thought of another uncomfortable, emotional breakdown in the terminal. Letting go of Baba would be by far the worst of all goodbyes.

That morning, we had breakfast together one last time. At the end of the meal, I packed my backpack and got ready for school. Baba accompanied me to Addison Street, firmly holding my hand as we made our final trek to the corner together.

I could hear my heart beating in my ears as Baba said his final goodbye. "Pendar Jan, this is the end of the line" he began, "I'm so incredibly proud of you. You have been so brave, and strong throughout our long trip. Now it's time for me to go back home."

"This has been the wildest ride of my life and one of the hardest things I've ever done," he said. "I'm just glad you were there by my side. You inspired me to continue, not take no for an answer, to never give up."

My eyes welled up with tears, and I fought the urge to break down. I didn't want my father's last image of me to be a crying mess. I forced myself to focus on his words and kept my emotions at bay.

"We finally did it," he continued, "and no one can ever take that away from us. Be safe and take good care. I want you to know that Maman and I will be thinking of you every minute of every day."

I wrapped my arms around my father and held on tight. "Kiss and hug Maman, Donya and Amin for me," I said. "I'll be missing you every day, too."

My face twisted and strained, I bit my lip, fighting back outright hysterical crying. I hadn't prepared myself for this moment, unwilling to imagine the dreadful moment I'd be forced to separate from my father, but the reality was sinking in.

I felt myself withering from sorrow, but at the same time, I recognized that this was the best decision for our family, a bittersweet moment of progress and separation wrapped in one.

We embraced and squeezed one another tight for a long time before finally letting go. Baba firmly and affectionately kissed my cheeks and forehead.

Compelled to say goodbye, I slowly pulled away from him before taking one last huge whiff of his unmistakable scent.

"Good luck, son, I wish you happiness and prosperity in your life," he continued, "I know you're going to accomplish anything you put your mind to. I'll be watching from a distance and adoring you every step of the way!" he said lovingly.

He shrugged, lifted his face, looked straight at me, and whispered, "You'll always be in my prayers." Now he was crying softly, which broke my heart more.

"Goodbye Baba, I love you and I'm going to miss you very much!" Tears were abundant, but I kept my cool and said goodbye in a calm demeanor. My whole life, I had been his son, but now he was leaving me, indefinitely.

He couldn't be my guiding light anymore; I'd have to find my own way. The thought of doing it alone terrified me. I felt like an orphan, abandoned by his parents. I experienced a saddening pain that began in the pit of my stomach and spread to every cell of my body. It was as if my very heart and guts were being ripped out. I was nauseous, with a raging inferno burning inside me, caught between sadness, regret, and anger.

I reluctantly tore away and started walking towards school. I looked back after every few steps to find that he was still standing there silently watching me. I waved to him from afar and he blew kisses back at me. I caught one final blurry glimpse of him standing on that street corner, still waving. Once he was completely out of my sight, I broke down and started to cry uncontrollably, hyperventilating as tears streamed down my cheeks.

In that moment, I contemplated my future and what was to become of me. At thirteen, I was certainly going to miss my family, but I knew that my education took precedence over my feelings.

I whimpered the rest of the way to school that day, thinking about the meaningless war now raging back in Iran; this was the reason I had been forced to abandon my home and family. The invisible force that followed me, just like the dark, black cloud of unfortunate events that had befallen us during our months-long journey. I had to pay the ultimate price by losing my family and everything I knew to escape its grasp.

War didn't discriminate, destroying the lives of innocent men, women, and children for years throughout history.

I was one of the fortunate ones and escaped to freedom, lucky to have survived. War is a reality for those like me who are forced to run from it, and for those who are compelled to join the fight, like my friend Mohammad.

I had spent months struggling to enter America, somehow convinced that everything would be better once I arrived. In fact, what I would soon discover is that the challenge of survival had only just begun. I had not asked to be disconnected from my family. It had all happened so quickly, and the outcome would turn out to be a far cry from what I had anticipated.

TWENTY-NINE
I PLEDGE ALLEGIANCE

SHERMAN OAKS, SPRING 1987

L ife in the United States was not at all how I imagined it. For starters, I believed that everything would simply fall into place. I would live with Amoo Hafez in his apartment, attend school, make friends and be happy.

Often, I felt like E.T. "The Extra Terrestrial" just wanting to "PHONE HOME" after being left behind on an alien planet by my spaceship. Unfortunately, Amoo Hafez was just as lost as I was in this strange, new land. He didn't even speak English and at fifty-six, he wasn't interested in learning. Living with him took some getting used to, our routine was more like two bachelors. We kept different schedules, I went to school, he went to work.

We lived a moderate and frugal existence, with money always a concern for my uncle.

I recognized the financial responsibilities that came with running a household early on and didn't pressure Amoo Hafez for extras. Still, it was difficult coming home from school every afternoon to an empty apartment and an empty refrigerator. No Papa Jahan waving to me from his apartment window, no Maman in the kitchen cooking up a delicious meal, there was no playtime with my siblings and no conversations about cars and movies with Baba in the evenings.

Attending school in America was also challenging, and struggling as an immigrant, and an undocumented one at that, was no walk in the

park. I could only pray that God would give me the strength to persevere against all odds.

My days began with the difficult walk past the street corner where
I'd said my final goodbye to Baba. Every morning, I'd look back and
imagine him standing there, waving to me for weeks and months after
his departure.

I felt numb, void of feelings. It seemed the only way to remedy my
lonely heart was to slowly forget about the past and concentrate on my
future in what felt like solitary confinement. Nobody could fill the void
in my life, there was no substitute for the family I missed so dearly.

Junior high school in the United States was vastly different from
what I was accustomed to back in Tehran. I confronted challenges I had
not thought about. Much of what I knew about America was based on
what I had seen in the movies. But what I was experiencing couldn't
have been further from that reality.

One of the first things I had to learn and memorize was the *Pledge of
Allegiance*, which we had to recite each morning, while putting the palm
of my hand over my heart and facing the American flag. I remember it
to this day, all the kids saying the pledge out loud, *I pledge allegiance to
the flag of the United States of America, and to the republic for which it stands,
one nation under God, indivisible, with liberty and justice for all.*

A few years earlier, I was screaming words like, "Death to America."
at school in Tehran. Now, I was pledging allegiance to the very flag I had
witnessed being burned in many bonfires during the Iranian revolution.
To my surprise, students in America did not fear their teachers, as we did
back in Iran. One boy in particular kept speaking out of turn and inter-
rupting our teacher, a mild-mannered, middle-aged woman, who would
say, "SHASH" to quiet him down. "SHASH" means "urine" in Farsi,
every time she'd say it, I'd giggle inside. I was bewildered that her
admonishments did little to deter him. Back at my old school, especially in
Mr. Hakimi's classes, this kid would have received the beating of his life.
But here in America, the worst thing that could happen was a visit to the
dean or principal's office. Another big change was that boys and girls
were not separated in junior high school. Not only that, but "boyfriends"
and "girlfriends" were outwardly affectionate. I was shocked the first time
I spotted a couple making out in the hallway next to my locker, seemingly
unconcerned that their public display would be called out or punished.
Yet, I found it awkward to speak to the opposite sex and was intimidated
at the sight of any pretty girl. I didn't know how to act around them.

In addition, I quickly learned that your social standing depended on
the group you belonged to or hung out with. There were the upperclass-

men, the jocks, the pretty popular girls, the rich kids, the brainiacs, and lots of middle-class students who kept to themselves and strived for good grades. But the least popular kids were the geeks or nerds, and the ESL (English as a Second Language) students like me.

The foreign students were drawn to one another and tended to hang together. We struggled to fit in and were often bullied. My first few months were particularly challenging when it came to bullying, made even harder because of my concerns over my "illegal" status in the country. Being undocumented was unsettling and made me feel "less than." I was constantly worried about being found out. *Would I eventually be caught and arrested? Hauled off to jail?* This, combined with the stress of being far from my home and family made me rethink my future in America.

But daily, and without constraint, I unwittingly reminisced about my old life, and how it had now been reduced to nothing. My life had turned one hundred eighty degrees upside down and everything was the opposite of what I remembered. In Tehran, I had my own comfortable bed but now was adjusting to sleeping on two folded up blankets on the floor, my makeshift bed. Growing up, my parents showered me with the best and most updated toys. And Baba's work in film ensured access to many foreign movies. In America, my uncle hooked up a second-hand T.V. set in our apartment, which is how I escaped reality by watching a variety of television shows.

Back home, I had a big closet with an expansive wardrobe, shoes and accessories for every occasion. But now, I was left with a couple of old T-shirts, shorts and pants. When my parents and I had initially spoken about coming to America, I could never have imagined it would be under these circumstances. I missed Maman picking out my clothes every day, and lovingly placing them on my bed. I missed her dearly, for cooking up a scrumptious dinner for our family, or even accompanying her on a shopping spree. Without her advice, I made many bad fashion choices, and my schoolmates were not shy to make me aware of them all.

In the afternoons, I found reprieve with Star and her daughter Darya. I'd walk to their apartment, do my homework quickly, then hurry to play with my friends, who lived just downstairs from them. Star was kind and showed me the basics of cooking. Chopping and frying of onions and garlic. Cooking and steaming rice, along with traditional Mexican dishes. Azad was an accountant and got home in the late afternoon from the office to join family dinner, much like Baba did back in Tehran. The scenario was reminiscent of home, but I was now experiencing it with people I hardly knew. On certain nights, Star forced me to help with the dishes, as one of my chores, something I had never done back home and even more reluctant to do now. Most nights, Amoo Hafez got home around 7 p.m. Once I knew he was home, I'd return to our apartment, a five-minute walk on the same block. My uncle and legal guardians Star and Azad made me feel comfortable and safe, but I was often ashamed to share about my struggles at school. It was as if I was lost in my own world. I didn't want them to frown upon it, or worse, report back to my parents about my troubles of not fitting in or adjusting to my new life. I kept many things to myself thinking it was in my own best interest, maybe a desperate attempt to protect myself. But over time, it got harder and harder to communicate my true feelings with anyone.

Life brightened just a little when Amoo Hafez came home from work one evening with a surprise. Someone had abandoned an inoperable portable audio cassette player at his repair shop. It was called a Walkman (today's version of an iPod). He was able to fix it, and he passed it on to me as a gift. The Walkman became my best friend and a new way to escape from my reality. I fell in love with music and started to lose myself in it, similarly to how I loved movies. I walked to school with headphones on my ears, initially listening to the Top 100 pop hits on the radio. That is until one of my classmates asked me if I had any cassette tapes for my Walkman.

"No," I said, "I just got it and I'm saving money to buy a couple of cassettes."

"I have a few bootleg copies, I'll bring you one tomorrow," he told me.

Bootleg, meaning an illegal reproduction of the original. The next day, he arrived with a cassette tape with a handwritten sticker on it that read, "METALLICA, MASTER OF PUPPETS."

I had no idea what to think of it, but I happily accepted the offer. After school, I put it in my Walkman and began my walk home. That was a life changing experience, I had never been so invigorated, excited, energized, or had this much adrenaline rushing through my veins while listening to any other type of music. I was instantly hooked and wanted more of it. I barely went back to the radio, listening to the entire album every day, over and over.

On weekends, I accompanied Azad and Star to family parties, hosted by Star's many relatives. She had a large extended Mexican family in the L.A. area, including her mom Norma, who lived in Hollywood. They were a big group, much like my family, with many uncles, aunts, cousins, siblings, and grandparents who were affectionate and loving patriarchs. They welcomed me with open arms and treated me like one of their own. I envied the close-knit family and longed to have mine back. Often, I sat separated from the group like an outsider, watching the family mingle, joke around, interact, and relish being in each other's presence. I found myself crying inwardly at those moments, tears pooling in my eyes as memories of my own big family touched me viscerally. I missed my parents, the adoration, the unconditional love that my family had for me, especially how Baba proudly gazed at me with his endearing smile. I missed watching Papa Jahan drawing puzzles in his office or going to the local pastry shop with Mama Goli. The family trips to Seaside, the large weekly gatherings, was all nothing but a memory now, images in my head that conjured uncomfortable and unwelcomed feelings.

I never felt so lonely in all my life, no longer the center of attention, only a mere afterthought. My only gratification came from witnessing the joy and happiness that was apparent on the faces of Star's entire family.

I graduated the ninth grade in June of 1988. To mark the occasion, Star and her sister Elena pitched in and kindly bought me a business suit to wear to the ceremony. I wore the suit proudly, for the first time, feeling confident about my wardrobe. Azad, Star and her giant extended family went out of their way to help me feel better about my new life, always making an extra effort for which I was very appreciative of.

THIRTY
GOING IT ALONE

After graduating junior high, I wrote down several goals for myself. I intended to participate in team sports, go steady with a girl, and learn a new skill. I wanted the financial freedom to buy a Nintendo entertainment system without having to ask Amoo Hafez. We were not living in a lap of luxury, often struggling to make ends meet and to contribute, I found a part time job. Amoo Hafez knew the owner of a pizza shop in North Hollywood, and he recommended me for the open position. After a quick interview, I was offered an entry level summer job, and was paid under the table, and off the records to avoid my illegal status.

My motivation also derived from being bullied all throughout junior high school. I knew that being a foreigner and an immigrant was frowned upon by many Americans, let alone an illegal alien. This was something I was truly ashamed and embarrassed by and didn't divulge that information to anyone. I kept the details of our tortuous journey a secret and brushed it under the carpet like it never happened.

My first assignment was to deliver flyers to local homes and apartments nearby. My training included instructions on how to zig-zag up and down every street to hang flyers.

I was dropped off at 8:00 am, with a massive stack of flyers and directions on where to begin my walk. I made sure to grab extras to show I could take on additional work. It was my first day on the job and I wanted to impress the owner of the pizza shop.

I walked the neighborhoods of North Hollywood, blaring the energizing music of Metallica, Guns N Roses, Motley Crue, and Def Leppard on my Walkman, filling my ears with exhilarating music. I was excited to pass out flyers, yearning to prove myself, even though it was considered an entry level position that paid $4 an hour, but it was cash!

I had never held a job in any capacity, and it felt unexpectedly gratifying. I continued working through the week, but every day I fell short of my goal and had a lump of leftover flyers. That didn't please me, but I vowed to work harder.

I needed to figure out a smarter way to finish passing out the full stack of flyers by the end of my shift. The biggest challenge in the following week materialized when I was dropped off one morning, on a street that consisted of enormous, multi-level apartment buildings with tight security.

The building complexes housed numerous units, which meant I could dispose of a substantial number of flyers. The challenge was how to penetrate the mighty fortified forts; most possessed sizable security gates and were not accessible to the public.

At the first building I came across, luck was on my side, the parking security gates magically opened in front of me just as a resident was leaving the parking garage.

I waited until the car made its way onto the street, and with my head on a swivel, I sneaked in, just before the parking gate closed behind me. I passed out numerous flyers, making sure every door was tagged.

This went against every sign that was posted on every fence and secured door. Signs like, "No trespassing," "NO soliciting," "NO Unauthorized Entry," "Violators Will be Prosecuted," and my favorite, "Beware of Dogs. "The next set of apartment buildings on the same street presented a similar challenge, but none of the residents were coming or going. I walked up to the towering front gate and stared it down, contemplating for only a second. Without hesitation or thinking twice, I started climbing the tall security gate of the building. After all, the only thing holding me back was my own good judgment, which had a funny way of deserting me, especially when it came to reaching my goals.

My focus fixated on the disappearing stack of flyers and nothing else. The goal of finishing my daily supply of flyers had become like a nagging sickness or disease, a thorn in my side I couldn't ignore.

It became a personal challenge to jump every fence, gaining entry to every building on the block. Stacks upon stacks of flyers were melting away in a matter of minutes, which would have normally taken an hour or two. With an 'I don't give a crap' attitude, and to achieve my summer goals, I scaled every locked security fence on the block, gaining unauthorized access to every building.

In hindsight, if all the border patrol agents, barbed-wire fences, and Mexican police couldn't keep me away from America, then surely these insignificant fences were not going to stand in the way of accomplishing my goals.

That day, I passed out the whole stack of flyers and proudly walked back to the pizza shop in the late afternoon with my hands empty for a change. I spotted the owner standing in front of the shop, arms crossed, pacing back and forth, his body language indicating his agitated state. I could see the veins popping out of his head from a distance.

Once back, he said, "Come to my office!" As we walked toward the back of the shop, I noticed the grim expression on his face and was certain it spelled trouble.

He turned to me, narrowing his eyes accusingly, "I need to speak to you," he continued, furiously slamming the door to his office.

Suddenly, I felt as though I'd been busted. I was overwhelmed with shame and embarrassment. The air let out of my chest as I hunched over on the chair.

"I've had several phone calls today," he began. "Different managers of apartment buildings are complaining about a young boy passing out flyers, I assume that's all about you?" he asked with frustration.

I looked down at the ground, filled with remorse. I couldn't believe I'd already messed up at work.

"The complaints aren't only from managers, but residents too," he continued.

My heart started to beat loud enough that I could hear it thumping in my head, and I thought the worst. *Was he going to fire me?* I broke out in a drenching sweat. Beads dripped from my forehead and onto my eyebrows and rolled down my nose.

"I've got the whole neighborhood complaining about you illegally trespassing on their property and passing out flyers. Are all these complaints about you?" he went on.

How do I explain to my boss that I engaged in the reported "ILLEGAL TRESPASSING"? I hesitated to answer but figured the best course of action was to be truthful. I took a deep breath through my nose, "Yes sir, that's all true, it was me, I did it," I admitted nervously and regretfully.

We sat in an uncomfortable silence for a moment while I tried to remain calm and unaffected by his furious stare. The second hand of the clock loudly echoed in the room. Blood thudded in my temples, thoughts flying around my head, a part of me knowing I had screwed up and now came the punishment. I maintained my cool when suddenly, a smirk started to slowly creep across his lips.

"You know what? I was mad at first and still am, a little, because right after the complaints finished, the phone kept ringing and orders started pouring in. All of them asking for the 2 large pizzas special for $9.99," he was proud about his coupon special on the flyer. "We've already tripled our lunch business today, all orders coming from the apartments which we've never delivered to before," he continued.

I started to smile, but stopped myself, waiting for the disappointment or a "but" to follow.

"Let me tell you something," he continued.

Oh boy, here it comes.

"I think you're doing a great job and want you to continue," he said.

"But what about the complaints?" I asked him.

"Let me worry about the complaints, I'll deal with them. And tonight, take a large pizza home, with every topping, on the house. It's your bonus for doing a good job." He smiled an ear-to-ear grin.

On my way out, he was counting the overstuffed cash register from lunch and looked forward to a record-breaking dinner rush. The delivery driver later overheard the owner say, "That was one of his biggest single day records of making a profit at the pizza shop, ever!"

I felt feelings of accomplishment, making me tear up in happiness. For the first time, I felt blessed with the same perseverance I observed in Baba throughout our travels. My father also had a singular goal and he achieved it, no matter what. It was my turn to be the panther now and climb the impossible mountain of life, in solitary. It dawned on me that my actions mirrored those of Baba's when he was accomplishing his own goal of getting me to America. Over the months, I'd thought of him often, how I liked burying my face in his chest when he held me against it, how his cologne smelled in the morning, and how his beard tickled my face.

Baba had clearly shown me with his actions that you can accomplish anything you set your mind to, if you are willing to work hard enough for it, and as always, never to give up or take no for an answer.

I was elated about the compliments from my boss and called Amoo Hafez to pick me up. Walking home with a large pizza was going to be challenging. I was also given a week's pay, nearly two hundred dollars in cash. It was a lot of money for a fifteen-year-old.

For the first time I had my own money, hard earned while sweating in the heat, with an extra effort to achieve my goals. That summer, while most of my friends were going to the beach or hanging out at the public swimming pool, I was working hard, concentrating solely on my goals.

To fend for myself was a huge sense of accomplishment and fulfilled my needs like nothing else. When Amoo Hafez arrived to pick me up, he immediately questioned me about the giant pizza. "Did you order that pizza? How much did it cost?" He was always concerned about the cost of everything.

"The owner gave me the pizza for free as a bonus," I proudly told him.

"Amoo, can you take us to the movie rental store down the street?" I requested politely. "I want to rent a movie, with my own money."

We arrived at the store marked by a bright sign that looked like a blue ticket stub for a movie theater with bright yellow borders and letters that read, "BLOCKBUSTER VIDEO". A giant warehouse of movie rentals. Once inside, I was like a kid in a candy store. There were an extensive number of movies in every category, covering every wall and shelf.

Amoo Hafez wandered off, gazing at older films in the classic section, the ones from his era. I scanned the racks, searching for an entertaining movie to rent.

I had forgotten how exciting it was to watch a good movie. Just then my eyes caught a familiar title and an image that immediately brought tears to my eyes. My lips started to quiver; I began whimpering. Inhaling a deep breath, I removed the movie from the shelf, deliberately running my fingers across the cover. The movie was *Jaws,* and seeing it immediately brought back memories of that evening in 1977 when Baba treated Maman and me to the cinema. I was fixated on the movie cover, the image alone, transporting me right back to the sparkling lights of the marquee. I vividly remembered skipping to the theater, holding my parents' hands.

The tears were rolling down my face and onto my shirt, but I couldn't control myself.

Just then Amoo Hafez came around the corner and spotted me sobbing. "What's wrong, Pendar Jan? Why are you crying?" he asked with concern.

"This is the first film I'd ever watched in the movie theaters with Maman and Baba. It's bringing back memories and I realize how much I miss them!" I said with a heavy heart.

"It's alright, Azizam," he said in a soothing voice. "I know it's diffi-cult to grow up without your family. I promise you that it will get easier with time.

"Be patient, God had bigger plans for you." He sighed through his nose and closed his eyes, feeling my anguish.

We embraced for a minute until I caught my breath, wiping the tears off my face. Once home I quickly inserted the video cassette into the VCR. Sitting on the couch, enjoying my well-earned pizza, watching my favorite movie of all time – reliving one of the best moments of my life.

Even the bone chilling scenes brought back fond memories of my parents' love and affection, which I missed so profoundly. I'd seen *Jaws* with my parents more than ten years ago, but it felt like yesterday.

I thoroughly missed the comfort of our family gatherings, the security I felt being surrounded by my loved ones.

Often, feelings of regret inundated me. I felt as if I had taken my previous life for granted and wished for it to somehow be reversed, to wake up from this bad dream in the safety of my parents' home.

That nagging feeling of having done something wrong began to surface, but I shoved it down with idealistic thoughts of the American Dream. I had arrived, I'll figure it out, I kept telling myself. Just like my father, I would reach my dreams and goals no matter what challenges lay ahead. I would climb the mountain and hope that someday I could be just like Baba, just like the relentless Panther that had appeared at the bottom of his cup back at Seaside when the psychic read his fortune using Turkish coffee grinds.

I had left behind everything from my previous life, constantly working hard was all I could do to keep my mind off my struggles. I longed to have a home and a family of my own someday. The future was uncertain, and I had many doubts about the way my life would eventually turn out. *How would I ever get a regular job?* I didn't have any legal documentation! *How would I navigate through this lonely life with no one to lean on?*

The future became another unpaved road without headlights, and this time, Baba was not there to help or guide me along the way. He had succeeded in removing me from the certainty of turmoil, but unexpectedly dropped me in a turmoil of uncertainty.

I felt content with a belly full of pizza, watching *Jaws,* but how was it all going to end for me? I pondered with tears in my eyes and a strong wave of emotions. I wondered; will I ever truly feel free from the pain of my history? Or would I constantly feel that I was trying to escape an existence that may be out of my control?

High school certainly had its own challenges, but I maneuvered through, not making the same mistakes I had made in junior high. I overachieved in sports, eventually playing on the varsity football team as a kicker and the varsity soccer team as the goalkeeper. I also ran cross country and track and field in four events.

That exceeded my own and everyone else's expectations to play on four different team sports. Many of my fellow students and players never thought much of me but envied how I managed to pull off this tremendous feat. In my junior year, I even bought a letterman's jacket with my last name embroidered on the back, something I had coveted since the first day I entered high school.

I went steady with a girl just as planned and attended the high school prom dressed in a tuxedo with her on my arm. I also learned a new skill and took cooking classes to be competent enough to fix a meal for myself. I even saved up enough money to buy a Nintendo Entertainment system. I created the best possible life for myself by working hard, an ethic I have continued throughout my life.

I was terrified a great deal of the time, afraid of what I'd done, nervous of what I was doing, and helpless of what I might have to do to survive in this country. It wasn't what you'd call a crippling fear, in fact it was just the opposite. I thrived on the feeling and found myself craving it at times.

Sometimes, it felt like I needed that overpowering rush of terror to get me out of bed in the mornings and to summon the courage to move forward. What I realized is that it is part of my DNA, my very existence, something I had thankfully inherited from my beloved father. When a storm came, some hid, some ran away, but I used the powerful force of the wind to spread my wings and fly through the storm.

THIRTY-ONE
RETURNING HOME

Life for my family resumed in Iran without me. In 1989, two years after my arrival in the United States, the Iran-Iraq war ended. In early 1990, my parents and siblings traveled to Spain, and successfully secured visitors' visas, with the secret hope of remaining in America, even after their visas had expired.

Amoo Hafez drove us to LAX on the day of their arrival. I was so excited; I was jumping out of my skin. I had longed to be back in the embrace of my parents and to be reunited with my family. I was overwhelmed with a wave of emotions, especially when I held Baba in my arms. I was taller now and buried my head on his shoulder instead of in his chest and wept like a baby. Our emotional reunion triggered tears of happiness.

My sister Donya was now seven, and my baby brother, Amin, was five. I remember trying to pick them up in a collective hug and struggling to embrace them both in my arms. They had grown tremendously since I'd seen them last.

Maman gazed at us with a look of relief, ecstatic to see her three children back together again. She had shoved her headscarf and *manto* into her carryon case long before arriving at LAX and looked lovely in her blouse, skirt and fashionable, yet comfortable flat shoes. We hugged for a long time and an abundance of tears flowed. Our family was finally reunited.

My parents and siblings would stay with us at Amoo Hafez's one bedroom apartment with the hope of Baba eventually finding us a place of our own. Once everyone was settled in, Maman went into the kitchen and got to work. I had missed her cooking and happily devoured the many meals she prepared for us. She relished the freedom of expression that had been taken away from her after the revolution in Iran and was thoroughly entertained by a visit to the supermarket and a day of browsing the shops and department stores at the nearby Fashion Square Mall.

My siblings were also enjoying themselves. Like me, they had only experienced America through movies and were excited when they learned that Baba had arranged for us to visit Disneyland, with me serving as the family tour guide for our day at the "happiest place on Earth."

Baba relished being able to go to a movie theater once again. He was enjoying the freedoms that America offered, but it was a stressful time for him. Arranging to move our family to the other side of the world presented many challenges. I yearned for them to stay, but soon realized that Baba would be making many significant sacrifices back home. He would need to sell all his assets to provide a comfortable life for our family in California. That meant he'd need to sell his business, both of his homes, his vehicles, and all the family's worldly possessions to start anew as a forty-year-old immigrant who did not speak English. It would be a tremendous roll of the dice, a huge risk with no guarantee of success.

After months of deliberation, Baba made the heart wrenching decision to return home to Iran and not risk it all for the American dream. Fate and destiny got in the way once more.

My parents offered me the burdensome choice of returning to Iran with them. But by then, I had been living in the United States for over three years and had grown accustomed to the freedoms afforded me here. I also didn't want to disappoint my father. He had fought so valiantly to get me here, and I was determined to prove that his mighty efforts had not been in vain. I feared expressing a desire to return with them would be viewed as defeat, both his and mine, and that was the last thing I wanted.

There were other factors at play. For one, I was now a teenager. Attending a coed school would not be possible in Tehran. Here I had the freedom to not only attend classes with girls, but to socialize and even date them. They were not required to hide behind a scarf and *manto*. I had also become enamored with the idea that all was possible with hard work and perseverance.

Here in the States, I was introduced to nice cars, fancy clothing, and upscale homes. I was convinced that if I worked hard, I could achieve some of these goals, opportunities that existed here that I didn't see for myself back home. I was determined to build a life for myself, and to prove that my father made the right decision in bringing me here.

My mother and siblings preferred the lifestyle in America, but they also missed home, family, friends, and schoolmates. In retrospect, this is exactly how I'd felt when I first arrived in the States. Ultimately, I decided to remain in America without my family. In my hands lay the American promise, something that has always set this country apart from the rest. It was the promise that says each of us has the freedom to make our own lives what we will. And that's exactly what I was determined to achieve, to cash in on that promise.

I knew saying goodbye to my parents and siblings would be excruciating, but I had a renewed determination to succeed on my own. The lonely road ahead would not be simple. But this time, it was my decision to stay.

In the coming years, I would be confronted and possessed by my own demons, often wondering if they would drive me to the life of a wanderer, to a rootless existence in a foreign land as an illegal immigrant without my family to anchor me. I had made my decision and was now on my own with no other choice but to persevere.

My parents stayed in close touch. They often mailed me family portraits that featured the four of them with one of my siblings holding a framed picture of me. It was a remembrance, a way of including me. I appreciated the sentiment but looking at those photos often brought me to tears.

Many times, it was more convenient to shut down emotionally, to escape my solitary existence. Still, I vowed not to squander the opportunity I had been given, to make something of my life. I was determined to make my father proud and had a voracious appetite to build a successful life for myself.

I graduated high school in Van Nuys, California in 1991. The occasion was bittersweet. I had accomplished the first of my many goals and was proud to wear the navy-blue cap and gown to collect my diploma. But I was sad not to share the joyous occasion with my parents, siblings, grandparents and many aunts, uncles, and cousins to celebrate with me. This was just one of life's many milestones that I wished to have them by my side.

I was barely out of high school when a spur of the moment decision I made culminated in my arrest. The incident happened just a few months after my eighteenth birthday, which made me an adult in the eyes of the law. My teenage "accomplices" were American citizens, and our youthful indiscretion did not hold the same weighty consequences for them.

I was placed in a holding cell at the police station in Van Nuys, terrified that my skeletons would escape from the closet, and my illegal status would rear its ugly head. To my relief, after four days I was released on my own recognizance, ordered to serve 100 hours of community service and 30 days of Caltrans, cleaning the freeways. It was a close call; things could have gone a different way and I could have ended up being deported.

Considering my love of movies and to follow in my father's footsteps, I started my first official job at a Blockbuster video where I worked as a customer service rep.

After graduating from high school, I worked a series of odd jobs before entering the car business as a salesperson in 1992; a delivery driver at an Ameci's Pizza and a cashier at a fried chicken restaurant. I even sold knee braces for a sports medicine company before finally finding my calling—the automotive industry.

I was excited to be selling cars. I'd had a love affair with automobiles all my life. When I started, nobody had ever heard of my name and since 'Pendar' was considered unusual by most, management recommended I change it to an American name, which would be easier for clients to remember."

Later, I found out this was a popular solution for immigrants working at the dealership. I, Pendar, became Andy, the name of my best friend in high school.

"Andy" became more than a name, it became my alter ego, my other personality, taking on a meaning of its own. I liked differentiating the two, but somehow, over the years, Pendar disappeared more and more, while Andy thrived on in the car business. My justification for this— If anyone knew about my past, or who the real Pendar was, the person hiding beneath the persona I worked so hard to portray—I might not have made it as far at work or in life. Often my conscience bothered me; I was living in shameful deceit. Worse, if anyone found out about my secret journey across the border, not only could I be fired, but possibly turned over to the authorities.

I was two years into my career when my poor decision to not complete the court ordered sentence came back to haunt me. And after a missed court appearance, a bench warrant was issued for my arrest. One night after playing billiards with a coworker, I was pulled over by the police for a broken taillight. While checking my driver's license, the officer discovered the outstanding warrant and placed me under arrest.

When the judge found out that I had only completed a few hours of my previous sentence, he ordered that I be incarcerated for 30 days in the L.A. County Jail. I survived a long eighteen days of hell, serving my time in overly packed jail cells with hardened criminals. I had seen this terrifying experience in movies, and now I was living it. I managed to keep to myself, but upon my release, I encountered additional trouble.

The last step to my freedom was an encounter with an INS officer, (now Homeland Security), asking for my social security number. At that moment, my heart started to beat out of control with memories of the fear I'd felt dodging immigration officials while traversing the Mexican desert upon first entering America.

I had provided a fake social security number when I'd begun working in the early nineties, done out of a necessity to survive and to provide for myself. I had no other choice and reluctantly gave the officer the bogus social security number I had been using.

I watched as the uniformed official punched the number into the keyboard, then took his eyes off the computer screen to look at me. I could tell from his expression that he believed he had busted me in a lie. My suspicion was confirmed when he ordered me to another holding cell.

From there, my cellmates and I were placed on a bus, and driven to an immigration jail in San Pedro. Amoo Hafez eventually bailed me out, but only after I'd endured several days of misery, and multiple sleepless nights, filled with dread and uncertainty.

Once back in immigration court, I was ordered for deportation within 30 days; it was an awful predicament that required me to hire an attorney who filed an appeal for my stay. Time was running out, but with renewed hope and the possibility of legally staying in America, I worked harder and thrived on in the car business.

In 1995, I was promoted to the position of finance manager, and for the first time, I started making well over six figures annually, which was a lot of money for a twenty-two-year-old immigrant. Yet, unbeknownst to everyone, I was existing among them as an illegal alien.

My immigration issues were finally resolved in 1996, when I married my now ex-wife, an American citizen. Our marriage was not one of convenience, but of mutual love.

I was now legally permitted to stay in the country, but it took a few more years for my immigration status to be resolved. Financially, I was doing very well and in 1997, I fulfilled my dream of becoming a home-owner. A few months later, my first daughter Blossom was born. My second daughter Julia arrived two years later.

I had climbed the ladder at work once again and was promoted to the sales manager position in the early 2000's, where my responsibilities were multiplied, and I found myself having to manage employees of multiple ethnicities and some who were twice my own age. In 2002, I finally became a U.S. citizen and received my own American passport, fulfilling a long-held childhood dream. Holding the blue passport with the gold eagle embossed on its cover, I thought back to my time in Frankfurt when I'd held Shirley's American passport in my hands and caressed it with wonder. Now, I was a proud American citizen and ecstatic to have one of my own.

Having an American passport was magical because it opened doors and afforded me opportunities like never before. I was now able to travel abroad, and I chose Iran as my first destination. It had been sixteen years since I'd left Iran as a thirteen-year-old boy. Now, in 2003, I was coming back as a thirty-year-old man.

Landing in Tehran, I was overjoyed to find all the family members who had seen me off in 1986 present at the airport to welcome me home. Sadly, Papa Jahan, his mother Maman Bozorg, and Amoo Sasan, Baba's youngest half-brother, had all passed away by then. It was hardest to embrace my grandmother, Mama Goli, absent of my grandfather, who'd always proudly stood by her side.

Being amongst my family, receiving many hugs and various members tussling my hair, reminded me of the day I'd left Tehran with Baba in pursuit of a visa to enter the United States.

My sister Donya was now twenty-one, a confident, outspoken woman and no longer the shy, adolescent girl I remembered. Amin, too, was all grown up. At nineteen, he was now my height with broad shoulders. He smothered me in a hefty hug, lifting me off the ground as I had done to him during our previous reunion at LAX.

Being back in Tehran felt strange. I was now a visitor in a place I used to call home. The streets of the city remained unchanged, but they felt more congested with traffic. The best part was visiting with various family members. Some had gained weight, some were now gray-haired, some had lost their hair, some seemed shorter, but the biggest difference was the sixteen-year age gap. The children I remembered were now adults, particularly my siblings.

My trip lasted less than three weeks, but we made every minute count with visits to everyone's home and our villa in Seaside. My parents had moved out of the A.S.P. Apartments, so there was nothing familiar about their new place.

But Seaside still felt like home. Other than overgrown trees and brush around the community, it was unchanged, although the pier had rotted away completely into the Caspian Sea from years of corrosion and lack of maintenance. In our neighborhood, I was inundated with familiarity, and gawked at the tranquility of the resort where I'd spent most of my childhood.

In 2005, I returned to Iran for a second visit, this time accompanied by my wife and two daughters, who would be meeting most of my family members for the first time. Blossom was now eight and Julia was six, and neither girl knew what to expect as the picture many Americans have of my country is a negative one.

Boarding the plane, they were brave and excited, not scared, or intimidated. They had heard many rumors about Iran, that it was an unsafe place inhabited by American haters. What they found was anything but. The Iran they discovered was the place where family lived, a place we went to vacation. And a place where I witnessed many curious Iranian citizens taking an interest in my American kids. While in public, they'd often stop us and ask many questions, even conversing with my daughters in English. All were very cordial and complimentary, some even excited and surprised to see Americans in their city. They always reminded us, "We love the American people, it's our governments who don't get along!" I strongly agree with this sentiment.

To my delight, my parents threw an extravagant birthday party for both of my daughters to make up for all the years of not being able to celebrate with them. The event was like a wedding with more than a hundred attendees in dress attire and enough gifts and praise to even make me jealous. Together, we got to visit Seaside and re-lived many of my childhood memories, including jumping off the high diving board at the community pool. Although this time I was the guiding hand for my daughter Julia, ascending the same stairs I had climbed with my father almost thirty years earlier.

Knowing how much I loved my Honda Z50 minibike, Baba didn't have the heart to dispose of it. It was kept under a pile of debris in the storage of our villa. I got to ride on the same exact bike, on the same exact streets, which is the most nostalgic thing I've ever done in my life. Julia and I went on a ride, as she was small enough to sit on the gas tank. My daughters have accompanied me back to Iran on three different occasions since.

Unfortunately, my siblings have not been able to visit us in America and it's not for a lack of trying. As adults, Donya and Amin tried for years to come to the United States, visiting American embassies in the Philippines, Spain and even Turkey, where my journey first began, unable to secure even a visitor's visa.

As adults, they both left Iran and are now living with their families in Ankara, Turkey. My parents have remained in Iran, making frequent visits to Turkey to see their children and grandchildren.

Over the years, my parents have made several more visits to America. With help from me, an American citizen, they now have Green Cards and permanent residency status, which means they no longer need to go through the arduous process of securing a visa to travel to the States.

When Baba visits me in Los Angeles, I treat him to fancy dinners at some of the best restaurants in the city, reminiscent of our adventures on the journey. But at the end of an expensive meal, he always remarks, "How is it that I get the same feeling of satisfaction from eating a hot dog at Costco than when you spoil me and spend hundreds of dollars for a fancy meal?"

Ironically, I agree with him more than I like to admit.

I am very much like my father, relentless in many ways, just like him. Growing up alone in America, I refused to give up under any circumstance, even as friends and family shook their heads in dismay at my stubborn ways. When I succeeded, those same people shook their heads in awe at my triumphant ways. I am certainly blessed with a gift, thanks to my father.

Unbeknownst to everyone, and despite my outward successes, I spent much of my time in the States plagued by feelings of self-doubt. Since arriving at the age of thirteen, I had been plowing full steam ahead, never stopping to consider the impact this journey had on me or the toll it took. I was so focused on proving that my father's decision to bring me to America was the right one that I never allowed myself to mourn all I had lost. My inability to recognize my struggle ultimately seeped into every aspect of my life.

Burying my pain caused me to suffer catastrophic failures. My marriage floundered in 2012 and, at thirty-nine years old, I found myself newly single and living away from my beloved daughters.

In 2017, I was faced with the possibility of another failed relationship, this time with Bita, my Persian goddess and the woman I wanted to spend the rest of my life with, that I finally began to look inward and realized I needed to seek help.

Agreeing to see a therapist was a hard step, but I knew I had no other choice. If Tony Soprano, a powerful, albeit fictitious mafia boss, could see a shrink, then so could I, I reasoned. During my two years of therapy with Dr. RJ, I was often brought to tears recounting the events that had brought me to this point. It felt good to finally acknowledge all the fear and self-doubt I'd been keeping bottled up.

Leaning back in his chair, Dr. RJ asked, "So, what's the reason you called my office?"

I sat for a moment, unsure how to respond. Tears pooled in my eyes as I gulped, struggling to swallow. "I feel ashamed and embarrassed by the true person I've been hiding all these years, even from my own kids."

I buried my face into my hands. I knew I needed to share the details of how I came to be in America and the shameful secret I'd been hiding for over thirty years. But that meant I had to be completely honest and revisit painful memories, including details of that fateful Wednesday, March 4, 1987, a date stamped in the back of my brain, one I think about and mourn every year when I open my eyes in the morning.

I'd come a long way since then, further than many thought or expected. But, in the end, it didn't matter. I was scared to death of the consequences of bringing up those old memories. My history was like a lump stuck in my throat and I struggled to keep my composure.

Considering the tale I was about to tell—living through the Iranian Revolution and the Iran/Iraq War, running from bombs and being exiled from my homeland, the prospect of immigrating to another country, being separated from your family, and relying on a 'coyote' to enter the U.S. illegally —one could only imagine it would be a strenuous proposition to speak with a therapist.

But over the next two years, I would tell Dr. RJ my deepest, darkest secrets. And despite my fear to the contrary, I would not only survive, but I would also thrive.

To my surprise, I was a patient of Dr. RJ's for a little over two years in 2019 when he informed me that our sessions were coming to an end. I had done the hard work, and I was ready to proceed without him. I met his pronouncement with excitement but also trepidation. It felt good to finally confront my demons in the safety of his office.

As our final session was winding down, I asked, "Now what, Doctor?"

With a hint of melancholy in his voice, he replied, "This whole affair hasn't played itself out yet. I suggest you go on and tell your story. Share it with everyone you know, your kids, colleagues, and friends. You should no longer be ashamed or embarrassed, you should be proud and celebrate your many accomplishments. The difficult journey is what has shaped you into the man you are today."

Drawing on his words of encouragement, that's exactly what I did. I stopped hiding and started living. What therapy did for me was bring all the buried secrets of my past to the surface; it certainly made me more self-aware. It was a testament to the journey I had given little or no credence to previously, and the lessons I learned from it on how to endure life's many ups and downs. It was a major turning point in my life and set me up on a new and better path.

It was my love for Bita that finally pushed me to face my demons, to examine my life and revisit many of my most difficult and challenging memories.

Bita and I got married in 2020. She is a fantastic life partner, and our union brings me peace and happiness. I have her to thank for threatening to leave me if I didn't seek help, and I have Dr. RJ to thank for helping me find my way. He showed me a new perspective, and much to my surprise and delight, I am more enlightened about my life after my two years in treatment. Without it, I would not have had the courage to be so open and honest about my journey.

Even all these years later, I have found that with adversity comes opportunity. In early 2020, when the nation shut down due to the COVID-19 pandemic, I was furloughed from work for nearly three months. Instead of panicking, I used it as an opportunity to finish writing the first draft of my memoirs.

Sadly, my grandmother, Mama Goli, died in 2021 and a year later, my beloved 91-year-old uncle, Amoo Hafez, who was like a second father to me, passed away in his sleep in a convalescent home.

Finding my way in America has been a long journey, and even all these years later, I haven't a notion of how I managed to keep my life together despite all the challenges I've faced. This book is my atonement, my confession and through the writing, I hope to earn redemption for all my faults and mistakes. Now my life is like an open book for the whole world to read.

Today, I am striving to live my best life while living the American dream. It was not until I finished therapy that I realized one thing; true freedom doesn't come from a document, a stamp, material things, or even an eagle on a passport. It comes from within, and only *you* hold the key.

EPILOGUE

After my work with Dr. RJ, my life began to move forward again like a slow, dusty, old train. He had helped me come to terms with my past and the secret that I had harbored for so long. But I realized that the shame of being an immigrant still lingered. Yes, I had begun to stop hiding my Iranian heritage and my humble beginnings in America, but I did not feel very patriotic. That all changed in September of 2022.

It was a beautiful Saturday morning when I arrived in the overcrowded parking lot at the corner of 6th and Hope Street. Walking towards Pershing Square to attend the peaceful protests, I spotted several compatriots who were proudly waving the Iranian flag.

I could hear the rumble of the crowd from a distance, and I was mesmerized by the humongous gathering of thousands of Iranians who were carrying the Iranian flag, homemade signs, and the relentless passionate chants which echoed through the tightly packed building structures of downtown Los Angeles.

The immense crowd was chanting slogans like, "Death to the dictator", "Death to the Islamic Republic", "Freedom for Iran", and "Women, life, freedom". I had joined several of the previous protests, attending for the first time in Westwood, near the federal building on Wilshire Boulevard.

At first, I was timid and embarrassed, even hesitant to participate in the relentless chants of the immense crowd. As time passed, I was soon chanting with the crowd in solidarity. Over time I felt different, overcome by emotions, and compelled to passionately join the rest of the demonstrators. The one chant everyone was emotionally screaming at the top of their lungs and with tears in their eyes at every protest, was the name of a young 22-year-old Iranian woman, who while on vacation in Tehran, was arrested on September the 13th, 2022.

Her name was "Mahsa Amini" and her image was placed all over flags, T-shirts, hats, and banners at every protest. She was detained by the guidance patrol or morality police in Tehran, which is a law enforcement command of the Islamic Republic of Iran and is tasked with arresting citizens who violate the dress code, usually concerning the wearing of hijabs by women.

Their primary role is to enforce religious laws in Iran such as strict rules on dress, behavior, and mixing between men and women in public. Punishment can take several different forms from a simple warning to imprisonment, or even physical beatings. Mahsa Amini mysteriously fell into a coma shortly after collapsing at the Vozara Detention Center, where she subsequently passed away in custody three days after her arrest on September the 16th.

The authorities insisted that Mahsa Amini died of natural causes and that her prior health conditions are what resulted in heart failure. Her family disagreed and feared the government was attempting to cover up what actually happened to Mahsa and soon their fears were confirmed. That's when the medical examiner's report and witness reports were leaked, which proved otherwise.

It was reported that Mahsa Amini was severely and viciously beaten on the head with a baton, and she was slammed against a vehicle by the morality police, causing blunt force trauma to her head, resulting in her collapsing into a coma from injuries that eventually caused her death. Her only crime for being beaten to death was for reportedly wearing her hijab too loosely. She broke the discriminatory compulsory veiling law which has been enforced in Iran since the Iranian Revolution of 1979.

Mahsa Amini's death stunned the global community, and the outpouring of rage and empathy could be found across all news outlets and social media platforms. Her death served as the catalyst to bring the entire country of Iran together and out into the streets. But more importantly, it awakened a deep fundamental desire for the women in Iran, who sparked an uprising that could not be silenced or ignored by the international community.

The single unfortunate and unnecessary event of Mahsa's death marked the start of mass protests which spread across major cities in Iran, and around the world. The streets of Tehran came to life with cries of liberty and the cheers of courageous individuals who were willing to sacrifice their lives.

The courageous young women in Iran started to burn their hijabs and cut their hair in public. They were not only fighting for women's rights and fundamental human rights, but for their own lives.

The young men, women and children of Iran will ultimately be held responsible for another major Iranian revolution. By now and months into worldwide demonstrations, it's reported that more than a million protestors had gathered in major cities all around the world.

From Los Angeles to the Bay, Toronto, Vancouver, Germany, France, Sweden, and the UK who united in one voice to bring awareness to a good cause. What the protestors were also asking for and what started as a response to Mahsa Amini's death, transformed into a bigger movement, calling for an end to the laws and systems who oppress women, and minorities in Iranian society. And an end to the overwhelming control of the country by an unelected, often uneducated minority.

The citizens of Iran see the government as completely oblivious to the interest of the Iranian population and are asking for a regime change. The protests were all calling for the end of the theocracy.

The Islamic Republic of Iran has to end the violence against its own citizens. Over the last 43 years, the regime has subjected the Iranian citizens to violence, theft, torture, sexual assault, political repression, extrajudicial executions, and unlawful killings amongst other crimes. The regime is being accused of robbing the country blind in order to line their own pockets, while the Iranian people continue to struggle with poverty, inflation, and high unemployment rates. The regime has a long history of practicing cruelties and violence towards its own female population.

The absurdity of Mahsa Amini's death will surely be the final nail in the coffin for the Islamic Republic. As usual, the Iranian authorities have responded with violent and deadly force in an effort to dissipate the ever-growing crowds. There is evidence of the security forces' unlawful use of birdshots or other metal pellets, teargas, water cannons, and beatings with batons to disperse protestors. But lately, live bullets fired against the crowds by the government forces have left hundreds dead, with many more injured and or imprisoned.

The protests in Iran may be disorganized, disjointed and working in a haphazard fashion, but that's partly because for years in the past, any opposition groups that began to rise in Iran were quickly and aggressively crushed. The government seems to have only one response to protests, which is to use brute force and suppress dissent.

They intentionally blocked social media and other communications to suppress information of the crimes committed against the people of Iran. Even after mass arrests, internet blackouts, and protestors being

killed every day by Iranian security forces, they continue to seek democracy, freedom, and prosperity. Because of the size and momentum of
this movement, the bell has been rung. It's the Islamic Republic for
whom the bell tolls.

The regime does not have the support of the Iranian public, or many
other segments of Iranian society, therefore the time has come to meet
the grievances of the public which is widespread, or the regime will face
an upheaval of this kind over and over which has been the case in the
past. The courage of the young women in Iran was awe inspiring to
witness and demonstrated the incredible bravery and resilience,
including junior high school students as young as fourteen years old
who were standing up to the brutal regime, standing up for their rights,
and setting an example for girls and women across the world. What the
women of Iran were doing was unprecedented in any previous uprising
or revolution.

Unfortunately, while the protests were raging on, my brother Amin
was lucky to only be hit in the thigh by a metal pellet, but my aunt who
lives in Tehran was not so lucky and was arrested while demonstrating
without her headscarf and imprisoned indefinitely. Our entire family
was worried sick about her, but she was not accused of a crime, nor was
she given a date to appear in court. Although worried, I was incredibly
proud of my aunt and all the other brave Iranian men and women who
have taken to the streets. It makes me very proud to call myself an
Iranian, but that's not how I've always felt.

I hid my true personality, that of an Iranian immigrant like a coward,
afraid of the dire consequences, but for good reason. That day, attending
the downtown Los Angeles protests, I was forty-nine-years-old and
surrounded by doctors, engineers, lawyers, celebrities, influencers, and
other outstanding members of the Iranian community, with me amongst
them as a corporate executive in marketing.

But what did all the demonstrators have in common? We shared the
importance of this monumental movement, despite being so far away
from our many loved ones, who still live in Iran.

History has a funny way of repeating itself, because the protests I
was attending in Los Angeles, triggered vivid memories of the
protests I'd attended a long time ago in Iran. The images brought
flashbacks of what I witnessed firsthand as a young boy riding in the
back seat of my father's car as protesters called for the Shah to be
deposed. As a six-year-old boy, I saw the American flag being burned
in the streets of Tehran with Iranian citizens demanding a change in
regime, chanting slogans like, "Death to America!" and "Death to the

Shah!" If I close my eyes, I can still hear these words ringing loudly in my ears.

It is my belief that the calls for justice and equality will continue on a global scale until the Islamic Republic is removed and no longer in power, which for many will bring closure to Mahsa Amini's death.

———

As of this writing, the 65th Annual Grammy Awards have just concluded. For the first time in history, an Iranian singer-songwriter by the name of Shervin Hajipour won the first-ever Special Merit Award for Best Song for Social Change. Remarkably, the announcement was made on live television by U.S. First Lady Jill Biden, a meaningful and important gesture.

Shervin Halipour's song, "Baraye" which means "For" or "Because of," is widely-known as the anthem of the protests and best portrays the emotions of the Iranian people around the globe. The song was inspired by the death of Mahsa Amini and has gained worldwide attention.

Less than a week later, on February 11, 2023, I attended another protest in Los Angeles, this one to mark the 44th Anniversary of the 1979 Iranian Revolution, which drew a record estimated to exceed 80,000 protestors. The immense crowd was surprised and joyous to see Reza Pahlavi, the exiled son of the Shah of Iran, speak at the event.

Reza Pahlavi has been profoundly involved with the revolutionary movement in Iran for many years and has now become the face of the movement, a symbol of freedom for many Iranians who were exiled and are now living abroad.

Thankfully, after spending 133 days in prison for the crime of protesting, my aunt was finally freed.

As of this writing, the protests in Iran have resulted in more than 500 reported deaths, over 20,000 imprisoned, and several unfortunate protestors who have been executed.

With millions of Iranians protesting across the world and the brave ones fighting in Iran, it is my belief that the end is near for the brutal regime of the Islamic Republic. This is an uprising where Iranians worldwide are demanding that my birth nation be like my new home, America, indivisible, with liberty and justice for all.

I hope and pray to see that day in the near future; I can only hope.

Printed in the USA
CPSIA information can be obtained
at www.ICGtesting.com
LVHW050720261023
761976LV00006B/148

9 781637 774437